Social Hi

G

Social History in Perspective is a series of in-depth studies of the
many topics in social, cultural and religious history for students. They
also give the student clear surveys of the subject and present
the most recent research in an accessible way.

PUBLISHED

FORTHCOMING

Titles continued overleaf

List continued from previous page

Anne Hardy   *Health and Medicine since 1860*
Steve Hindle   *The Poorer Sort of People in Seventeenth-Century England*
David Hirst   *Welfare and Society, 1832–1939*
Anne Kettle   *Social Structure in the Middle Ages*
Peter Kirby and S. A. King   *British Living Standards, 1700–1870*
Arthur J. McIvor   *Working in Britain 1880–1950*
Anthony Milton   *Church and Religion in England, 1603–1642*
Christine Peters   *Women in Early Modern Britain, 1450–1660*
Barry Reay   *Rural Workers, 1830–1930*
Richard Rex   *Heresy and Dissent in England, 1360–1560*
John Rule   *Labour and the State, 1700–1875*
Pamela Sharpe   *Population and Society in Britain, 1750–1900*
Benjamin Thompson   *Feudalism or Lordship and Politics in Medieval England*
R. E. Tyson   *Population in Pre-Industrial Britain, 1500–1750*
Garthine Walker   *Crime, Law and Society in Early Modern England*
Andy Wood   *The Crowd and Popular Politics in Early Modern England*

Please note that a sister series, *British History in Perspective*, is available which covers all the key topics in British political history.

Social History in Perspective
Series Standing Order
ISBN 0–333–71694–9 hardcover
ISBN 0–333–69336–1 paperback

(*outside North America only*)

You can receive future titles in this series as they are published by placing a standing order. Please contact your bookseller or, in case of difficulty, write to us at the address below with your name and address, the title of the series and the ISBN quoted above.

Customer Services Department, Macmillan Distribution Ltd
Houndmills, Basingstoke, Hampshire RG21 6XS, England

STATE, SOCIETY AND THE POOR

IN NINETEENTH-CENTURY ENGLAND

Alan Kidd
Reader in History
Manchester Metropolitan University

First published in Great Britain 1999 by
MACMILLAN PRESS LTD
Houndmills, Basingstoke, Hampshire RG21 6XS and London
Companies and representatives throughout the world

A catalogue record for this book is available from the British Library.

ISBN 0–333–63253–2 hardcover
ISBN 0–333–63254–0 paperback

 First published in the United States of America 1999 by
ST. MARTIN'S PRESS, INC.,
Scholarly and Reference Division,
175 Fifth Avenue, New York, N.Y. 10010

ISBN 0–312–22363–3

Library of Congress Cataloging-in-Publication Data
Kidd, Alan J.
State, society and the poor in nineteenth-century England / Alan
Kidd.
p. cm.
Includes bibliographical references and index.
ISBN 0–312–22363–3 (cloth)
1. Public welfare—England—History. 2. Charities—England–
–History. 3. Poor—England—History. 4. Poor laws—England–
–History. I. Title.
HV249.E89K53 1999
362.5'0942'09034—dc21 99–21777
CIP

This book is printed on paper suitable for recycling and made from fully managed and
sustained forest sources.

10 9 8 7 6 5 4 3 2 1
08 07 06 05 04 03 02 01 00 99

Printed in Hong Kong

In Memory of
Richard Kenneth May
1917–1993

Father-in-Law and Friend

Previously published books by Alan Kidd

Gender, Civic Culture and Consumerism, edited with D. Nicholls (1999)
The Making of the British Middle Class?, edited with D. Nicholls (1998)
Manchester (1996)
City, Class and Culture, edited with K. W. Roberts (1985)

CONTENTS

ACKNOWLEDGEMENTS

Few books are written without the support and assistance of others in what amounts to a mutual-aid network. In the first place, Michael Rose set me out on my initial researches on the Poor Law over twenty years ago and gave wise counsel during the supervision of two research degrees and beyond. Also, I have benefited from many discussions over the years with Stephen Davies, with whom I do not always agree but from whom I have learned much. Equally, a decade and more of undergraduate and research students at Manchester Metropolitan University have contributed to my knowledge of poverty and welfare, particularly those who asked awkward questions. The particular shape taken by this book crystallised in the stimulating environment of the Anstey conference organised by Hugh Cunningham at the University of Kent at Canterbury in January 1997. I would like to thank Joanna Innes and Steve King for allowing me to see copies of papers prior to publication. Additionally, I want to show my appreciation to Terry Wyke and Peter Shapely for their very helpful comments on an earlier draft and to acknowledge that the errors which remain are entirely my own responsibility. Finally, the greatest support of all has come from my family, especially Elaine whose sound advice and loving patience has been indispensable. In the interests of reciprocity it is her turn now.

1

A MIXED ECONOMY OF WELFARE

The growth of central government provision of health and welfare services for all citizens, financed from the revenues of national taxation, has been a significant feature of the histories of the industrialised nations in the twentieth century. Britain's welfare state owes most to the combination of social ideals and political will that crystallised during and after the Second World War, finding expression in the Beveridge Report of 1942 and the Labour reforms of 1945–51. By contrast, in the nineteenth century the social welfare obligations of the state were limited to assisting the destitute and much was expected of voluntary welfare services and agencies operating outside the sphere of state competence. This pluralistic approach to social provision and the much more restricted character of public welfare it involved reflected a quite different pattern of state responsibility.

For a start, there was considerably less central control of government functions than today. Much state authority was locally based. The raising of finance and the day-to-day administration of the official welfare agency, the Poor Law, was in local hands. Finance was through the poor rate collected in each parish (Poor Law union after 1865) rather than via national taxation, and parish overseers and Poor Law guardians enjoyed a significant degree of autonomy from central state control. There were financial constraints on state provision flowing from this balance between central and local authority. Low taxation was a key tenet of government fiscal policy and ratepayer concerns for economy were a constant pressure downwards on costs. There was little contest over this degree of local control nor over the confined character of state responsibility within society as a whole. Indeed, the limited sphere allotted central government was a deliberate political

1

intention. In Victorian society, the broadly agreed aim of government itself was to provide a basic framework within which civil society could function freely. Good government was limited government.[1] The ideal of restrained and decentralised government was a key element in the 'liberal state' which had emerged by the mid-nineteenth century. It was accompanied by political and social ideas which conceived liberty in terms of freedom from constraint. A pivotal tenet of Victorian liberalism was the development of a freely choosing and self-reliant people. Voluntary activity, undertaken as it was by freely associating individuals, was regarded as an intrinsic and permanent element in the corporate life of society. Far from being rivals, state action and voluntary action were deemed to be complementary. The role of central government was generally envisaged as that of an 'enabler', facilitating the actions of enlightened individuals. It was the conventional wisdom that self help was superior to state help and that private action was better than government interference, and therefore 'solutions to social problems were . . . seen to lie in voluntary and local initiative rather than in statutory and centralised agencies.'[2] It was only in the 1880s and 1890s that alternative visions of welfare started to gain credibility and only during the first two decades of the twentieth century that the conception of the limited, 'liberal' state was seriously undermined as central governments increasingly intervened in fields formerly confined to the 'private sphere'.

The expanded role of the state in welfare provision in the twentieth century has served to obscure the extent to which there exists a 'mixed economy of welfare' in which the state is only one of several constituent parts.[3] Tax-funded public welfare benefits and services stand alongside the commercial provision of private goods such as savings, insurance and pensions; voluntary non-profit agencies organised on a philanthropic or mutual-aid basis, and the informal welfare networks and services of household, kin and community. Looked at in less institutional terms, survival for the poor means making the best of an 'economy of makeshifts': mixing earned income (of all sorts) with savings and loans, the support of family and neighbours, the claiming of welfare benefits and the help of charity. This array of agencies and practices within the economy of welfare can be found in most of western Europe since at least the sixteenth century, although the relative balance of forces has varied from age to age.[4]

If we bear in mind this notion of a 'mixed economy of welfare', we will be better placed to understand the particular blend of public and private that characterised social welfare in the nineteenth century. In the Poor Law, especially as reformed in 1834 with its workhouses and outdoor relief, the state provided little more than a safety net for the poorest. Above this safety net a panoply of self-help and mutual-aid strategies existed, the result of working-class endeavour, commercial enterprise and middle-class benevolence. The more prudent or better paid worker could obtain a degree of social security by investing in a savings bank or, more commonly, through membership of a friendly society or trade union, whilst surviving bouts of poverty might depend upon such things as the availability of credit from shopkeepers and the support of family, friends and neighbours. Charity worked between the safety net of the Poor Law and the activities of self-help organisations and community-support networks. Much of this involved the encouragement of self-reliance among the able-bodied poor but, additionally, charitable effort was focused on the care of the sick and infirm and the welfare of children. Some of this voluntary work was the forerunner of today's personal social services.

'Poverty' is not a universal concept. Its usage and meaning differs across time. However, its modern configuration as an economic phenomenon, along with various discourses about it, originated with the rise of the market in western Europe from around the sixteenth century. In market societies, individuals are economically vulnerable when their material resources are insufficient for their needs (however defined). This can occur at any time, but is particularly associated with certain points in the life cycle and with particular risks. Thus childhood, unemployment, sickness, disability and old age can be especially precarious moments and events in the lives of individuals and communities. Each of them is characterised by a loss of resources and a potential or actual dependency upon others. These moments and events are most likely to pose a threat to survival if the individual is unprotected by attachment to a group with conventions about, and mechanisms for, assistance in times of need. This group can be as confined as the family or as inclusive as the welfare state. It is the exclusion from all such attachments which makes the individual most vulnerable. Thus in the 'economy of makeshifts', it is best to possess as many attachments as possible. It is clear from this that exposure to want is a cultural condition as well as an economic phenomenon. A society's approach to the welfare of others is determined by such things as its ideas of economic causation and individual rights, or the dominance of certain versions of these. In the twentieth century, the balance of welfare has come to cede the state a large role as an inclusive mechanism for the public good. In general, this is underpinned by notions of poverty which (for various reasons) emphasise the need to include individuals as citizens with social rights.

For most of the nineteenth century, the state persisted in defining poverty in terms of the problem of pauperism. Social attitudes in nineteenth-century England were dominated by ideas and assumptions derived chiefly from the writings of the classical political economists and the doctrines and teachings of evangelical religion. In terms of policies towards the poor, this implied an emphasis upon a framework of individualism and self-help, plus a determinedly moralistic approach to social problems. A distinction was drawn in official theory between the economic phenomenon of poverty and the moral responsibility of the individual to avoid welfare dependency. This did not imply a refusal to assist the poor, but a desire to be selective about who was helped and on what terms that help was offered. Thus there grew up the ambition to reduce the assistance offered to those considered able to provide for themselves and to shift resources away from compulsory provision, with its implications of legal entitlement, and towards voluntary care in which the help offered was a gift to be bestowed not a right to be claimed. The contraction in state welfare which this implied can be dated to the Poor Law reform of 1834 and was in sharp contrast to the more paternalistic and comparatively generous philosophy which underpinned much public provision under the Poor Law in the eighteenth century.

The nineteenth century was a period of rapid industrial advance and unprecedented urban growth; of major shifts in patterns of occupation (chiefly from agricultural to industrial and service) and of economic insecurity for many. It was an era which saw the formation of new social classes, new ideologies and novel forms of politics and government. It is not surprising that such a 'revolutionary' period should also be accompanied by a reformulation of social policy. The most important moment in the history of welfare in the nineteenth century was the passage of the Poor Law Amendment Act of 1834, which marked the demise of a relief system which originated in the early seventeenth century, thereafter designated the 'Old Poor Law', and its replacement by a new system, based on broadly new principles, known (not surprisingly) as the 'New Poor Law'. Unusually in welfare history, this Act was intended to reduce state provision. Its key ideas were derived from the report of a Commission of Enquiry into the Poor Laws, the famous Poor Law Report of 1834. With its statement of welfare principles (chiefly 'less eligibility' and the 'workhouse test'), it established the theoretical framework and practical strategies for a new approach to social welfare. The Poor Law Report of 1834 has been described as 'one of the classic documents of western social history'.[5] What is meant by such a claim? There had been schemes for poor relief for centuries, but the New Poor Law of 1834 was intended to do more than simply relieve the needs of the poor. It represented a new view of both society and economy in an era of rapid change.

In economic terms, the Poor Law Amendment Act of 1834 has been seen as the advent of 'liberal capitalism'. It marks the 'liberal break' with the past: the measure which ushered in a free market in labour, or at least signalled the intent of the propertied classes to facilitate its creation. Its key principles were designed to supersede the paternalistic ethos of the traditional 'country ideology' and the mutuality of the 'moral economy'; replacing both with the rigours of the market economy already established in the shape of capitalistic forms of commerce, industry and agriculture.[6] The phenomenon of pauperism and the ideal of limited state provision, the importance of charity and the virtue of individual responsibility, although challenged by economic crisis and change and by new social and political ideas, remained central to welfare policy for the rest of the century.[7] However, by the 1880s rising real wages and spreading notions of respectability were leading to new distinctions between the working classes and the 'poor'. New concepts such as 'unemployment' were enabling economists to develop an understanding of poverty as a social problem concentrated in particular groups and identified with distinct issues. The crudities of the 'liberal break' were being modified by new social knowledge, the prospect of a working-class electorate and the anxieties created by international rivalry and an imperial role. In the twentieth century, this would result in new legislation and a further revolution in social welfare, with a greatly expanded role for government and a reduced contribution from voluntarism and mutuality.

The pattern of welfare in modern society cannot be understood without first appreciating the role of the state. However, whilst it is essential to understand the broader significance of changes in social policy, it does not follow that our interests should stop there. In fact, histories of poverty and welfare before the twentieth century have too often adopted a teleological perspective, seeking the origins of modern welfare services, and therefore have concentrated over much upon state provision. The historiographical roots of this lie, to some extent, in the massive histories of the Poor Law constructed between 1905 and 1930 by Sidney and Beatrice Webb, themselves among the architects of the modern welfare system. There were sound political reasons why the Webbs took the approach they did. They were out not only to write history, but to use it to directly influence the social policies of their times and we should be aware of the political context in which their books were written.[8] However, the Webbs's priorities – rooted as they were in the social reform era of the Edwardian period and after – sufficiently anticipated the welfare philosophy of the middle decades of the twentieth century to remain persuasive for almost half a century. Historians subsequently have been far more concerned to examine state approaches to poverty than they have the welfare alternatives of charity and self-help. This has remained true even as the extent of non-state provision before 1900 has become apparent. It remains rare for histories of the post-1800 period to attempt a synthesis in which the 'mixed economy of welfare' is studied as a whole.[9]

In writing this book, there were a number of options about its structure. First of all, a word about the selected time frame. Most studies of social welfare in the nineteenth century follow the story through to at least 1914 and very often up to the era of the welfare state after the Second World War, which is usually seen as a culmination, an ending to which the past has lead. In the process, the balance of welfare in the nineteenth century, with its leaning towards voluntarism and the mutual-aid strategies of the working class, has been subordinated to narratives of the 'rise' of the welfare state, searching for its 'origins' and charting its 'evolution'. The organisation of this volume is a deliberate attempt to focus attention on the era before the emergence of modern state-centred welfare systems, when official expenditure on social security was channelled overwhelmingly through the Poor Law and voluntary charity and self-help remained essential ingredients in the welfare package. It was only after 1906 with the emergence of statutory social services outside the poor-relief system (pensions for the elderly, meals and medical examinations for schoolchildren, and unemployment and health insurance for adult males) that a rising proportion of the population once more looked to the state as a provider of social security.

Second, it might have been possible to adopt an approach which focused upon welfare outcomes. Thus chapters and sections might have been organised around the needs and strategies of different groups: women, children, the elderly, the able-bodied, the sick and so on. The relative welfare product for each could have been considered. However, such an approach does have its drawbacks. It is difficult enough to disaggregate the experience of particular groups from the collective in this way. For example, the elderly are often also the infirm; alternatively, in the absence of any clear definition of old age for much of the nineteenth century, they might also be regarded as able-bodied and employable until quite old. However, despite the different experiences and situations between them, it would be possible to discuss the common outcomes for certain groups, this would certainly be the case for women who were more likely to suffer a disadvantageous position for the whole of the century. But there are also other drawbacks to this approach. It would make it less easy to identify the ideological and institutional configurations which I considered to be important for an understanding of why welfare outcomes were as they were. Moreover, a central argument of this book is the extent to which the experiences of individuals, and their fates at times of hardship and deprivation, are influenced by the balance of ideas, social knowledge and state policies. Although the informal and private mechanisms may be the first port of call for those in poverty, the degree to which they are also the last depends on the responsibilities assumed by the state.

Thus this book is structured in such a way as to enable me to consider the ideas and policies of public welfare in Chapter 2, the philosophy and patterns of private charity in Chapter 3, and the institutional and informal strategies of prevention and survival developed by the working classes in Chapter 4. Finally, Chapter 5 considers the extent to which state provision and social theory transcended the Poor Law before 1900 and brings discussion of the 'mixed economy of welfare' into the twentieth century.

2

THE STATE AND PAUPERISM

For much of the nineteenth century the state relieved only a minority of the poor. Moreover, its welfare role was a declining one with both the costs of poor relief and the numbers assisted consistently falling after 1850. This was a deliberate consequence of the policy set out in the Poor Law Report of 1834 and enacted through the New Poor Law. However, it was far from being uniformly enforced. Considering the extent to which the exercise of authority was a matter of negotiation between the central and the local state, it is not surprising that there was a great deal of diversity in poor–relief practice across the country. This very diversity has helped shape the historian's picture of the Poor Law, in which contradictory generalisations are often made according to the evidence from particular local case studies. None the less, it is possible to discern a broad pattern across time. In essence, there were two Poor Laws, one operating up to (and possibly beyond) 1834 and derived from centuries old notions of entitlement which were relatively broad and inclusive. The second gradually replacing the old system during the middle decades of the century and based upon a narrower and increasingly more punitive approach to adult applicants for relief. However, almost by default, this second system found itself responsible for a range of welfare services for the sick and infirm and for children. Furthermore, the chief institutional innovation of the new system – the workhouse – was transformed from the purely deterrent mechanism of its creators to something approaching a state hospital system by the end of the century.

The history of the Poor Law in the nineteenth century must be understood in its ideological and socioeconomic context. A society's values can be judged by its approach to welfare. Thus it is important

8

to understand the arguments against state responsibility and in favour of individual responsibility which came to hold such sway by the Victorian era. The combination of new thinking, which provided the rationale for the New Poor Law (classical political economy, utilitarianism and evangelicalism), set the values and standards for the 'liberal state' of the mid-nineteenth century. Although challenged in the later nineteenth century by new intellectual approaches which looked for broader based state welfare, this particular combination retained considerable potency down to 1900 and beyond. However, the socioeconomic climate in which these ideas surfaced was to change dramatically as the century wore on. The New Poor Law was created to deal with the problem of rural unemployment. The parliament which enacted the legislation was still overwhelmingly representative of the landed classes. Yet the main pattern of economic change in the nineteenth century was a shift from rural to urban. At the beginning of the century, approaching 40 per cent of families were involved in agriculture and, although this had fallen to about one third by 1831, farming remained the single largest occupational category for adult males in 1851. Yet by 1871 only 15 per cent of the working population were employed in agriculture, falling to a mere 7.6 per cent in 1911. The life-cycle crises which brought people to apply to the Poor Law authorities may have changed little, but the context was increasingly urban rather than rural, and the sheer size of the problem escalated dramatically as the population of England and Wales multiplied four-fold during the century.

Beginning with the pattern of relief across the century, this chapter will proceed to a consideration of the Old Poor Law and the key areas of debate between historians. The intellectual roots of the reformed system are examined and also the controversy over the extent to which it altered the treatment of the able-bodied adult male. The development of the New Poor Law will be followed chronologically, looking at policy towards women, the sick, the elderly and the young in the period 1834–60. A relief crisis in the 1860s aided a restructuring in which certain groups were more harshly treated whilst others were approached more favourably, thus out-relief was further curtailed, affecting mostly women applicants, whereas the sick and children were among those for whom provision could be said to have improved in the later Victorian period. Finally, the chapter will conclude with a consideration of the extent to which the state had adopted a welfare role beyond the Poor Law prior to 1900, as well as the impact of new thinking on the responsibilities of government as the state prepared to expand its welfare functions, side stepping the issue of further Poor Law reform, with the liberal reforms of 1906–11.

Declining State Welfare

English poor relief was probably the most generous in Europe in the late eighteenth and the early nineteenth centuries, absorbing around 2 per cent of the national product.[1] However, from the mid-1830s, the trend was downwards costing ratepayers less and involving a declining expenditure per head of population (see Table A1 in the Appendix). A comparison of the average expenditure per head for 1830–33 (9s. 10d.) with that for 1840–43 (6s. 1d.) reveals a fall of more than one third in per capita costs over a ten-year period. In 1831, with a population in England and Wales of almost 14 million, the total cost of poor relief was £6.7 million. By 1841 the population had risen to 16 million and yet the cost of poor relief had fallen to £4.8 million. In terms of the amount spent by the state on the welfare of the poor, the mid-1830s has the appearance of a watershed. Whereas between 1813 and 1833 costs per head had ranged from 9s. 1d. to 13s., from a low of 5s. 5d. in 1837, annual per capita costs rose above seven shillings on only six more occasions before 1900. Poor relief in England and Wales cost the nation over £7 million in 1832. Although the population virtually doubled over the next 40 years, it took until 1868 before the £7 million total was reached once more. In as much as tax-based social welfare is redistributive (transferring income from taxpayers to the poor), this element was at its highest in the decades preceding 1834 and at its lowest in the mid to late nineteenth century. The level of per capita expenditure on poor relief reached between 1813 and 1822 and in the early 1830s was not to return until the 1920s, when the use of poor relief to deal with the mass unemployment of the interwar years caused a rapid escalation in costs. In between these twin peaks, the average per capita cost during the Victorian era was less than half the figure for the second decade of the nineteenth century.

Declining levels of expenditure in the face of rising population figures could represent reduction in relief provision rather than a fall in the number of paupers (persons in receipt of poor relief from the state). It might simply mean that less was being spent on the same pauper aggregate. In fact, the available statistics suggest that the proportion of the population assisted by state welfare also declined. Unfortunately, the evidence of numbers relieved is less reliable than the figures for relief expenditure.[2] Before 1834, there was no central agency to gather relief statistics and only *ad hoc* returns exist, such as those for 1802–3 and for 1813. There is evidence from the 1840s of the total number of relief applications over particular three month periods, but these must have involved much double counting of individuals and families who repeatedly applied for relief. The situation is much better for the second half of the century. From 1849 an annual survey was undertaken, consisting of twice-yearly counts of all paupers relieved on a single day (on the first days of January and July each year). The mean annual totals for this series are reproduced in Table A2 in the Appendix. This is a only a guide to the numbers in receipt of state assistance and remains essentially a snapshot view. Inevitably, it fails to distinguish between the permanent pauper and those temporarily on poor relief. Nevertheless, it does say something about trends across time, suggesting a consistent pattern of declining numbers receiving poor relief from the state. The ratio of paupers per hundred of total population follows a clear course downwards with 6.3 per cent receiving state welfare in 1849, falling to 2.5 by 1900. In fact, apart from the worst year of the Cotton Famine in 1863, the ratio never rose above 5 per cent after 1852. However, these figures may underestimate the size of the pauper host. Whole-year calculations were undertaken in 1892 and in 1907 which, arguably, can give a fuller picture. These suggest that the real annual totals for those years may have been at least double the figures derived from the twice-yearly day counts.[3] If this ratio was extrapolated to the rest of the years recorded in Table A2, it would have the effect of doubling both the annual totals and the ratio of paupers per hundred of population. If such a calculation is considered valid, it would follow that in 1849 a possible 12 per cent of the population might have been in receipt of poor relief at some time during the year, a figure which would decline to 5 per cent by 1900. None the less, although the numbers on relief would be greater, the impression would remain that the English Poor Law was of diminishing significance in the 'economy of makeshifts' by which the poor survived.

But can these statistics perhaps be taken as evidence of declining poverty as living standards rose? Might they reflect the impact of long-term increases in wage rates and declining grain prices, for example?

It would be a mistake to jump to such a conclusion too easily, however, since the figures are an estimate of the number of paupers and not a measure of the number of people existing in poverty. Indeed, it is unwise to treat statistics of poor relief as a simple measure of poverty levels. The impact of the trade cycle on the pattern of relief was variable, depending on the willingness of the authorities to expand assistance at such times. Per capita costs rose during periods of high unemployment, such as the second decade of the century and the late 1840s, and fell again during better periods, like the mid 1820s, the late 1830s and the 1850s, but this trend becomes less noticeable as the century progresses and the economic depression of the last quarter of the century had no impact upon the numbers relieved. In other words, welfare policies are culturally determined, they reflect changing notions of relief entitlement. A reduction in poverty cannot simply be 'read off' from a fall in the size of the welfare budget.

It is a more reasonable assumption that, as a proportion of the population, the poor were a much larger group than the recorded number of paupers, however calculated. This is not 'provable' in any quantifiable sense. There were no systematic attempts to measure poverty, as opposed to pauperism, until the surveys conducted at the end of the nineteenth century by Charles Booth and Seebohm Rowntree in London and York respectively. However, each of these surveys identified around 30 per cent of the population to be living in poverty. There is no reason to presume that the extent of poverty was greater in the 1890s than it had been earlier in the century. Thus the numbers receiving state help during the nineteenth century consistently fell below the likely levels of poverty. In the 1890s, whilst, according to Booth and Rowntree, approaching one third of the population were poor, there were no more than 2.7 per cent in receipt of poor relief in any one year. For all its attention from contemporaries, and from the historians ever since, in terms of numbers affected the Poor Law was more often the junior partner to self-help, mutual aid and voluntary charity. Only in the generation before the reform of 1834 could it be said that the state was the first recourse for the poor and even here, as we shall see, the pattern of support varied considerably from region to region.

Poor Law before 1834

Old Poor Law in Crisis

England was unusual in eighteenth-century Europe in possessing statutory-based poor relief financed by taxation. According to Peter Solar, the distinctive features of English poor relief were its uniformity and comprehensiveness compared to European relief systems, which were more honoured in the breach than in the practice; the financial base of the English system in a local property tax (the poor rate) and the services of unpaid local officials; and (up to 1834) the relative certainty and generosity of relief.[4] The key piece of legislation had been the great 'Elizabethan Poor Law' of 1601, which enshrined the twin purposes of assisting the 'impotent' (the old, the sick and the infirm) whilst setting the 'able-bodied' poor to work.[5] What became known after 1834 as the 'Old Poor Law' was highly decentralised, based as it was on the parish as the basic unit of organisation, tempered by the supervisory eye of the county magistracy and only ultimately responsible to Parliament.[6] In terms of relief practice, its chief hallmark was its 'face to face' character. Overseers of the poor usually knew those they relieved, especially in the small village communities that generally made up the 15 000, mostly rural, parishes. Magistrates were responsible for ensuring that the Poor Law was enforced according to statute. They ruled on disputes between parishes, for example over rating levels, but also frequently gave specific orders for the relief of individuals.

The Poor Law was a pivotal social institution in England during the seventeenth and eighteenth centuries: 'providing relief, enforcing discipline, an expression of communal responsibility yet a potent reminder of social distance'.[7] Corresponding to communal responsibilities were communal rights. Such an intimate social exchange generated expectations both among the relieved and those in charge of relief grants: 'It was assumed, by magistrates, managers and the poor themselves, that the poor were entitled to relief if they required it.'[8] This notion of entitlement was less a legalistic interpretation of the statutes and more a question of a moral right of access to the 'necessities' of life. The assumption of community responsibility meant that the poor were more often an integral rather than marginal element in society, and some arguments see parish relief expanding in the seventeenth and eighteenth centuries at the expense of more informal sources of support.[9]

Deference and reciprocity were at the heart of this system of social security and the whole was underwritten by the ideology of paternalism. Yet economic changes in the later eighteenth and early nineteenth centuries were to create a crisis of paternalism, in which the future of the Poor Law was conceived as a major problem.

It was inevitable that the advancing commercialism and economic uncertainties of the late eighteenth and early nineteenth centuries would have an impact on a system of social security designed for an age of paternalism. A population of approximately six million in 1750, which had risen to almost nine million by the time of the first official census in 1801, had more than doubled by 1831. Accompanying this population growth was the rapid expansion of employment in the industrial towns of the West Midlands and the North. Meanwhile, in the arable farmlands of the predominantly agricultural counties of the South Midlands, the South and the South East long-term increase in wheat prices between 1760 and 1815 encouraged landowners to seek the enclosure of previously marginal land such as wastes and commons. Two thousand or so enclosure acts involved the loss of centuries-old common rights of grazing and gathering vital to the economy of the poor. The situation for the agricultural labourer was exacerbated by two further developments. First, a decline in the availability of allotments on which food could be grown to supplement wage income. Second, the decay of cottage industries, especially those of hand-spinning and weaving, in the face of competition from mechanised production in factory towns. Domestic manufacture had provided employment for men during the slack winter period of the rural economy and for women and children the year round. Constraints imposed by the Revolutionary and Napoleonic war, and the impact of the post-war depression made matters worse.

These issues help to explain why the Poor Laws entered a period of crisis from the later eighteenth century onwards, and also why the crisis centred on the poverty of the adult rural labourer, who was increasingly left with little alternative to the wages paid for farm work. Reduced employment opportunities combined with a decline in alternative sources of income created a problem of rural unemployment, or more accurately, of seasonal employment or under-employment which dogged the rural economy of southern England until well into the nineteenth century. In the view of prevalent assumptions about the right to relief, a deterioration in the economic conditions of the labourers might be expected to lead to an expansion of provision.

The Poor Law authorities in most rural parishes in the south of England responded to the problem of under-employment with an expansion of out-relief to the able-bodied. A variety of expedients were adopted at different times and in different places. An over-concentration on the so-called 'Speenhamland System' in the Report of the Royal Commission on the Poor Laws in 1834, and in the accounts of an earlier generation of historians, has tended to obscure the complexities of poor relief before 1834. But, beginning with Blaug's ground-breaking analysis in the early 1960s, historians have generally moved away from the view that the Speenhamland-style practices characterised poor relief, and recent accounts draw attention to a range of outdoor relief mechanisms.[10] Boyer identifies six methods used by rural parishes to relieve poor able-bodied labourers between 1780 and 1834: allowances-in-aid-of-wages; payments to labourers with large families; payments to seasonally unemployed agricultural labourers; the roundsmen system; the labour rate; and, finally, the workhouse.[11]

Allowances-in-aid-of-wages were potentially the most generous of these since they were intended to subsidise the weekly income of labourers' families (both employed and unemployed), adjusted according to the price of bread and the number of children in the family. The most famous example of the allowance mechanism was the bread scale adopted by the magistrates at Speenhamland in Berkshire, in May 1795. It was not, however, the first instance nor was it the beginning of an era of Speenhamland-style relief lasting up to 1834. In fact, allowances were a temporary expedient adopted during subsistence crises brought on by harvest failures and high food prices, and were preferred by farmers as an alternative to raising labourers' wages. The use of allowances-in-aid-of-wages may well have peaked in the late 1790s, have been in marked decline after 1815 and enjoyed a revival in the early 1820s, only to have virtually disappeared by 1832. Whilst over 40 per cent of parishes were reportedly subsidising wages out of rates in a parliamentary return for 1824, by the time of the *Rural Queries* in the Royal Commission enquiry of 1832, the proportion had fallen to just 7 per cent. Much more common were child allowances, typically paid to labourers' families with four or more children. In the parliamentary return of 1824, 90 per cent of parishes reported giving child allowances and even in the *Rural Queries* of 1832, the figure remained as high as 55 per cent, rising to 69 per cent in the agricultural counties.[12]

However, according to Boyer, the major function of poor relief in rural parishes from 1795 to 1834 was the payment of unemployment benefit to seasonally unemployed agricultural labourers. This, rather than Speenhamland bread scales, characterised the system of relief, at least in the agricultural South. The amount paid was often predetermined and fixed somewhat below the going-wage rate. Variant forms of unemployment benefit were the so-called roundsmen system and the labour rate. The roundsmen system became widespread from the 1780s and generally involved the offer of seasonally unemployed labourers to farmers at reduced wage rates, with the parish making up the deficit to subsistence levels. The labour rate did not become common until the mid 1820s; it allowed farmers to employ pauper labour in lieu of the payment of the poor rate. Of the strategies to deal with the able-bodied, the workhouse was the least important before 1834. Of the total of one million paupers recorded in the return for 1802–3, only 83 468 or 8 per cent were reported as resident in a workhouse and this figure covered all categories, including the old, the infirm and children. The able-bodied were rarely found in workhouses under the Old Poor Law.

The Report of the Royal Commission on the Poor Laws of 1834, in its critique of the prevailing system, concentrated on this issue of outdoor relief to the able-bodied, on the grounds that out-relief to the impotent was subject to less abuse.[13] To a great extent, the agenda for historical discussion of the Old Poor Law between 1795 and 1834 has been set by this critique, and much has been written over the years for and against the views of the 1834 Commissioners and much energy has been expended in the 'testing' of hypotheses about the operation and economic and moral impact of the relief mechanisms identified above. We will return to these arguments below. However, a pertinent question at this time, and one masked by the over-concentration on the able-bodied, is the extent to which there was a difference in quality as well as quantity of poor relief between the pre- and post-1834 systems. It is worthwhile to ask whether, in 1834, we lost a social security system which, in the words of Marc Blaug, constituted a 'welfare state in miniature'.[14]

Solar's point about the 'certainty and generosity' of English poor relief (see above) is drawn partly from a comparison with European relief systems, but also from a body of literature since the 1960s which has stressed the broad welfare function of the Old Poor Law. In this literature, relief to the able-bodied is only part of the equation. According to the national return of 1802–3, children accounted for 30 per cent of persons relieved, and the old and infirm constituted 16 per cent. Many studies suggest that poor relief was used to sustain individuals and families at various points in the life cycle: childhood, widowhood, infirmity and old age. Moreover, the relief that was given is regarded as more than basic. It appeared designed to restore the relative status of individuals in the community rather than providing only a bare minimum of subsistence. Besides unemployment relief and pensions for the elderly, eighteenth-century overseers' accounts commonly contain payments for rent, food, fuel (coals), boots and shoes, clothing, lying-in expenses (such as childbed linen and payments to the midwife) and burial costs (laying-out, shrouds, grave digging). A picture emerges of a wide-ranging paternalism which extended to the management of the local labour market, the fixing of wage rates, the fostering of parish orphans, the apprenticing of young persons and the support of single-parent families.[15]

But how accurate is this picture? Or more precisely, how accurate is it as a national picture and to what extent was its generosity tempered by the crisis of paternalism in the generation before 1834? To take the question of national diversity first – King and Gritt have argued that the image of a generous welfare system is derived from research heavily biased towards the rural South and the South East which underplays the significance of regional and urban variations in the practice of poor relief.[16] Elsewhere in the country the situation could be quite different. On the basis of research in Lancashire, they conclude that:

> . . . in some of the agricultural and industrialising townships of the north of England, the administration of the Old Poor Law was not, and was not designed to be, either flexible, sensitive or supportive. On the contrary, it was used to control lives, exploit the poor and to minimise the growing burden of poor relief . . . there was a constant tendency . . . to err on the side of harshness and exclusivity.[17]

It has been clear for some time that per capita relief expenditures were lower in the 'high-wage/pastoral' counties than in the 'low-wage/arable' counties. Following Caird's agricultural map of England in 1850–51, these correspond roughly to the North and West of the country on the one hand, and the South and East on the other. Per capita relief expenditure in the South, extending over the half century and more preceding 1834, outstripped that in the North by anything between 80 and 100 per cent, a distinction that may have persisted beyond 1834.[18] An analysis of the county totals in the return for 1802–3, if compared to population figures, reveals that Lancashire had the lowest pauper:population ratio in the country at 6.7 per cent. At the other end of the spectrum came the Speenhamland county itself, Berkshire, with a ratio of 20 per cent, exceeded only by Sussex at 22.6 per cent and Wiltshire at 22.1 per cent.[19] In fact, the Old Poor Law in Lancashire looks very much like the New Poor Law after 1834, with low expenditure and limited relief numbers.

It is not so much this phenomenon itself as the explanation for it that King and Gritt are challenging. A hypothesis based on economic evidence would point to the fact that agricultural wage rates were higher and that there was less seasonality in employment patterns in this predominantly pastoral region than in the arable farmlands of the South. Moreover, there were more alternatives to poor relief in Lancashire, such as allotments and small holdings, plus greater employment opportunities in cottage industries even before the advent of factory production. However, King and Gritt maintain that in certain Lancashire townships and villages, where there was a scarcity of alternative earning opportunities and where the problem of endemic poverty was as acute as in any southern parish, poor relief policies remained comparatively harsh. Thus, they argue, the explanation for regional variations (and for variations within regions) is less the incidence of need and more the attitude of those in charge of the relief system. In parts of the North, instead of paternalism and generosity, there already existed a climate of opinion in which overseers and elites encouraged a culture of self-reliance to minimise relief expenditure. Poor relief was a short-term, selective mechanism and long-term welfare dependency was discouraged even before the reform of 1834.

What conclusions are to be drawn from these conflicting portraits of relief practice under the Old Poor Law? One is the difficulty of basing generalisations about a national system on the basis of a few local or even regional examples, whether they are drawn from the South or the North of the country. A second is the considerable diversity of outcome one is likely to find in such a decentralised, locally financed welfare system, especially where the unit of administration (the parish) was so small. It would be more surprising if there were not wide variations between regions and parishes. There truly was a welfare patchwork. This might be the case for economic reasons, but equally, cultural or political factors might explain some of the diver-

gence in relief strategies. There is certainly good reason not to eulo-
gise the Old Poor Law. Equally, however, it is clear from more general
evidence on the cost of relief and the broad pattern of numbers in
receipt of relief that there is a margin of difference between the Old
and the New Poor Laws in need of explanation.

The second issue of the chronology of relief patterns goes to the
heart of the debate over the origins of the reform of 1834. The apparent shift within the relief system towards providing social security
for unemployed men and their families and subsidising the family
income of those on low wages may have made sense in terms of the
traditions of reciprocity and deference, but it was an affront to the
moral, as well as economic, sensibilities of a new generation which
increasingly accepted the new philosophy we now know as 'Classical
Political Economy'. Under the influence of new ideas, many contemporaries came to regard the English Poor Law as dangerously
generous. The Report of the Royal Commission on the Poor Laws in
1834 complained that whilst most countries had felt the need to relieve the indigent, in no other country in Europe had the state
attempted to relieve poverty itself. This, it was claimed, was the result of an abuse of out-relief through allowances-in-aid-of-wages that
was 'destructive to the morals of the most numerous class, and to the
welfare of all'.[20] Thus the 1834 Report set the allowance system and
relief to the able-bodied at the heart of the debate over Poor Law
reform. This analysis was not new, it had been at the centre of a hotly
contested debate over the effects of the Poor Law conducted since the
last decades of the eighteenth century. It was a debate in which the
deficiencies of the welfare system seemed apparent, but in which a
satisfactory solution never seemed to be at hand, at least until the
1834 Report came along and swept all opposition before it.

From Poverty to Pauperism

From Joseph Townsend's hostile *Dissertation on the Poor Laws* (1786)
onwards, a debate raged which taxed the minds of some of the greatest intellectuals of the day, such as Edmund Burke, Thomas Malthus
and Jeremy Bentham, plus a host of pamphleteers and essayists.
Through writers such as these a sustained critique of the Poor Law
evolved.[21] In the course of this debate, the concept of 'pauperism' rather than poverty emerged as the central issue. 'Poverty' was regarded as

the 'natural' state of the majority of mankind required to labour for
subsistence, this was an immutable condition not a proper subject for
human assistance. It was only those unable to labour for their subsistence who should be relieved as paupers. Pauperism emerged as a moral
as well as economic problem: how to relieve the genuinely indigent
without discouraging self-reliance and demoralising the labourer? This
was nothing less than the application of market values to the ancient
traditions of poor relief.

The debate leading up to 1834 took place in an intellectual climate
in which the ideas of Adam Smith (famously espoused in *The Wealth of
Nations* of 1776) and of the political economists who followed in his
wake were forging economic doctrines for a commercial society.[22] Influenced by Smith's notions of economic liberty, Burke endeavoured
to achieve a mental separation between the terms 'labourer' and 'poor'.
Objecting to the prevalence of the term 'labouring poor' during the
food scarcity of 1795–96, he rejected what he saw as sentimental attitudes to the unemployed and the low paid:

> We have heard many plans for the relief of the 'labouring poor'. This puling
> jargon is not as innocent as it is foolish . . . .. Hitherto the name of poor (in
> the sense in which it is used to excite compassion) has not been used for
> those who can, but for those who cannot labour – for the sick and infirm,
> for orphan infancy, for languishing and decrepit age; but when we affect to
> pity, as poor, those who must labour or the world cannot exist, we are tri-
> fling with the condition of mankind. It is the common doom of man that
> he must eat his bread by the sweat of his brow . . . .. This affected pity only
> tends to dissatisfy them with their condition, and to teach them to seek
> resources where no resources are to be found, in something else other than
> their own industry, and frugality, and sobriety.[23]

Burke's distinction between 'labourers' and the 'poor' only took hold
in general discourse in the wake of Thomas Malthus's famous *An Essay on the Principles of Population* (1798 and editions thereafter). Malthus
replaced earlier mercantilist optimism about the relationship between
an increasing population and the creation of national wealth with
dismal predictions about the tendency of population growth to out-
strip the means of subsistence unless checked by 'misery' (war, famine,
disease) or 'vice' (abortion, infanticide, birth control). In a second
edition of his *Essay* in 1803, succumbing to criticism that he had been
unduly negative, he added the 'preventive check' of 'moral restraint'

(later marriages and sexual continence before marriage). The implications for the Poor Law were apparent from the outset, although Malthus elaborated his theme in successive editions up to 1826. Not only allowances to the able-bodied, but all poor relief was condemned for its presumed contribution to population growth and its other harmful economic and moral effects. The 'first obvious tendency [of the Poor Laws] is to increase population without increasing the food or its support. A poor man may marry with little or no prospect of being able to support a family without parish assistance. They may be said, therefore, to create the poor which they maintain.'[24] He displayed a characteristically low opinion of the labouring population and determined that it was in their self-interest that poor relief should be curtailed: 'The poor laws . . . diminish both the power and the will to save among the common people, and thus . . . weaken one of the strongest incentives to sobriety and industry, and consequently to happiness.'[25]

The Malthusian critique evolved into an argument for the eventual abolition of poor relief, starting with the next generation of children so as gradually to nurture prudential habits as opposed to habitual dependency. This could be assisted by discriminating charity but the chief resource of the poor would be themselves:

> When the poor were once taught, by the abolition of the poor laws, and a proper knowledge of their real situation, to depend more upon themselves, we might rest secure that they would be fruitful enough in resources, and that the evils which were absolutely irremediable, they would bear with the fortitude of men, and the resignations of Christians.[26]

The Malthusian argument was taken up by numerous other critics and dominated the debate from the post-war period to the 1830s. When his population principle was combined with particular doctrines of Classical Political Economy, such as the wages-fund theory it proved a lethal weapon in the hands of those hostile to poor relief.

Parallel to the Malthusian critique and the argument of the political economists were the ideas on poverty and pauperism emerging from the revival of evangelical thought, what Boyd Hilton has called 'Christian Economics'.[27] According to Hilton, the approach to social issues in the early nineteenth century included a model of the economy which explicitly linked competition and the market to moral and spiritual growth. Although opinion was influenced by Malthus and the broader teachings of political economy, it envisaged an alternative list of priorities: 'Its psychological premise was not self-interest but the supremacy of economic conscience, the latter innate in man yet needing to be nurtured into a habitude through the mechanism of the free market, with its constant operation of temptation, trial and exemplary suffering.'[28] The operation of the natural laws of the market was about moral lessons and spiritual growth not economic prosperity. Since the individual was personally responsible for his own salvation, the sustenance of the labourer merely because of his poverty was in contravention of the laws of God. To remove this unthinking paternalism would be to restore the natural order and to foster self-denial, spiritual growth and moral virtue.

The language of 'self-help' and 'independence' issued naturally from evangelicalism and nowhere was it more clearly expressed than in the influential views of the Scottish divine, Thomas Chalmers. Chalmers's ideas came to prominence in England after articles on pauperism in the *Edinburgh Review* in 1817 and 1818. To his mind, the 'invention of pauperism' threatened to engulf the wellsprings of benevolence and godly endeavour. To abolish the compulsory poor rate and to remove the phenomenon of pauperism would be to release 'four fountains . . . now frozen or locked up by the hand of legislation'. The 'four fountains' were the 'frugality and providential habits of our labouring classes'; 'the kindness of relatives'; 'the sympathy of the wealthier for the poorer classes of society'; and 'the sympathy of the poor for the poor'.[29] The evangelicals were a major influence in the development of charity and, at least till 1834, there was a common presumption, shared with the Malthusians, that discriminating Christian charity was infinitely superior to the Poor Law. According to Peter Mandler, this combination of natural theology and political economy influenced the politics of liberal Toryism which gave parliamentary support to the Whig reform of the Poor Laws in 1834.[30] From the mid century, the evangelical 'economic conscience', with its emphasis upon moral restraint and tendency towards pessimism, was gradually undermined by the optimistic economics of John Stuart Mill and the development of evolutionary theories of the natural and human worlds. But this resolution was still in the future when Poor Law reform was the key social issue in the 1830s.

In the eyes of its critics, the Poor Laws of England were responsible for a variety of evils. Outdoor relief in general, and allowances-in-aid-of-wages in particular, were the prime target. Rising poor rates,

increasing unemployment, falling wage rates, higher food prices, im-
provident marriages and a rising birth rate were among the charges
against a system that came under attack as an 'engine of pauperisa-
tion'. Since the 1960s, economic historians (often using economic
theory and an armoury of econometric techniques) have largely refut-
ed these criticisms of the effects of the Old Poor Law. As we have seen
already, allowances-in-aid-of-wages were less widespread than contemporaries thought, they were rarely the main form of outdoor relief to
the able-bodied. Moreover, Blaug maintained that allowances were too
meagre to constitute a viable alternative to gainful employment and
McCloskey used economic theory to undermine the idea that outdoor relief eroded wage rates. Blaug's chief point was that the Old
Poor Law, 'with its use of outdoor relief to assist the underpaid and to
relieve the unemployed was, in essence, a device for dealing with the
problem of surplus labour in the lagging rural sector of a rapidly expanding but still underdeveloped economy.'[31] Rather than causing
economic dislocation, poor relief developed in response to economic
circumstances.

Baugh produced evidence to support this contention, showing that,
in the counties he studied (Essex, Sussex and Kent), relief expenditures fluctuated and relief policies changed in correspondence with
unemployment levels. Finally, Huzel turned the Malthusian link between child allowances and population growth 'on its head', although,
using regression analysis, Boyer has arrived at different conclusions
arguing that there is a correlation between variations in the use of
child allowances and the pattern of fertility, as Malthus had argued.[32]
Much of the analysis that has led to these conclusions has its roots in
the school of positive economics, with its use of economic models to
formulate and test hypotheses. But the application of economic theory
in such a way has been seriously challenged. Karel Williams has condemned such 'empiricist scientificity' which 'cannot and will not work
in philosophy or history' since it 'naturalises' economic concepts which
are not universal scientific laws, but cultural products likely to change
across time. This is a powerful argument which must be taken into
account when considering the value of much of the analysis of the Old
Poor Law.[33]

Whatever the conclusions of the modern economic historians, contemporary opinion assumed that the administration of relief rather
than the underlying economic conditions was behind the rising tide
of pauperism. The critical literature on the unreformed Poor Law was

taken seriously at the highest levels. There were several parliamentary enquiries into the practice of poor relief before that appointed in
1832. The most influential document arising from this flurry of parliamentary interest was the report of the Select Committee of the
House of Commons of 1817. It fully accepted the demoralisation thesis
about out-relief and, following Malthus, came close to recommending abolition, but held back on grounds of practical expediency rather
than on any principled defence of a discredited system. However, the
parliamentary reception of the 1817 Report was mixed and the government response was positive but cautious. As Poynter notes: 'The
growth of abolitionist opinion after 1815 may have been spectacular,
but it did not sweep all before it.'[34] Finally, it fell to the writers of the
1834 Report to come up with a scheme which offered to meet the
aspirations of the abolitionists, whilst satisfying the doubts of those
who feared such a drastic solution.

New Poor Law between 1834 and the 1860s

1834 Reform

Why did reform of the Poor Laws (rather than abolition) become such
an urgent political issue in the 1830s, leading to the appointment of a
Royal Commission and the introduction of a new system of public relief? Historians do not agree on the balance of factors involved. But it
is useful to distinguish between the long-term critique of the Poor Laws
which drew attention to its perceived deficits, but was of itself insufficient to lead to either abolition or reform, and those short-term factors
which can help to explain why the case for reform became irresistible
by the early 1830s. Poynter's is the most complete discussion of the
debate between the intellectuals, but covers the broader economic
and social context less well. Dunkley provides what is probably the
most comprehensive account of the search for reform. Brundage has
refocused attention on the political dimension and, along with Mandler and Hilton (although with different conclusions), has emphasised
the importance of understanding landed opinion and the views of its
representatives in Parliament.[35] Factors which all mention are the
mounting rates burden and the fear of unrest following the 'Captain
Swing' agricultural labourers' riots of 1830–31. What sense are we to
make of this?

There was certainly increasing financial pressure from the rates, although, on the face of it, costs had peaked long before the 1830s. The national poor rate rose from £5.3 million in 1802–3 to a high point of £9.3 million in 1817–18. Lower levels in the 1820s were followed by a further rise to £8.6 million in 1831–32. However, the poor rate may have bitten disproportionately hard in agricultural districts because the values of gross rental of farm land, which were related to many assessments for the poor rate, had risen much more slowly.[36] Tenant farmers were the main body of ratepayers, but they may have been able to shift some of the burden on to the landowners through lower rents. Allied with anxiety about an expanding relief system, this loss of rental income might explain why the landed class was anxious to find a lower cost solution to the problem of poor relief. But it is unlikely that this, on its own, was a sufficient issue to persuade Parliament of the need for Poor Law reform. It was also a question of public order and class relations on the land.

The immediate catalyst for Poor Law reform was the last great agricultural labourers' revolt, the so-called Captain Swing disturbances of 1830–31, which affected well over 1400 parishes, mainly in southern and eastern England. Riots, machine-breaking and rick-burnings, accompanied by petitions and protests over wages and poor relief levels, as well as against the introduction of new machinery (threshing machines threatened the winter employment provided by hand threshing), spread across the southern counties. The Captain Swing riots were precipitated by a sharp decline in the economic conditions of the agricultural labourer following the hard winter of 1829–30. There is evidence of reductions in out-relief payments and a more deterrent approach to all relief at a time of falling living standards.[37] Local negotiations over wages and poor relief often led to temporary increases in both. It was the fact that the smashing of threshing machines and of acts of incendiarism were concentrated in counties with high per capita relief expenditure which most worried contemporaries and convinced them that reform of the relief system might restore social stability by disciplining an increasingly unruly agricultural labour force.[38] Assertions by labourers that they had a right to an 'adequate' or 'fair' subsistence caused particular alarm. It was a point emphasised (by Edwin Chadwick) in the Poor Law Report of 1834.[39] Poor Law reform seemed a way of preventing further outbreaks of rural unrest. According to Dunkley it was the 'prevailing sense of urgency and impending disaster' which provided the 'ground swell of support that greeted the New Poor Law'.[40]

In the wake of the Swing riots, which had been harshly punished with imprisonments, executions and transportations, and immediately following the passage of the momentous Parliamentary Reform Bill of 1832, the reforming Whig ministry of Earl Grey appointed a Royal Commission for Inquiring into the Administration and Practical Operation of the Poor Laws. Two years later, the widely read Report of the Poor Law Commission won Parliament's approval and was the inspiration behind the New Poor Law of 1834. The New Poor Law was one of several political and social reforms which, over a seven-year period in the 1830s, expanded central government responsibility in various fields such as factories, police and education, as well as poor relief. However, local government did not become subordinated to a centralised state. Utilitarian notions of rational centralised administration superseding management by local community elites were repeatedly thwarted in the 1830s to 1850s. The administrative structure of the New Poor Law is the prime example of the nineteenth-century tendency to devise corporate structures on the basis of a partnership between local and central.

The Royal Commission of 1832–34 comprised nine men, supported by 26 assistant commissioners. The Royal Commission's researches depended jointly on the local investigations and reports of the assistant commissioners, plus the return of questionnaires sent out to parish officials. Of the questionnaires, only 10 per cent were returned, although this amounted to a mass of evidence. However, despite the apparent empiricism of the Inquiry, the Report made only selective and anecdotal use of its evidence (Blaug dubbed it 'wildly unstatistical'). Most historians believe this was because the outcome was preconceived and the particular shape of the reform was decided early on in the Commission's enquiry. It was Nassau Senior, the Oxford Professor of Political Economy, and Edwin Chadwick, Bentham's former secretary and protégé, who between them wrote the Poor Law Report produced in 1834. Benthamite influence on the Report is inescapable, at least in the broad sense of utilitarian ideas about achieving the 'greatest happiness of the greatest number' through the laying down of general rules and administrative structures for their implementation. Moreover, the hedonistic view of human nature implicit in Benthamism (seeking pleasure and shunning pain) could be said to be at work in the principles of the New Poor Law. More specifically, it is claimed that the shape of the reform in 1834 closely resembled Bentham's own

Pauper Plan of the 1790s, even to the use of the term 'less eligibility'. None of this came about because Bentham's ideas were widely known, for they were not, but because his influence worked through the individuals on the Commission. But the Webbs's claim about Benthamite personnel among the Commissioners and Assistant Commissioners is counterbalanced by Mandler's allegation that at least as many were 'Christian Economists'. In any case, given the common ground between both groups: 'it is not surprising that both the diagnosis of and remedies for the Old Poor Law's ills were agreed upon within six months of the Commission's appointment.'[41]

The Poor Law Report of 1834 is a consistent polemic against the out-relief of the able-bodied male. It pays scant attention to other categories – the sick, the elderly, children, and so on. However, rather than the pessimism of the Malthusians, the Report expresses an optimism about the possibilities of reforming the system to achieve the same ends. None the less, much of its rhetoric would have been familiar to those who had read the critical literature on the Poor Laws. For example, the Report is at pains to draw a distinction between poverty and pauperism. Poor relief was to be confined to the 'indigent', it was not to apply to the merely poor, that is, those forced to labour for their subsistence. Thus any benefits paid to those in work were to cease. Indeed, it was to reinforce the necessity to labour in any job at any wage that this distinction between the employed and the unemployed was drawn so clearly and the other principles of the Report follow from it. By such means it was believed paupers would be transformed into independent labourers, surplus labour in the South would be dispersed and a national free market in labour would be encouraged.

The Report endorses much of the Malthusian critique, but the case for abolition is rejected since the 'evils . . . connected with the relief of the able-bodied' were not 'necessarily incidental to the compulsory relief of the able-bodied . . . under strict regulations, adequately enforced, such relief may be afforded safely and even beneficially'. Thus the relief of the unemployed was to be allowed but only 'under strict regulations'. Conditions were to be imposed on the receipt of relief, the chief of which was that it should not contravene the principle of 'less eligibility': that the 'situation' of the pauper 'on the whole shall not be made really or apparently so eligible as the situation of the independent labourer of the lowest class'.[42]

This desire to restore a differential between benefit and employment was hardly new, nor was the mechanism by which it was to be achieved, although the completeness of the system was entirely novel. There was to be a sharp line drawn between the type of relief available to the impotent and that offered the able-bodied male. Whilst out-relief would continue to be given to the former, the only relief to be offered the latter was entry to a 'well-regulated' workhouse. In order to enforce 'less eligibility', conditions in the 'well-regulated' workhouse would, of necessity, have to be a less acceptable alternative to seeking work at the wages and conditions available to 'the independent labourer of the lowest class'. It would perforce need to be a repellent institution, designed to deter all but the most necessitous from applying for relief. However, it was not through poor food or harsh living conditions in the workhouse that the principle of less eligibility should be enforced, but through hard labour and 'strict discipline' which would be 'intolerable to the indolent and disorderly'.[43] The offer of the well-regulated workhouse as the only legal relief of the able-bodied was conceived as a self-acting test of an applicant's destitution, in true utilitarian terms, aligning the self-interest of freely choosing individuals with the greater happiness of society as a whole. There was a clear target for the Report's remedies. The Report constantly returns to the able-bodied male with a family, just the class of person they believed had become dependent upon the allowance system. Thus, except for medical attendance: 'all relief whatever to able-bodied persons or to their families otherwise than in well-regulated workhouses . . . shall be declared unlawful . . . and all relief afforded in respect of children under the age of 16 shall be considered as afforded to their parents.'[44]

In addition to its key principles, the Report outlined an administrative machinery for enforcing the new system. A Central Board was recommended 'to control the administration of the Poor Laws', supported by assistant commissioners who would 'frame and enforce' workhouse regulations for the whole country. Parishes should be grouped together for the purpose of workhouse construction.[45] It was intended that this should be a national and a uniform system, but the degree of centralisation only went so far. Only minor amendments were suggested to the system of rating. The funding and day-to-day running of poor relief was to stay in local hands, this was a much less centrally run proposal than that of a regime run directly by paid inspectors, which Nassau Senior had started out with and been forced to abandon as too extreme.[46] The Report, moreover, was not a complete overhaul of poor relief. The sense of crisis in which it operated, and the obsession with the able-bodied it demonstrated, marginalised other areas of reform. Apart from some minor proposals on the law of settlement and bastardy legislation, there were no further recommendations of substance. The impact of the Report may have been heightened by this very clarity of purpose. Its message was clear and simple on the relief of the able-bodied and unlikely to be obscured by controversy over other reform proposals that might arouse opposition in themselves.[47]

Implementing the New Poor Law

The 1834 Poor Law Amendment Act set up the machinery to implement the Report's key principles of reform. A three-man Poor Law Commission, independent of Parliament, was authorised to issue orders and regulations on relief practice to boards of guardians. But the powers of the Poor Law Commissioners were only sanctioned for a period of five years and parliament was to receive an annual report on the working of the new system. The 15 000 parishes of England and Wales were to be grouped together into some 600 Poor Law Unions. The process, which took several years to complete, was undertaken by assistant commissioners in co-operation with local employers, magistrates and landowners. The guardians succeeded the parish overseers (who none the less survived) as the central figures in the local operation of the Poor Law after 1834. Guardians were elected on a property qualification with multiple votes for the larger proprietors. The influence of the county magistrates over poor relief was considerably reduced, although they remained as *ex officio* guardians until the law was changed in 1894.

Despite the reorganisation into unions, each parish remained the place of settlement and retained responsibility for the cost of its own paupers which, until the Union Chargeability Act of 1865 spread the expense across the whole union, meant inequity in the share of the financial burden between rich and poor parishes. The administrative machinery set up in 1834 was to last, in substance at least, until the Local Government Act of 1929 abolished the boards of guardians.[48] However, the Poor Law Amendment Act did not simply translate the 1834 Report into practice. Despite the intentions of the reformers, subsequent official policy was the result of compromises between central and local interests which varied *between* regions and, as had been the case before 1834, also varied *within* regions. This does not mean there were no national trends, but that national characteristics were not to be found uniformly expressed across the country. Due to the absence of completely reliable central statistics of relief, there remains the great temptation to generalise from local studies, a common feature of Poor Law historiography.

The Poor Law Commission began its work in the mid 1830s, steadily at first, establishing the union structures and issuing orders and regulations. But the administrative history of the New Poor Law in its first 20 years is one of conflict and compromise. In part, the compromise between central and local control represented in the New Poor Law is characteristic of the approach to government responsibility in the nineteenth century. But equally, there was a mismatch between the intentions of the central authority and the interests of many localities, especially in the industrial North (the focus of an Anti-Poor Law campaign) and in Wales, but also sporadically across East Anglia, the South and the South-West. Dissent was fuelled by a diligent press campaign of Poor Law 'horror stories' in which *The Times* took the lead. In the case of a number of towns in Lancashire and the West Riding of Yorkshire, employer opposition accompanied worker hostility to the discipline of the new workhouses – the 'bastilles' – and there were several anti-Poor Law riots.

In the eyes of the working-class radicals, the New Poor Law was yet another Whig attack on the interests of labour and the campaign was one of the roots of Chartism. The resistance movement in Wales was more violent and inflamed by anti-English sentiments. This perhaps explains the lack of any links to resistance elsewhere and the confined nature of the Welsh movement. Secret meetings and attacks on workhouses under construction culminated in the Rebecca Riots of 1842–43, in which the New Poor Law was a focus of discontent.[49] Eighteen unions had failed to build workhouses 20 years after the 1834 Act, ten of which were in Wales. Even those hostile unions *with* workhouses remained objects of concern to the central authority. As late as 1858, the workhouses in Rochdale, Lancashire, were reported to be 'more in the nature of almshouses'.[50] Among the consequences of resistance of this sort was a system which, whilst centrally organised in principle, by modern standards retained great potential for local autonomy in practice. This inevitably resulted in the significant disparity in relief policy between and within regions which is at the heart of any attempt to understand the repercussions of the reform of social welfare in 1834.

Able-bodied Males

Historians are by no means in agreement about the impact of the New Poor Law, especially over the first 30 years or so of its operation. A central issue is the extent to which the reformed system was successful in achieving its primary aim, the abolition of out-relief to the able-bodied male. In particular, a series of local studies since the 1960s have apparently undermined notions about the revolutionary achievements of '1834'.[51] They have stressed the continuity between the pre- and post-1834 periods; emphasising the absence of uniformity in the New Poor Law, highlighting the range of local variation, and the continued possibility of localised interests to subvert as well as resist the orders of the central authority in London. Secondly, they have pointed to the persistence of pre-1834 practices after the mid century, including precisely those so severely criticised in the Poor Law Report. Thus despite the best intentions of the reformers, local autonomy meant the survival of out-relief. Michael Rose found the allowance system operating in the West Riding of Yorkshire and, according to G. R. Boyer, granting relief to seasonally unemployed farm labourers in the grain-producing South of England made as much economic sense after as before 1834. Moreover, even when the workhouse test was being enforced, this may have concealed relief to the unemployed masquerading as something else. Thus guardians used a variety of subterfuges to get round the new restrictions, such as funding relief to the unemployed through the highways rate not the poor rate and granting out-relief to the able-bodied under the guise of sickness benefit. According to Anne Digby, this element of continuity was 'more striking than any differences which the 1834 Act had made'.[52]

The chief dissenting voice to this new orthodoxy has been a particularly strident one. Karel Williams has castigated Rose, Digby and others for what he classes their confused understanding of the aims of 1834. Local variations cannot be regarded as sufficiently significant to undermine the central point that 'a line of exclusion was drawn against able-bodied men after 1850 . . . unemployment related relief was virtually abolished by the middle of the century'. Certainly, the official statistics support Williams's contention since those relieved as 'in want of work' soon became a tiny minority of the outdoor poor.[53] Whether this means the Poor Law Commission were successful in excluding the able-bodied male applicant depends on how widespread the various alternative devices were of relieving the unemployed, undoubtedly adopted in some areas.

The diversity of relief practice under the New Poor Law was partly a consequence of concessions over the crucial issue of out-relief to the able-bodied made in the 1840s and 1850s. General Orders prohibiting out-relief to the adult able-bodied were issued to most rural unions in the early 1840s. These were consolidated in the Outdoor Relief Prohibitory Order of 1844, which required that the able-bodied be relieved only in workhouses, with some important exceptions including 'cases of sudden and urgent necessity', and widows with dependent children. Meanwhile, in view of large-scale unemployment and opposition to the New Poor Law in the industrial districts, the Poor Law Commissioners had issued an alternative order which allowed guardians to grant relief to able-bodied men on condition they completed a task of work. This Outdoor Labour Test Order of 1842 was not a return to pre-1834 principles, although it did recognise that the 'workhouse test' was not always appropriate. It was an attempt to maintain 'less eligibility' without the workhouse; tasks were to be monotonous and hard (such as stone breaking and oakum picking) and must not interfere with the labour market.[54] None the less, it was a significant concession.

By 1847, when the Poor Law Board became the central authority, although most rural areas and southern towns outside London had been issued the more stringent 1844 Outdoor Relief Prohibitory Order, 142 unions (comprising one fifth of the total) were allowed the Outdoor Labour Test Order of 1842, either on its own or in tandem with the Prohibitory Order. Moreover, in large parts of the North and in London, as well as in surviving pre-1834 incorporations, there was no Order in force at all.[55] An attempt to restrict the forms and duration of all out-relief, the Outdoor Relief Regulation Order of August 1852, was challenged by an orchestrated campaign of protest, which caused the Board to issue a revised version of the Order in December 1852. This was another instance of the ability of local opposition to frustrate centralising ambitions. Policy was a compromise between central authority intention and the exigencies of local practice. There was no entirely consistent or uniform national Poor Law. The treatment accorded applicants might vary from area to area, and even from union to union. The Poor Law Board issued no further general orders on out-relief during the 1850s and 1860s. It was not until the 1870s that the central authority was once more to return to the workhouse test in the shape of the so-called 'crusade against out-relief'.

The perceived gap between the desire of the reformers and the reality of local practice is a commonplace of Poor Law historiography. Local studies reinforce the impression of a considerable variety of practice. However, they do not always serve to undermine the 'revolutionary' model of 1834. Whilst the researches of Digby and Rose point to continuity in relief practice, one of the most detailed local studies of the immediate post-1834 period has concluded that in rural Bedfordshire: 'the relentless reduction of relief expenditure in these years . . . had to have been achieved almost wholly at the expense of able-bodied paupers.' This 'alone precludes the possibility that social policy was worked out after 1834 within a framework of traditional assumptions and practices.' It is suggested that: 'Bedfordshire's Poor Law officials, ratepayers and common folk would have been astonished at such an idea.'[56] This is more than just another instance of conflict of interpretation between national generalisation and local exception, it supports the notion of an 'organised diversity' of practice with considerable leeway for local discretion. There are examples of over-zealous boards of guardians whose strictness had to be tempered by the central authority, as well as those where the Poor Law Commission's writ held little sway.[57] Thus although the local case study has been used to explain relief continuities, it can also illustrate the significance of 1834. However, the case for the latter lies chiefly in the downward trend of relief expenditure and relief rolls, and also on the new assumptions and attitudes represented in the reformed Poor Law.

As we have seen, the official statistics on poor relief do not allow a comparison of pre- and post-1849 figures. However, they imply a steady reduction in the ratio of paupers to population for most of the second half of the century. But the chronology of reformed practice in the decade or so following 1834 remains unclear and much depends upon comparisons of data collected in different ways. As the evidence of the struggle between the Poor Law Commission and some local boards suggests, it was a story of compromise in which regulations were adapted to local circumstances. In such a situation, and in the context of the economic crisis of the 1840s, immediate large-scale reductions in relief were less likely, although as Dunkley's study of the New Poor Law in the North East suggests, the new welfare ideology allowed a crackdown on relief rolls where this was desired.[58]

The Workhouse System

There is less disagreement amongst historians about other aspects of poor relief after 1834. Although the workhouse became a familiar feature of the New Poor Law, it only ever accommodated a minority of paupers. As before 1834, out-relief remained the central mechanism. In 1849, of the recorded relief total of over one million, 88 per cent were being assisted without entry to the workhouse. Twenty years later, in 1869, the position was similar, with 84 per cent on out-relief. Even in 1900, after a period of reducing out-relief rolls the proportion of outdoor to total paupers was as high as 73 per cent. Thus even though the mean number of indoor paupers grew steadily during the second half of the century (whilst that of the outdoor poor remained fairly constant before the 1870s, only to fall sharply thereafter), less than one person in 100 entered a workhouse at any time during 1849, a ratio which remained virtually the same at the end of the century.[59]

None of this undermines the deterrent role envisaged for the 'well-regulated workhouse' in the 1834 Report. Its purpose was to deter poor-relief applications and not to become a 'pauper palace'. However, although 'less eligibility' was mainly aimed at the able-bodied, the decision in the mid 1830s to adopt the general, mixed workhouse meant its application to all classes. Original plans for a series of specialist workhouse institutions according to the category of inmate (able-bodied, elderly, children etc.) were abandoned in preference for segregation within one workhouse building. This was one of the many battles which Chadwick lost as Secretary to the Poor Law Commission. He may have accepted this as a transitional stage towards a reformed system, but never abandoned his preference for specialised institutions. The prison-like regime of the workhouse was intended to enforce less eligibility by psychological means rather than through physical cruelty; hence the emphasis upon uniformity and discipline, the monotony of the routine, the uselessness of the task-work, and the segregation of inmates. Segregation was according to a classification of indoor paupers issued by the Poor Law Commission in 1836 and revised in 1847. There were to be seven classes divided by age and gender, and to be housed and treated separately:

1.   Aged or infirm men.
2.   Able-bodied men and youths aged over 13 years.
3.   Youths and boys aged over seven and under 13 years.

4. Aged or infirm women.
5. Able-bodied women and girls aged over 16 years.
6. Girls aged over seven and under 16 years.
7. Children aged under seven years.

'To each class shall be assigned by the board of guardians that apartment or separate building which may be best fitted for the reception of such class, and in which they shall respectively remain, without communication, unless as is hereinafter provided.'[60] This system of segregation, uniformity and discipline found expression in the model-workhouse plans the Commissioners included in their early annual reports.[61] The principle of less eligibility was embodied in the division of space within the workhouse, as well as through its controlled, mechanistic regimen. 'Receiving wards', work rooms, exercise yards, dormitories and sick wards were all to be segregated by gender and by age; only the dining hall and chapel were to be communal. Since the able-bodied adult could not be relieved without their families entering the workhouse, this meant the separation of husband and wife, parents and children. A standard daily discipline was laid down, involving ten hours' work in the summer and nine in the winter for all except the sick, the aged, the infirm and young children. Meal intervals were to be notified 'by the ringing of a bell' and to be eaten in silence.

Does the workhouse system have any broader significance? It was part of a move towards institutional treatment common to nineteenth-century Europe and America. Prisons, asylums, hospitals, schools and workhouses were all specialised institutions providing a range of regulated treatments of criminals, lunatics, the sick, children and paupers. Michel Foucault has seen the new prison system of this era as marking the transformation of punishment of the criminal from public violence to the body, to private control of the mind under a regime of constant surveillance and individual discipline. This 'strategy of domination' is seen as a model for modern society.[62] However, the workhouse was no Panopticon, despite its similarity in design to Bentham's idealised institution and to the new reformed prisons of the 1830s, like Pentonville. There were neither the arrangements nor the possibility of constant surveillance. From this point of view, the workhouse was an anonymous institution which deprived inmates both of identity and dignity. The workhouse's punitive character could be justified on moral, as well as utilitarian grounds, since each inmate had applied to enter:

workhouse paupers were not prisoners. The whole idea of the workhouse as a deterrent establishment required that as well as repelling potential applicants, experience of it should propel able-bodied inmates back into the labour market, thus the stipulation was that: 'Any pauper may quit the workhouse, upon giving the master three hours notice of his wish to do so' with the proviso that the whole family be similarly released.[63] Although there were later additions and exceptions to workhouse rules, such as provision for elderly married couples, for imbecile, fever and lying-in wards, and specialised vagrant accommodation, the system of classification and segregation introduced in 1836 remained the basis of workhouse organisation for the rest of the century.

Did workhouses conform to the rules and regulations laid down? The workhouse system was not run by a profession of workhouse administrators with standardised training and procedures, it was maintained and managed as an aspect of local government. Moreover, as with the administration of out-relief much depended upon local-central relations. The possibilities for a diversity of treatment were present regardless of central authority regulation or inspection. As with out-relief, the central authority eventually stopped trying to impose a rigidly uniform system, although they still aimed at uniform standards through lengthy correspondence with each union. These records of local-central negotiations and struggles survive in huge numbers in the Public Record Office and in county archives as a testament to the diversity of pauper experience. As Ann Crowther has observed: 'If the Commissioners' regulations were obeyed, the pauper would live in semi-penal conditions separated from his family; but his children would be educated, his diet sufficient, and his body reasonably warm and comfortable' although he would be subject to 'intolerably mean-spirited' rules. 'On the other hand, a pauper in one of the northern workhouses where the Commissioners' writ did not run, was likely to have more of the comforts dear to the poor – some liberty of movement, a more varied diet, tea (and sometimes beer), and easier access to his family and the opposite sex.' Sanitary conditions in the latter might, however, be a danger to health and life.[64]

Women

The reformers of 1834 were obsessed with male able-bodied pauperism but in reality, the adult male was the best placed to become self-reliant. The bulk of welfare dependency arose among other groups: women, children, the aged and infirm. It was these categories which dominated the relief rolls of the mid century. In what proportions were they granted poor relief? There are problems in answering this question with any degree of precision since it is difficult to disaggregate the statistical returns on poor relief into meaningful subgroups of categories relieved. However, it is a safe assumption that, across all the categories, women comprised the majority of adult recipients of poor relief, both indoor and outdoor, throughout the history of the New Poor Law. The fixation on male labourers in the 1834 Report, combined with patriarchal assumptions about the dependency of women, caused it to say little about female poverty. Welfare was conceived in family terms and assumed to be solely the husband's responsibility. The role of wives as contributors to the family income was not considered. However, if the 1834 Report gave scant regard to married women because they were classed as non-wage earning dependants of their husbands, it was even less interested in the poverty of women without men and has nothing to say about widows, deserted wives, the wives of the absentee soldier or sailor, and the like, whether with or without dependent children.

The neglect of women is all the more striking since women generally had fewer defences against poverty than men. Their more limited work opportunities and their uniformly lower wages made them more vulnerable. Moreover, women's work involved much more part-time and short-time working, and many were doing 'sweated' labour at home. Since they earned less and were more often paid irregularly, women generally could not afford the self-help strategies available to the better-off male worker. Women's vulnerability to poverty was multiplied by marriage breakdown or the death of their partner. Responsibility for children increased their burden. They lived longer than men, yet were generally less able to accumulate resources against old age. Although women developed their own survival strategies and mutual-aid networks (see Chapter 4), it is little wonder that destitute single mothers, chiefly widows and deserted wives, and elderly poor women often turned to poor relief or charity.

As the operation of the New Poor Law unfolded, its implications for women became more clear. From the outset, official policy was that the relief of a married woman was to be determined by the position of her husband. A wife had no independent status as an applicant for poor relief. If her husband entered the workhouse, she was bound to follow. She could neither leave without him nor obtain admittance on account of her own destitution. If he was classed as non-able bodied, so was she – regardless of her own physical condition.[65] The law of settlement and removal embodied women's dependent status. The law as revised in 1834 gave a married woman's settlement in her husband's place of birth. This meant that a destitute widow or a deserted wife could find herself removed to the only place legally required to consider her application for poor relief, the parish of her husband's birth. The position regarding widows with children was made clearer by legislation in 1846, forbidding removal within twelve months of the husband's death or during sickness, and allowing settlement after five years' continuous residence (shortened to three years and then one year in the 1860s).[66]

Widows with children appear as a particularly large group in the statistics of those relieved, making up between 10 and 20 per cent of the pauper total between 1849 and 1900. Even more striking, comparison with the census suggests that as many as one in three widows between the ages of 20 and 45 were assisted by the Poor Law in the 1850s and 1860s, a proportion which had fallen by the 1880s as a result of changed policies on out-relief.[67] However – as with much out-relief – the assistance widows received mostly 'consisted of meagre doles which had to be supplemented from other sources' such as charring, taking in washing or forms of 'homework'. Between 1839 and 1846, 80 per cent of widows receiving out-relief were assisted because of insufficient earnings.[68]

The Poor Law Report of 1834 was markedly unsympathetic to the position of unmarried mothers and guardians were granted no rights to pursue the father for maintenance. Moral responsibility was held to lay with the woman or her parents. Despite this, destitute unmarried mothers were relieved, although they were generally refused out-relief in preference for the workhouse. The cost of such relief to the ratepayers, plus the moral inequity involved, led to a change in the law in 1844 which allowed affiliation suits in the courts and the suing of the father by the guardians for support of both wife and child. The lowly moral status of unmarried mothers was underlined by the Poor Law Board in 1851 when it required that they do onerous task-work, such as oakum picking, rather than the domestic tasks normally assigned to female inmates.[69]

The Elderly

A significant number of the women dependent on poor relief were elderly. It has been argued by David Thomson that the English Poor Law provided the main source of financial support for the elderly poor in the 1830s and 1840s, thus continuing a long-established practice arising from the cultural expectation that children would offer only limited maintenance to their parents in old age. Accordingly, he maintains, inter-generational support for the elderly was slight and the so-called 'liable relatives clause' (the law which allowed magistrates to enforce family responsibilities to the elderly under certain circumstances) was rarely enforced until the 1870s, when state responsibility was deliberately reduced. This view and the evidence upon which it is based (law digests and the limited scope of his local studies) has been challenged by Pat Thane, who argues that co-residence, close-residence and other non-monetary forms of 'inter-generational exchange', although impossible to quantify, were much more common in the support of the elderly than Thomson allows for.[70] The Poor Law was much more a source of residual or subsidiary maintenance when family resources were inadequate or absent. Guardians were often willing to make payments to poor families so that elderly folk could be helped without the whole family becoming destitute. Moreover, she argues, only a small minority of the elderly poor received full subsistence from poor relief, most grants were small and the majority of the elderly received no assistance at all from the Poor Law. There were regional variations but, 'poor relief . . . made an important but not dominant contribution to the incomes of the aged poor; and . . . families contributed more, not necessarily in cash, than has been recognised.'[71] The official relief statistics may offer support for Thane's contention.

Although we should not underestimate the numbers of the elderly helped by state support before the 1870s, they probably did not constitute anything like a majority of the aged, even in the 1840s and 1850s. This has to be inferred, however, since it is not generally possible to determine the proportion nor, indeed, to separate out the elderly at all for most of the century. This is partly because, in itself, old age was neither clearly defined nor understood as a social problem until the end of the century. There was no fixed age at which being elderly became an entitlement for relief. Old people were relieved in large numbers because they were more likely to be destitute and incapable of support without aid rather than because of their age as such. Thus they were not separately recorded in the statistics until the 1890s. Instead, the returns combine several types of pauper into a broad classification, 'the aged and infirm'. This was the age-old category of the 'impotent' in different guise. As far as the officials were concerned, their chief characteristic was not being able-bodied: that is, those who were permanently incapacitated from obtaining paid employment, whether from old age, physical defect or chronic debility. According to the available figures, the 'aged and infirm' comprised between 42 and 49 per cent of paupers during the second half of the century.

The elderly are not entirely lost within this category, however. It is possible to determine separate figures for elderly workhouse paupers from the census returns. Thus in 1851, 19.8 per cent of the 'indoor' poor were aged 65 and over. This was only 3 per cent of the age group for the entire population. These figures rose as the century proceeded. However, most elderly paupers received out-relief and the statistics do not allow us to number these until 1890 when, in a special return (a one-day count), around 22 per cent of the combined total of indoor and outdoor paupers was 65 years and over. This was 18 per cent of the population in this age group. As one might expect, the figure was higher for those over 70, with about 23 per cent of the population of 70 years and over in receipt of poor relief. A further return in 1892 (for the Royal Commission on the Aged Poor) provides the only hard evidence on the gender of the elderly poor. It suggests that over a twelve-month period, 58 per cent of the male poor over 65 years – as opposed to only 19 per cent of female paupers in the same age group – were in the workhouse.[72] This supports contemporary impressions across the century that elderly women paupers were more likely to be self-sufficient or maintained by relatives.

The Sick and Infirm

Sickness was a major cause of applications for poor relief. Those who could not afford to buy medicines or pay for medical treatment, and were unprotected from the costs of illness by sick club membership or who were rejected as unsuitable for assistance by the voluntary charities, might become clients of state relief. The Poor Law was legally bound to provide for the destitute sick, although the practice of providing treatment may only have arisen in the later eighteenth century. There was little specific discussion of medical relief in the 1834 Poor Law Report and the growth of medical services under the New Poor Law was unplanned. Although some have seen the origins of the National Health Service in this period,[73] the treatment of illness remained subordinated to the relief of destitution (and the need to watch the rates) until the later 1860s, when some separation of function was achieved in London at least. It is impossible to determine the precise proportion of poor relief granted directly and indirectly to assist cases of illness or infirmity at this time. Ill-health was often a precipitant but unrecorded cause of destitution, as well as being directly represented in the applicant's request for assistance. Moreover, there was no uniformity in the classification of cases of sickness and a number of the sick were classed as able-bodied both inside and outside the workhouse. However, of those relieved on grounds of sickness, around two thirds were given outdoor relief, although the sick were approaching one third of the workhouse population by the 1860s.[74]

The key development in Poor Law medical provision after 1834 was the division of unions into districts and the appointment of district medical officers. In 1842, the Poor Law Commission laid down minimum qualifications for these positions, and by 1844, there were over 2800 district medical officers in England and Wales. However, the service remained parsimonious and fraught with contradiction. The medical officers were paid very little and doctors were only willing to compete for the posts because their profession was overstocked and income had to be sought from a variety of sources. Parish work supplemented the fees of private patients. However, it was lowly work and the guardians generally regarded their medical officers as servants. They were paid little and were often obliged to provide medicines out of their own pockets. In addition, the prime rationale of medical relief remained the relief of destitution, it was not conceived as a health service. Hence the decision about whether an applicant for out-relief needed medical attention was generally made by the union's relieving officer and not its medical officer. It was, not surprisingly, a constant source of friction between doctors and guardians.[75]

The cost of relieving the sick poor was a small proportion of the whole relief bill. In a total expenditure of £4.5 million in 1840, only £150 000 went on medical relief. The situation had improved little by

1871, when medical relief accounted for a mere £300 000 out of a total of nearly £8 million.[76] It was not only the parsimony of boards of guardians, fearful of the expense to which medical care led, that retarded provision, but a prevalent assumption that therapeutic treatment was of little use and not worth the money. This reflected the belief that sanitary reform was more effective against disease; a not unreasonable supposition given the state of medical knowledge at the time. Most workhouses had sick wards. However, the doctors' only assistants were the pauper nurses; often elderly women rewarded with extra rations for their services, they were the mainstay of workhouse nursing. The central authority resisted the employment of professional nurses until the 1850s, but the newly trained nursing profession, for which Florence Nightingale was mostly responsible, was always poorly represented in the Victorian workhouse.

Children

If the medical services of the New Poor Law developed largely without the encouragement of central authority officials, the opposite is the case with the education of pauper children. This was one of the earliest examples of specialist provision within the workhouse system. The 1834 Report had assumed that workhouse children would be educated so as to render them 'industrious and valuable members of the community'. Accordingly, the Poor Law Commission included in its workhouse rules the stipulation that children were to be instructed for at least three hours a day: 'in reading, writing and the principles of the Christian religion; and such other instructions . . . as are calculated to train them to habits of usefulness, industry and virtue'.[77] The schooling of paupers required some justification. Apart from the army and prison, the workhouse school was the only direct incursion of the British state into the education of its citizens before the Education Act of 1870.

The main protagonist of workhouse education was the assistant commissioner, James Phillips Kay (later Sir James Kay-Shuttleworth), fourth annual report of the Poor Law Commissioners in 1839. Kay maintained that workhouse children (especially those orphan or deserted children for whom the guardians acted *in loco parentis*) had a claim 'not for food and clothing merely, but for that moral sustenance which may enable them . . . to attain independence'. He wished to exclude them from the rigours of less eligibility on the grounds that they were there 'not as a consequence of their errors but of their misfortunes'. Whilst their physical condition should not be elevated above that of the 'self-supported labourer', it was rational to regard education 'as one of the most important means of eradicating the germs of pauperism from the rising generation, and of securing in the minds and in the morals of the people the best protection for the institutions of society'. The education Kay advocated was to focus on industrial training, plus the kind of intellectual and moral curriculum found in voluntary schools. The value of this seemed self-evident: 'the duty of rearing these children in religion and industry, and of imparting to them such an amount of secular knowledge as may fit them to discharge the duties of their station, cannot be doubted.'[78]

Kay's preference was for large district schools serving several unions, but in practice few of these were built (those at Swinton in Manchester and Kirkdale in Liverpool were well-publicised examples outside London) due partly to limits imposed on size and costs, but also to political fears about ceding too much power to the central body. When the Poor Law Commission fell in 1847, a District Schools Act led to the formation of six more schools, but enthusiasm for the idea had waned and only a further three were established throughout the rest of the century. None the less, pauper education was on the agenda and its rationale of reducing pauperism in the next generation, linked to a cheaper welfare system and the prospect of social stability, was attractive to the propertied classes. The interest of historians in the arguments of those, like Kay, who advocated educational reform as a means of 'social control' is understandable and it is useful to set the Poor Law into a broader 'discourse of moral regulation' which emerged in the 1830s. However, the district-school principle became discredited, earning the epithet 'barrack school' for its regimented discipline and narrow curriculum. In any case the total numbers involved were small.[79]

More common was the individual workhouse school. Kay had the long-stay workhouse child in mind, especially those who were orphaned or deserted, but the 'ins and outs' (children in the workhouse with their destitute parents for short but often repeated stays) could be significant and often fluctuated with the pattern of seasonal employment. For example, Worcester workhouse had only 45 child inmates in June 1845 compared with 133 in March 1847.[80] Moreover, the workhouses continued to deal with pauper children in traditional ways. The most notable example was the practice of apprenticing children to outside employers (the fate of Oliver Twist), often at around nine or ten years of age. Placements were appropriate to pauper status. In Norwich, 80 per cent of the boys apprenticed between 1834 and 1863 had gone into shoe-making. Girls most commonly entered the lowest echelons of domestic service. Of those who took workhouse girls as servants in Rochdale between 1851 and 1870, and whose occupations are known, over half were manual workers.[81]

We know considerably less about the circumstances of the vast numbers of pauper children who were listed among those on out-relief. As a whole, children comprised between 30 and 40 per cent of total pauperism from the mid century onwards. Of these, the workhouse children were easily outnumbered by those relieved outdoors: in 1851, by a ratio of more than six to one. The child on outdoor relief remains obscure to us. The statistics cover a diversity of circumstances and conditions. Unlike their workhouse counterparts, they had little chance of receiving an education. Guardians routinely enquired of adult applicants if they had children of working age (nine or ten). However, some paid the 'school pence' of the outdoor poor. In 1855 this practice was legalised and, in 1876, was made a statutory requirement to assimilate the pauper child into the rate-aided elementary system. Even before this, an increasing number of outdoor pauper children attended some sort of school, by 1869 the national average was as high as 69 per cent.[82]

Between 1834 and 1860, the Poor Law had done little to step beyond its appointed task of reducing pauperism. Even the deliberate eschewing of 'less eligibility' in some aspects of the treatment of children had the long-term objective of 'dispauperisation'. The medical service for the sick poor was parsimonious and meagre, even by the standards of the day. But as a mechanism for deterring able-bodied males from relief applications, the medicine of the New Poor Law may well have proved an effective remedy by the 1850s. To many, the new system seemed to be working well. However, the economic and social character of the country was changing rapidly. The rural world of 1834 was vanishing. During the second half of the nineteenth century, urban growth and the decline of agricultural occupations was creating a new environment of poverty. Moreover, the return of unrest and disorder in the 1860s and after made the Poor Law seem less than successful. Removing pauperism was not the same as reducing poverty. However, the challenges facing the official relief system were complex. On the one hand, in the face of disquiet amongst medical professionals and campaigners about care of the sick poor, provision became more expansive and even aimed to provide a service for the working classes as a whole. Whilst, on the other hand, a key response to unrest and fears about the 'outcast' of the cities meant that relief options for many applicants actually got worse as the century progressed.

Later Victorian Poor Law

Crisis of the 1860s

Enthusiasm for the principles of the 1834 Poor Law was a feature of mid-nineteenth-century liberalism. Individual property rights, limited government, free trade and faith in the moral superiority of self-reliance over community responsibility were among its key features. Applauding the New Poor Law's mixture of local and central management, John Stuart Mill, the leading intellectual of the liberal state, believed it 'almost theoretically perfect'. The moral lessons it taught were the key to the future progress of the working classes, not simply by enabling some to rise above their station but, by its encouragement of the 'virtues of independence', it was a mechanism for 'raising the class itself in physical well-being and in self-estimation'.[83]

Optimism that 1834 had seen a final settlement of the pauper problem remained strong in the early 1860s. Yet opinion was about to change. Henry Fawcett, justifiably regarded as Mill's disciple, shared his optimism, declaring in the second edition of his *Manual of Political Economy* in 1865 that: 'The present poor law will probably remain permanent with few alterations . . . on the whole, it seems difficult to devise a better system of poor relief.'[84] However, in his 1870 lectures on pauperism, Fawcett was much more pessimistic. He did not doubt the principles of 1834, but attacked a 'leniency and want of firmness' in enforcing them, pointing to the predominance of out-relief over the workhouse and blaming 'false economy' or 'a mistaken kindness' which sentimentalised the poor. By then, Fawcett feared a return to the mass pauperism of the Old Poor Law. Rather than advancing as Mill had hoped, the working classes seemed just as imprudent as Malthus had found them. In fact: 'our existing Poor Law so powerfully encourages improvidence that until there is a radical change in the present method of administering relief, it is hopeless to expect any very general diffusion of prudence.'[85] This view was echoed by other classical economists such as Henry Sidgewick, who argued that even the prospect of the workhouse weakened 'the inducements to labour, forethought and thrift'. Indeed, the state organisation of charity might be preferable to 'the discouragement to thrift which . . . legally secured relief entails'.[86] What had happened in the 1860s to bring about this questioning of relief administration and revival of the Malthusian dictum that poor laws 'create the distresses which they seek to alleviate'?[87]

The 1860s can be justifiably seen as a watershed in the relief of poverty in a number of ways.[88] In particular, a sense of urban crisis emerged in this decade which provided the inescapable backdrop to most discussion of society's response to poverty for the rest of the century. It focused initially on the effectiveness of the Poor Law in dealing with its original target, the able-bodied, and resurrected anxieties about under-employment and the ability of the market to absorb surplus labour. This emerged most conspicuously in a series of relief crises in London during the winters of 1860–61, 1867–68 and 1868–69, when the casual and seasonal workers of London's East End were hit very hard by depressions in trade. Poor-relief applications soared and the union offices of the poorer districts were besieged with claimants. There was disorder and looting which went 'to the very verge of bread riots' and, in the face of overstretched state welfare, an outpouring of alms which critics regarded as 'swamping' the East End with 'indiscriminate charity'. Through it all, there emerged a spectre of an 'outcast London', immune to the rigours of self-help and living in a demoralised state, often in unimaginable poverty. The journalist, John Hollingshead, writing in January 1861, conveys the sense of alarm:

> The chief streets of the metropolis have been haunted for weeks by gaunt labourers . . . . The workhouses have been daily besieged by noisy and half-famished crowds; the clumsy poor-law system has notoriously broken down; . . . and all the varied machinery of British charity, have been strained to the utmost . . . either inadequate for the purposes to which it has been applied, or applied in the most wasteful and unskilful manner . . . . The metropolis, not to speak of other towns, is not 'managed', not cleansed, not relieved from the spectre of starvation which dances before us at our doors. We are evidently surrounded by a dense population, half buried in black kitchens

and sewer-like courts and alleys, who are not raised by any real or fancied advance in wages; whose way of life is steeped in ignorance, dirt and crime; and who are always ready to sink, even to death, at their usual period of want.[89]

The London relief crises of the 1860s had repercussions, both for public and private welfare, lasting the remainder of the century. The Poor Law was criticised for being too lenient and too expensive. Along with indiscriminate charity, it was blamed for an apparently widening gulf between the social classes. Moreover, competition between charity and the Poor Law to meet the demand for relief was said to be undermining the distinction between the deserving and the undeserving. Criticisms of relief administration were to lead to new policies in the 1870s which dramatically cut the numbers on out-relief. Anxiety about the 'deformation of the gift' led to a resurgence of 'organised charity', chiefly in the shape of the Charity Organisation Society. The economic context of these policy developments was the existence in London and most major cities of a pool of unskilled casual labour, living precariously on the margins of the labour market, growing in numbers and the first to apply for charity and poor relief at times of trade depression. Such under-employment was little understood by economists until the end of the century, and the tendency was to blame the 'irregular habits' of the casual worker for his poverty rather than the operation of the casual-labour market itself.[90]

However, the greatest single economic crisis of the 1860s, the Lancashire Cotton Famine, was an exceptional event, resulting from the curtailing of raw cotton supplies during the American Civil War and the laying-off of tens of thousands of cotton operatives. It proved once and for all that the Poor Law was inadequate to deal with the mass unemployment of the industrial economy. Applications for relief in the cotton districts reached a peak of over 270 000 in December 1862, a rise of 300 per cent over a normal year. Poor rates escalated from one shilling in the pound to more than ten shillings. As in London, charity stepped into the breach, although this time better organised, co-ordinating funds through a Central Relief Committee. But, again, neither Poor Law nor charity could cope with the crisis. The magnitude of the problem triggered government action in the shape of the Public Works (Manufacturing Districts) Act of 1863, providing cheap loans for local authorities to employ the laid-off factory workers in road digging and the like. An important conclusion which contemporaries drew from these twin relief crises of the 1860s was a presumed distinction between the 'deserving' Lancashire operative and the 'undeserving' denizen of London's slums. The former were regarded as the victims of events beyond their control – the 'involuntary poor' – whilst the latter were the architects of their own fate. These 'voluntary poor', were also the 'clever paupers', who exploited the charitable, defrauded the relief system and, through their pernicious example, threatened to demoralise the honest working class. The benevolent were said to 'stand aghast at the Pauper Frankenstein they had created'.[91]

During the later nineteenth century, there were to be several attempts to draw a distinction between the deserving and the undeserving, however defined, in the forms and availability of both public and private relief. This found expression in a readiness to reform and restructure the Poor Law to make it more discriminating; the acceptance of certain classes of indoor poor as deserving and the provision of better treatment for them (the sick, children and the aged); and attempts to encourage the use of mechanisms other than poor relief for a privileged section of the able-bodied. In all this, the Poor Law remained the central element in Victorian social policy.

The Crusade against Out-Relief

By the end of the 1860s, the central Poor Law authority had become alarmed. Rising national expenditure levels reinforced anxieties about the 'deformation of the gift' in London's East End. George Goschen, last president of the Poor Law Board, set the tone. In 1869, he issued a Minute to guardians in the capital, urging a division of responsibilities between the Poor Law and charity which would avoid the duplication of relief. Encouraged by the formation of the Charity Organisation Society (COS) in the same year and the hope of more efficient and discriminating voluntary giving, the intention was to encourage guardians and charitable societies to co-operate so as to confine poor relief to the truly destitute, whilst achieving a more discriminating charitable aid for the deserving:

> . . . the Poor Law authorities could not be allowed without public danger to extend their operations beyond those persons who are actually destitute, and for whom they are at present legally bound to provide. It would seem to

follow that charitable organisations, whose alms could in no case be claimed as a right, would find their most appropriate sphere in assisting those who have some, but insufficient means, and who, though on the verge of pauperism, are not actual paupers, leaving to the operation of the general law the provision for the totally destitute.[92]

In his report for 1870, Goschen focused on expenditure. Comparing the decades 1850–59 and 1860–69, he noted that average annual expenditure had risen by 12 per cent more than the increase in the number of paupers. Out-relief, absorbing around half of total expenditure in the 1860s, offered the chief prospect for economies.[93]

If out-relief rolls were to be reduced this was bound to affect women since they were the major beneficiaries. The Goschen Minute had specifically mentioned the case of widows and the point was pressed home in the stern tones of the circular on out-relief issued by the newly created Local Government Board in December 1871. This roundly condemned 'a too lax or indiscriminate system of administration'. Guardians were especially discouraged from giving relief outside the workhouse to able-bodied women, as well as men. Thus began the so-called 'crusade against out-relief'.[94] The objective was to enforce the workhouse test, which had officially applied to able-bodied males since the relief orders of the 1840s, for the first time to women claimants. However, it was also an attempt to indirectly influence the behaviour of men by reducing the relief options of their wives and children.[95] Thus the principal targets were wives of able-bodied men, single women without children (including widows), deserted wives, and wives with husbands in prison or the armed forces. The exclusion extended to outdoor medical relief, but although this was never specifically proscribed, it lessened in quantity and quality as part of a general contraction of domiciliary assistance. Applicants were to be encouraged to seek help from family and the 'liable relatives clause' was more often enforced.[96] The 'crusade' was remarkably successful in reducing out-relief rolls. In just five years between 1871 and 1876, despite rising population figures, the number of outdoor paupers fell by a third from 843 000 to 567 000, reducing the proportion of the total population drawing out-relief from 3.8 per cent to 2.4 per cent.[97]

In pursuing its policy against out-relief in the 1870s and 1880s, the Local Government Board relied on Circulars giving advice (albeit firmly pressed), and pressure on individual unions from the Poor Law inspectors, rather than on Orders issuing regulations as the Poor Law

Commission had done, to its cost, in the 1840s and early 1850s. For example, it recommended the adoption of particular out-relief codes, such as that devised by the Manchester guardians in 1875, and encouraged co-operation between guardians and the COS, although this was rarely achieved.[98] In some urban unions, the 'crusade' was embraced with great enthusiasm and the reduction in out-relief numbers could be striking. For instance, in Southampton the numbers of able-bodied females granted out-relief fell from around 1000 in 1871 to a mere 180 in 1881. However, it was not just women who were targeted. There was a general tightening of the conditions on which all out-relief was granted. Thus, whilst in Southampton an average of 550 able-bodied males had received out-relief half-yearly between 1863 and 1871, in the 1880s the number fell sharply to less than 50.[99]

The restriction of out-relief in the 1870s was conceived by the central authority and the inspectorate as a strategy to devise different policies for the deserving and the undeserving. This is clearest in Henry Longley's report on out-relief in London, and guardians were generally encouraged to make moral criteria more explicit in their relief decisions. It became common for unions to refuse out-relief on grounds of 'bad character' or 'improvidence'. In Birmingham during 1884, the first year in which the guardians operated a restrictive policy, of the 200 or so women whose relief was either removed altogether, or who were offered indoor instead of outdoor relief, approaching a third were refused on moral grounds such as drunkenness, having illegitimate children or living in 'filthy homes'. In Manchester and district, out-relief was denied on grounds of 'drunken or immoral habits' and destitution caused by 'improvidence'. There were also restrictions on residential grounds. Applicants from neighbourhoods with a bad reputation would be unlikely to be successful. Of course, such assessments were inevitably impressionistic, there could be no precise measure of 'respectability'. However, to enforce such decisions involved closer supervision of out-relief applicants by the relieving officers and occasionally by COS members on boards of guardians, although the active involvement of the latter was sporadic outside a few East End unions. Equally, there is evidence that whilst out-relief numbers were reduced, this might be complemented, as in Southampton, by higher grants for those who were considered deserving of the privilege of domiciliary assistance. This was the more selective and yet 'adequate' relief called for in the Goschen Minute and by the Charity Organisation Society.[100]

How uniform was the 'crusade against out-relief'? Although uniformity of practice across all unions was very unlikely, a large number of predominantly urban unions successfully reduced out-relief expenditures over a 20-year period between the 1870s and the 1890s. Why did its appeal to guardians and ratepayers extend beyond London, where the alarm about 'indiscriminate relief' originated? The crusade was strongest in the larger cities, precisely those areas where out-relief rolls had risen fastest in the 1860s and where the problems of the casual-labour market were most in evidence. Did these places take up the idea, promulgated by the Local Government Board and the COS, that out-relief should be used as a means of influencing working-class morals? The evidence cited above of particular penalties against 'improvidence', and so on, would suggest that this was the case. But Mary Mackinnon has argued that the generality of the policy suggests other more mundane motives. Chief amongst these was the desire to save money by reducing out-relief costs. This was made acute by changes in the rating system in the early 1860s, culminating in the Union Chargeability Act of 1865. This made the whole union rather than individual parishes responsible for the costs of poor relief, which was now apportioned on the basis of the rateable value per parish. These reforms are usually credited with giving unions a stronger financial base which, along with improved borrowing arrangements in 1869, facilitated an improvement in institutional provision in the later nineteenth century. This is often seen as the corollary of the crusade against out-relief. Mackinnon claims that whilst this was so, it also encouraged wealthier parishes to favour cost-cutting policies as they were unwilling to bear the cost of out-relief to the poor of other parishes.[101]

Whatever the rationale of the 'crusade', the consequence for all categories of the poor was that outdoor assistance became much less likely from the 1870s, especially in urban areas. In extreme cases, out-relief virtually disappeared, as in the East End union of St George's under the guidance of Augustus George Crowder, COS 'zealot' and dominant figure on the board of guardians from 1875 till 1911. Crowder was convinced that the policy had been a lesson in self-reliance. Looking back in 1909 he commented: 'the people have been systematically taught for many years by the practical abolition of outdoor relief not to look to the parish but to provide for themselves; hence in ordinary times applications for outdoor relief are rarely made.'[102] But the crusade did not solve the problems of poverty, it merely restricted the palliative of out-relief as all categories found outdoor assistance less easy to obtain. The denial of the supplement of out-relief damaged the 'economy of makeshifts' and forced the poor into even greater reliance upon other resources. With a tendency to penalise relief applications from neighbourhoods with a 'bad reputation', it would not be surprising if survival strategies, such as the women's mutual-aid networks discussed in Chapter 4, assumed an even greater importance. Equally, we might expect to find voluntary charities compensating for the out-relief cutbacks. Although, charity was never as 'indiscriminate' as the COS and other critics believed, there is strong evidence from some quarters that, from the 1870s to the 1890s, charitable resources played an increasingly important role in relieving categories of the poor, who would otherwise have applied to the guardians and ended up in the workhouse. This was even the case with able-bodied adult males, who found that applications for relief might be met with the offer of confinement in a designated 'test workhouse', set aside exclusively for the able-bodied (a separate, prison-like institution favoured by the inspectors, but introduced in only a handful of urban unions). Innumerable soup kitchens, shelters and refuges sprang up offering cheap or free assistance to the unemployed and homeless who preferred sleeping rough to the full rigours of the workhouse test.[103]

A Public Hospital System?

The 1860s also marked a significant watershed in the Poor Law medical service following a series of workhouse-infirmary scandals. Although the chief impact was confined to London, it marked a transition from the narrowly based parsimony of 1834, and held out the prospect of publicly funded hospitals for all the working class rather than merely beds for sick paupers. At a time of increasing confidence in the efficacy of medical treatment, the Poor Law was found wanting. The campaigns of the likes of Louisa Twining and the Workhouse Visiting Society, which had highlighted the inadequacies of the care of sick paupers, in the mid 1860s found support from the male establishment in the shape of investigations into the state of London's workhouses by the medical journal, the *Lancet*, and by an enquiry into provincial conditions conducted by inspectors of the Poor Law Board itself. Both were critical of the indoor medical service resulting largely from the lack of classification in the general mixed workhouse. Investigators reported widespread overcrowding, inadequate sanitation, little separation of cases (including those with infectious diseases), a paucity of qualified medical staff and a reliance on pauper nurses.[104] The *Lancet* report was followed by a concerted campaign of public agitation, chiefly organised by a newly formed Association for the Improvement of the London Workhouse Infirmaries (membership included Sir Thomas Watson, President of the Royal College of Physicians, Charles Dickens and John Stuart Mill).

The exposure to public criticism had an immediate effect, at least in terms of the capital's Poor Law system, in the shape of the Metropolitan Poor Act of 1867. Passed as an epidemic of scarlet fever swept across London, the first priority was the creation of isolation hospitals. But this was to be part of a broader attempt at classification and separate treatment in the state's care of the sick (and later across the whole workhouse system). In order to achieve this, the capital was to have a combination of hospitals and dispensaries separate from the workhouse. A Metropolitan Asylums Board, comprised of guardians and officials, was established as the managing authority for the treatment of typhus, smallpox and insanity, across the whole of 'greater' London. The cost was to be borne by a Metropolitan Common Poor Fund, financed by the unions according to their rateable value (not the number of their paupers). For other elements of medical relief, the unions were assembled in asylum districts to supply separate Poor Law hospitals for the non-infectious sick. The Poor Law Amendment Act of 1868 empowered provincial unions to provide separate infirmaries, but there was no financial stimulus as with the Metropolitan Common Poor Fund.

Publicly-funded hospitals amounted to the development of 'personal health services' for the poor without the stigma of pauperism. Even before the emergence of a working-class male electorate with the parliamentary reform acts of 1867 and 1884, it was becoming more difficult to sustain the principle of 'less eligibility' in the treatment of illness, but the Medical Relief (Disqualifications' Removal) Act of 1885 finally severed the legal connection between medical relief and pauperism by which, previously, the recipient had lost his voting rights (receipt of all other forms of poor relief still incurred this disqualification). This alone contributed much to the idea of social services provided by the state rather than exclusively for the pauper, and recognised the fact that, for the majority of the working class, the workhouse was the chief source of hospital care.[105] However, in reality, the transition across the country from workhouse sick ward to public hospital was limited. Although much was achieved in London, outside the capital there were only a dozen or so separate workhouse infirmaries by the 1890s. Despite the fact that approaching half the Poor Law unions had built infirmary blocks, only a small percentage were separately managed as hospitals. Only 17 per cent of beds in Poor Law institutions were in separate infirmaries by 1891,[106] and they were concentrated in the larger towns and cities. Some of them had been pioneering in the field of hospital design. The workhouse infirmaries in Manchester, built in the 1860s and 1870s on the pavilion system at Chorlton and Crumpsall, were considered models of their type.[107] It was the 20 years after 1891 which witnessed a greater period of expansion, with a third of beds in separate infirmaries by 1911. Even so, the persistence of the 'general mixed workhouse' as an impediment to classification and treatment, especially in rural areas, was a major point of criticism in the reports of the Royal Commission on the Poor Laws as late as 1909.

The principle behind the expansion in the workhouse hospital system was the recognition that much pauperism was not merely a question of individual responsibility and therefore should not be subject to the strictures of 'less eligibility'. This was evident by the 1860s. However, the decision to pursue this principle, largely through the institutional mechanism, was encouraged by increased hostility towards out-relief after 1870. Although there was no general order condemning it, domiciliary medical assistance was a casualty of the crusade against out-relief. The trend towards institutional treatment stifled attempts in the late 1860s to develop a network of free medical dispensaries in London and the provinces. However, the sea change in official opinion and the new hostility to most forms of out-relief by the mid 1870s, although it did not destroy the vision of a non-pauperising medical service, did ensure that the dispensary system was not to be its vehicle. Rather than rise with population, the number of dispensary orders fell steadily from 144 676 in 1873 to 102 470 in 1900. The opportunity for a network of state-funded outpatient clinics was lost and the Poor Law concentrated its resources into hospital provision. It was not that there was no need for a local dispensing service – provident dispensaries and other sick clubs continued to expand. However, with few exceptions those unable to contribute were excluded. This meant that free medical care was most frequently hospital care.[108]

From Deterrent Workhouse to Specialist Social Services?

Increasing specialisation within the workhouse system, at least in the larger urban areas, was a return to Chadwick's vision from the 1830s of a range of designated buildings for the sick, the aged, children, the insane and for the able-bodied. Hence from the 1860s, the central authority officials urged guardians to classify inmates more clearly, and to distinguish in treatment and diet between them on grounds of the causes of their poverty and assessments of their character. The result was a sharp increase in expenditure on workhouse construction which was maintained through to 1914, the decade of greatest outlay being the 1890s. Whilst up to the 1860s, the greater cost had been the construction of new workhouses, from the 1870s, most money went into additional blocks at existing workhouses. Specialised accommodation was authorised in a number of categories, chiefly infirmaries for the sick, but also casual wards for vagrants, homes for deserving children, segregated blocks for imbeciles, and separate accommodation for married couples and the elderly.[109]

The building of separate blocks, generally on the same site, allowed for sharper distinctions within the workhouse between the treatment of the deserving and the undeserving. This is amply illustrated by the different approaches adopted with regard to one of the largest groups of inmates, the aged, and one of the smallest, the vagrant. For the latter, there was an increasingly harsh policy as the century progressed. The construction of separate casual wards had been official policy since the 1840s. Their deterrent nature was intended to drive a wedge between the travelling artisan and the professional tramp. Onerous task-work, humiliating induction procedures, a meagre diet, and deliberately cramped and spartan sleeping accommodation made the casual ward the resort of the desperate or unimaginative. Legislation in 1871 (Pauper Inmates Discharge and Regulation Act) and 1882 (Casual Poor Act) increased the powers of guardians to detain casuals (pauper vagrants) for longer periods. This segregation for punishment inevitably deterred the vagrant, but did not remove the problem of vagrancy. Men genuinely in search of work were discharged from the casual wards too late in the day to find employment. Consequently, the vast majority of homeless wayfarers took refuge in dosshouses, charitable shelters and even preferred sleeping rough to a night in the casual ward. Despite attempts to assist the genuine traveller through a variety of 'way ticket' procedures and, by the 1890s, earlier release times, never more than a small minority of vagrants sought refuge in the workhouse and vagrants constituted less than 1 per cent of all paupers for all but six of the years between 1849 and 1900.[110]

By contrast the treatment of the elderly pauper became more generous, although only as the century drew to a close. The treatment of the elderly at the hands of the Poor Law may have actually deteriorated in the 1870s and 1880s as more were refused out-relief. This forced many into the workhouse and around a third of all indoor paupers were aged 65 or over by the 1890s, although percentages were highest in the big cities and lowest in the country districts. By this time, old age was becoming recognised as one of the single most significant causes of poverty and Charles Booth and others were conducting a campaign for an old-age pension. The Royal Commission on the Aged Poor reported in 1895 and the Select Committee on the Aged Deserving Poor in 1899. In this climate, the Local Government Board recommended a return to out-relief, where relevant, and an increase in the 'privileges' and 'comforts' of the elderly within the workhouse. These included wearing their own clothes rather than the pauper uniform, a preferential diet and additional rations of tobacco, tea and sugar. Separate sleeping accommodation and day rooms were to be provided and the daily routine relaxed for the elderly. Thus it took until the very end of the century for improvements in the condition of indoor paupers to become official policy and for the notion of 'less eligibility' to be superseded, at least as official policy. In many rural unions, there was little change in the workhouse experience for the elderly inmate. The notion of specialist social services for old age was still a thing of the future.[111]

An element in the medical responsibilities of the Poor Law, which expanded considerably in the second half of the century, was provision for the insane poor. One in a hundred workhouse inmates were classified as 'lunatics' in 1842. By the 1890s, the proportion had risen to around 10 per cent. Although certification procedures became more rigorous after the Lunacy Act of 1890, the legal and medical terminology used for much of the century often conflicted with, and certainly differed from, modern practice. In particular, a lack of clarity in the use of terms such as 'imbecile', 'idiot' and 'feeble-minded' allowed a large variety of poor persons with mental illnesses or mental disabilities to become institutionalised as long-stay residents. However, this was a movement broader than the workhouse system. The Lunacy Acts of 1845 and 1862 created a permanent board of

Lunacy Commissioners and allowed it to remove lunatics from workhouses with guardians' agreement. The county asylum became the chief repository for the insane poor by the early twentieth century. The nine county asylums of the 1820s had expanded in number to 91 by 1911, with over 94,000 inmates. However, in the same year, there were 18 000 insane housed in workhouses and in London's district asylums established under the Metropolitan Poor Act of 1867. But there remained considerable ambiguity over the responsibilities of the state, and research has affirmed the continuing role of communities and kinship in negotiating the terms of treatment. There was little in the way of an official policy for certain categories, notably the child lunatic, until the 1890s and the autonomy of the guardians remained strong. Despite the asylum movement, the shift away from the local authorities to a professionalised central state service only became clear by the beginning of the twentieth century.[112]

Similarly, although Poor Law provision for children changed during the later nineteenth century, it is regarded as occupying 'a transitional position between the state as the arbiter of rescue, reclamation and protection, and as the provider of services for children as publicly recognised citizens of the future': the 'social services state' of the Edwardian era.[113] After the Education Act of 1870, the tendency within the workhouse system was away from the large institutional strategies of the district school and towards smaller institutional arrangements and non-institutional care. Thus cottage homes, on the lines pioneered by voluntary societies like Barnado's, became a preferred policy from the 1870s. The more family-like arrangements of the 'scattered homes' pioneered by the Sheffield guardians were never very widely used. More central to the policy of the Local Government Board was 'boarding-out' (akin to fostering) children without families of their own. The children involved were usually orphans, the illegitimate and deserted, and those whose parents were convicts, insane or had emigrated.

The intention of these policies was to increase the element of personal care in the treatment of children, who were increasingly being seen as deprived rather than simply poor. However, this tendency should not be exaggerated. At the beginning of the twentieth century, whilst children made up approaching one third of the pauper total (210 000 in 1901) only around 30 per cent (c. 70 000) of these were in residential care. The rest were counted amongst those on out-relief. Of this latter figure, at any one time approximately 30 per cent would be in the general wards of workhouses on their way to more specialist care. Over half would be resident in various classes of homes and foster care. Here, ironically, the largest category was the 18 per cent or so in voluntary homes paid for out of the poor rates. Lastly, only 17 per cent were to be found in Poor Law schools.[114] By this time, the Poor Law was only one amongst several state agencies dealing with the needs of children. Moreover, as we shall see in the next chapter, under pressure from voluntary charities, like the National Society for the Prevention of Cruelty to Children, the state began to set standards in child welfare beginning with the 1889 Prevention of Cruelty to Children Act and culminating in the Children's Act of 1908.

Beyond Pauperism? Relief of the Unemployed

By the 1880s and 1890s, for those in work, wages and living conditions continued to rise. However, unemployment rates, even amongst skilled trade unionists, exceeded 10 per cent in 1886, and the economic circumstances of the casual or underemployed worker were far worse. This led to unrest and disorder on the streets. Unemployment demonstrations and riots occurred in most major cities with startling frequency between the 1880s and the 1900s. They tended to coincide with downswings in the trade cycle and, since they were focused on the most casualised employment – such as dock work and the building trades affected by lay offs during bad weather – unrest was most marked during the winter months. Often accompanied by the agitation of socialist groups, such as the Marxist inspired Social Democratic Federation, they appeared to constitute a political threat to property and the state. The most notable and among the largest of the disturbances were the Trafalgar Square riots of 'Black Monday' and 'Bloody Sunday' in 1886 and 1887, which fuelled public anxiety about urban degeneration and the 'residuum'.

The notion of a degenerate residuum resistant to the contagion of self-help had gained credence at the time of the 1867 Reform Act, amidst concern that the vote should only be extended to the respectable. By the mid 1880s the residuum seemed less a dwindling rump and more a spreading menace within the body of the working class. In practice, popular disturbances like these were treated as a police matter, a question of public order rather than social policy (public meetings in central London were banned for five years after 1887).

But they raised the spectre of respectable workers being 'demoralised' by unemployment and even joining forces with the 'outcast' of the cities. In the event, the political threat posed by unemployment was a chimera. The poverty and desperation of many among the casual workers led them to become the cannon fodder of street politics, but they were never a revolutionary force. None the less, the gathering of thousands of impoverished and unemployed men in the streets and squares of major cities stimulated the search for a policy to distinguish between the treatment of the so-called 'bona fide' unemployed workman and the undeserving 'residuum'.[115]

As President of the Local Government Board in 1886, Joseph Chamberlain sought a solution to the 'problem of the unemployed' outside the Poor Law. However, the spectre of Speenhamland still haunted the relief system. The difficulty, as Chamberlain saw it, was how to 'relieve artisans and others who have hitherto avoided poor law assistance, and who are temporarily deprived of employment' without relaxing the conditions of relief to adult males. To do this 'would be most disastrous, as tending directly to restore the condition of things which, before the reform of the Poor Law always destroyed the independence of the labouring classes and increased the poor rate until it became an almost insupportable burden.'[116] The answer in 1886 was to expedite relief works which did not involve the stigma of pauperism nor interfere with the normal operation of the labour market (that is, were not a form of cheap labour). The recommendation was for a variety of public works, such as road making or the laying out of recreation grounds, and the like, arranged so as to coincide with downturns in trade.

Despite this attempt to provide a non-stigmatising relief mechanism for the temporarily unemployed, there was to be no central finance and certainly no element of compulsion. The relief works were to be financed by local authority borrowing. In the late 1880s and through the 1890s, there were sporadic attempts to deploy such strategies in a number of towns and cities. Generally speaking, this was done by municipal authorities and Chamberlain's exhortation to guardians to co-operate fell on deaf ears. During the depression of 1892–95, in winter time when work became scarce and demonstrations of the unemployed filled the streets, several municipal authorities set up registers of the unemployed and allocated them to relief works. But in the terms set out in Chamberlain's original circular, they were an almost uniform failure. It was not the unemployed artisan who registered for relief works, but the casually under-employed who supplemented their income by this means. Skilled men would no more seek to obtain municipal unemployment relief by resorting to unskilled spade labour than they would toil in the guardians' own labour yard or seek entry to the workhouse. Both were equally degrading. However, from the Chamberlain Circular of 1886 through to the Unemployed Workmen Act of 1905, central government toyed with decentralised and voluntarist alternatives to the workhouse or the labour test for the 'respectable' among the unemployed. Labour registries, relief works and labour colonies were among the expedients tried. Voluntary as well as public agencies became involved. Indeed, as we shall see in the next chapter, by far the most imaginative and ambitious schemes were the result of private initiative, notably the 'home colonisation' plan of the Salvation Army. However, as a means for separating the 'bona fide' from the less respectable, they were each a distinct failure. None the less, they were a belated attempt to deal with the hardships caused by unemployment which 50 years of the New Poor Law had neglected.

From Pauperism to Poverty

Anxiety over the unemployed adult male, which had been at the heart of the Poor Law reform of 1834, thus returned to be at the centre of a broader rediscovery of poverty at the end of the century. In the process, theories were revised and new ideas generated. Firstly, the writings of moral activists and social investigators in the 1880s and 1890s implied that the combination of Poor Law and discriminating charity had been unable to remove the spectre of physical and moral degeneracy. Secondly, the thinking of some influential economists supported the conclusions of social investigators and focused attention on environmental causes of poverty, as well as individual ones. It was the housing crisis of the 1880s, combined with the spectacle of unemployed demonstrations, which revived religious and philanthropic alarm about the outcast of the cities. Much of this was expressed in the rhetoric of evangelicalism, from the Reverend Andrew Mearns, *The Bitter Cry of Outcast London* (1883), to General William Booth's Salvationist text, *In Darkest England and the Way Out* (1890).

The panic of the mid 1880s about the threat posed to property and the social order was short-lived, but the problem of poverty was once more at the top of the public's agenda. Moreover, it was being redefined in the process. Under the influence of evolutionary thought, the notion that society existed as a living organism had gained widespread credence among intellectuals. However, the language of evolution generally involved only an acceptance of the role of environment in character formation rather than of biological inheritance in the strict social-Darwinist sense. It fostered an organicist model of society which drew attention to social practices and industrial organisation as influences on individual behaviour.[117] This reinforced a sense of community and of community responsibility, and encouraged talk of 'national efficiency' in which structures and organisation were seen as the key to social adaptation. A result was the application of a more complex model of causation to the problem of poverty. In the 1890s, it was increasingly conceptualised as a series of specific conditions and misfortunes rather than through the blanket concept of destitution. In this, the traditional 'moral' conception of poverty had to accommodate 'environmental' explanations. However, the pace or completeness of the transition from moral to environmental models of poverty should not be overstated.

The 'moral' and the 'environmental' could be comfortable bedfellows. Charles Booth's poverty survey of 1889, which eventually formed the first part of his 17 volume *Life and Labour of the People of London*, began to define poverty in more quantitative terms, but his analysis of the condition of the 'very poor' (his classes 'A' and 'B') still employed the rhetoric of moral condemnation. His assessment that a third of London's population lived below a 'line of poverty' measurable in terms of a family income of around 18–21 shillings a week, and his identification of low and irregular earnings among the causes of poverty, drew attention to the vast numbers who remained poor although they did not figure in the statistics of those on poor relief. A decade later, Seebohm Rowntree's comparable study of York entitled starkly, *Poverty: A Study of Town Life*, reinforced Booth's insights with more clarity. Rowntree's poverty line was set deliberately low and was underpinned by nutritional data about the diet necessary for 'mere physical efficiency', yet he still classified approaching 30 per cent of York's population as poor. Rowntree's analysis of the causes of poverty, like that of Charles Booth before him, combined environmentalist and moral elements expressed most clearly in the distinction he drew between primary and secondary poverty, but his argument was unambiguous in identifying inadequate wages as the largest single cause of 'absolute want'. His elaboration of the 'cycle of poverty', through which individuals and families might pass according to the stage in their lives, undermined notions that the poor were a 'class apart', forever in want. Rather, poverty was a condition or circumstance which might be analysed and by implication might be alleviated or even eradicated. The constructions of the social investigators were reinforced by the theories of the economists. Alfred Marshall, whose *Principles of Economics* (1890) founded the modern discipline in England, demonstrated how involuntary unemployment could occur, and linked economic depression to poverty as a problem for the whole of society because of the lack of effective demand from the poorest. Marshall's view of poverty thus accepted the causal significance of environmental factors. However, as with Booth and Rowntree, this was not a simple displacement process. 'Character' remained central, but it could be degraded by physical poverty. The nature of a man's work, the size of his income and his living conditions could determine his moral nature.[118] This dual emphasis upon poverty as a problem affecting the whole of society and upon the coexistence of environmental and moral factors continued to distinguish the rhetoric of social reform into the early twentieth century.[119] The first point is exemplified in state-sponsored attempts to 'rationalise' the labour market and deal with unemployment through the Labour Exchanges Act of 1909 and the National Insurance Acts of 1911. The drift of the argument is exemplified in the title of William Beveridge's *Unemployment: A Problem of Modern Industry* (1908).

Secondly, as we have seen, the role of 'character' had been crucial in attempts since the 1860s to discriminate between the 'deserving' and the 'undeserving', both in terms of poor relief and charity. It continued to find its mark in the case for social reform into the 1900s, especially in the case of adult able-bodied unemployment, where, according to Beveridge, although 'industrial forces decide that a certain number of people shall be idle, personal considerations decide which individual workpeople shall be thrown out'.[120] Thus, whilst a redefinition both of poverty and of the responsibilities of the state towards the poor was under way before the close of the nineteenth century, we should not underestimate the continued importance of 'Victorian' ideas, especially the notion of 'moral character', in the social reform ideology of the early twentieth century, which was 'thoroughly permeated by the desire to provide decent treatment and social incentives to the respectable, and to separate them from the residuum'. The Liberal welfare reforms of 1906–11 were 'not an abandonment of individualism, but a reinterpretation'.[121]

Conclusion

The New Poor Law did not set out to become a provider of social services. Its rationale was always more limited. However, the increasing number of exceptions to the principle of 'less eligibility' (children, the sick, the elderly) complicated the simple solution of 1834. Designed to deal with the phenomenon of rural under-employment and to restore the social fabric in the countryside, it was the problems of structural unemployment, urban poverty and the casual-labour market which the relief system faced by the 1860s. In the 1840s and 1850s, traditional responsibilities for women, children and the aged poor were reinforced by the assumption that, although much out-relief to adults was in support of 'insufficient' earnings, they were marginal to the labour market. However, out-relief was to be restricted from the 1870s as part of a campaign to reduce costs and enforce the workhouse test on groups which even the 1834 Report never had in mind. Paradoxically, this was accompanied, in some of the larger towns and cities, by *more* expensive provision in larger pavilion-style workhouses which were turning the general mixed workhouse into a series of specialist institutions. In addition, separate foster-care facilities were approved for motherless children.

But this should not lead us to assume a simple model of change within the relief system from 'deterrence to treatment'. Specialisation could also be for punishment as was increasingly the case for the vagrant. Rather, it exemplifies an increasing diversity in approach according to the moral category in which classes of applicant were placed. Those moralising aspects we generally associate with Victorian attitudes to the poor were most explicit in official welfare policy after the 1860s. They evolved alongside the more utilitarian assumptions of 1834. Thus in the Goschen Minute of 1869, the workhouse test was reaffirmed and extended to women, but at the same time, guardians were advised to discriminate in dealing with reputable and disreputable claimants. Making character a factor in granting relief enhanced the stigma of pauperism and intensified hostility to poor relief among the working class. Poor Law officials and their supporters too readily judged success by declining numbers on relief, whilst evidence mounted of a vast reservoir of poverty which the Poor Law never touched. By the 1880s and 1890s, this was beginning to generate concern across society about the apparently intractable problem of poverty, for which the Poor Law seemed an increasingly inadequate instrument.

In any case, the intellectual climate was changing. The prominence of the rhetoric of character in social discourse from the 1860s, and of evolutionary metaphors from the 1880s, marked a turning away from the more mechanistic model of human nature which had determined the reform of 1834. Moreover, the increasing emphasis within the official discourse of poor relief upon 'character' and the need to distinguish between 'deserving' and 'undeserving' applicants implied that the poverty of the former was down to socioeconomic forces beyond their control. The apparent acceptance of this, even in the case of adult able-bodied unemployment, further undermined the utilitarian simplicities of 1834 and laid the foundations for broader conceptions of state responsibility in the future.

3

VOLUNTARY CHARITY AND THE POOR

A corollary of the limited duties assigned the state in the welfare of the poor was the importance placed upon voluntary action. Charity, which plays a supporting role in the welfare services of the present day, was considered by many in the nineteenth century to be the vital element in the welfare equation. Many of the statutory social services of the welfare state were pioneered by voluntary action in Victorian times. However, the place of charity then was as partner to state welfare rather than the subordinate position it has assumed during the twentieth century. The selective discretionary gift of charity was considered preferable by many to the notions of entitlement implicit in any legal machinery of relief, and many of the ablest social welfare minds of the nineteenth century sought solutions to social problems through voluntary rather than statutory action. Moreover, philanthropy flourished in the intellectual climate of an age in which the tenets of individualism were reinforced by the vitality of evangelical religion. To the charitable, saving souls was at least as important as healing bodies. But charity to the poor was not an invention of the nineteenth century.

Charitable giving is as old as civilisation. It can be found in a variety of structures and forms in most human societies down the ages. During the eighteenth century, however, charitable giving underwent a transformation as part of a broader social and cultural revolution. This included the expansion of urban society and increasing middle-class management of public affairs. A result was the flowering of civil institutions independent of the structures of both the state and the private sphere of family and household, including clubs, societies and associations in which private people (chiefly they were educated,

65

propertied men) could come together to act as a 'liberal public sphere'. The emergence of the voluntary society, formed by subscribing members as the typical means of charitable organisation, was part of this process. Up to the eighteenth century, the chief organisational form had been the charitable trust. Generally, this involved trustees managing the property bequest of a wealthy individual in the interests of the designated beneficiaries. Although the endowed trust survived, it was overtaken in the number and value of charitable gifts by the organised giving of those who wished to oversee the dispensation of their charity themselves, rather than rely on the posthumous efforts of trustees. Indeed, organised charity was the principal expression of middle-class resolve to manage the forces, as well as to alleviate the suffering created by urban growth and social change.[1]

It is the purpose of this chapter to examine the ideology, activities and development of voluntary charity to the poor in the late eighteenth and nineteenth centuries; to consider its place in the welfare culture of the age and the extent to which voluntarism was converging with state activity by the end of the period. Beginning with an assessment of the comparative financial value of charity and poor relief, and the range of charitable causes and charitable motives, the discussion proceeds to the intellectual roots of nineteenth-century philanthropy. The long history of the self-help and home-visiting charities from the 1780s onwards is followed by consideration of a key concern of the mid to late nineteenth century, the moral welfare of children and young women. The contribution of voluntarism to the development of medical services comes next and the extent to which they tended the health needs of the poor. Finally, space is given for an extended discussion of later Victorian charity, the significance of the Charity Organisation Society, and the continuing tension within voluntarism between the evangelical and the utilitarian springs of social action. Voluntarism developed professional standards in the provision of personal social services and yet, by the end of the century, there were many in the field of voluntary action who looked for statutory intervention in areas such as child welfare. Equally, there were others much more wary of extending state responsibility, but propelled by events towards reluctant co-operation as the priorities of state and society shifted towards more, not less, public welfare. However, just as the role of 'character' persisted in the social reform ideology of the Liberal 'social service state' so, too, the moral priorities of Victorian charity endured into the post-Victorian era and the emergence of the 'new philanthropy', along with more modern conceptions of voluntary service, was a slow process.

Charity and the Charitable

How significant was voluntary charity to the poor in the nineteenth century? We have no comparable run of statistics to put alongside those for poor relief. We will never know the full story for not only do historians have to contend with the problem of missing evidence, but much charitable giving went unrecorded. This includes not just the informal gift of alms, but the whole range of charitable gifts between individuals and the countless acts of the innumerable minor charitable bodies which left no permanent record of their work. Only the endowed charities had to register their accounts with an official body, charitable societies were accountable only to their members. Any estimate of their funds is at best a 'guestimate'. None the less, some historians claim that the receipts of the charities outweighed the total national costs of poor relief.[2] For example, gross expenditure on state poor relief in 1870 came to £7.7 million. This compares with a contemporary estimate that the annual sum devoted to charity in London alone lay somewhere between £5 million and £7.5 million. The imbalance between voluntary and public expenditure may have narrowed by the end of the century. In 1899, whilst the national cost of poor relief had spiralled to reach a total £11.2 million, the receipts of London's charities remained around the £6 million mark. Despite this narrowing of the gap, the figures could be construed to suggest that charitable giving was at least the equal of state welfare provision in the nineteenth century. Although it must be stressed that whilst we know that the Poor Law figures represent the money spent on poor relief, charity went to a variety of other causes as well as to the direct relief of poverty, including the gathering of funds to promote the spread of religion, numerous animal societies, worthy purposes such as the Lifeboat Society and charities to help humans not classifiable as poor, distressed gentlefolk and the like.

Any list of charitable causes tells us more about the priorities of the charitable than its does about the needs of the poor. In fact, the sheer range and variety of nineteenth-century charitable causes almost defies description. However, studies of nineteenth-century Bristol and Manchester have revealed the numerical preponderance of educational, medical, evangelical, 'rescue' and poor-relief charities. They confirm that the direct distribution of relief to the poor in cash and in kind was less well supported than the provision of institutions such as schools, hospitals and reformatory homes, and the work of the innumerable evangelical visiting societies and missions.[3]

The survival chances of a particular charity depended largely upon its ability to raise (and successfully manage) the necessary funds. In the nineteenth century, the income of voluntary societies generally fell into two categories; charitable gifts and income from other sources. Gifts to charitable societies generally came in the shape of the regular annual subscription, the occasional donation, the contribution to special appeals, the purchase made at a sale of work, and finally, the often looked for but unpredictable legacy. In terms of secure finance, the reliability of the regular subscription was preferred and, in the early years of a charity, it would be vital to secure adequate funds upon which to base a society's activities. The benefits of subscriber status were of some importance. Subscribers could vote in the affairs of the charity, chiefly the election of officers, notably presidents, treasurers and the like. The subscribers became the members of a voluntary society. In theory at least, the charity was owned by its members and the voluntary societies of the nineteenth century have been deemed 'subscriber democracies'.[4] But although subscribers 'owned' a charity, charitable gifts – even in the nineteenth century – were not the sole nor, in some cases, the main source of income. This was especially true of charities with institutions like hospitals to run, and large capital outlays and running costs to consider. There were always other sources of revenue. The interest from investments, from payments made by inmates and patients (e.g., from relatives, friendly societies, contributory schemes and boards of guardians), and the proceeds from the sale of goods and from other charitable events were essential to the finance of many benevolent societies. The balance between these various sources of income differed from society to society.

What can we say about the motives of the charitable? Why would individual men and women give to a charity and why would some take the further step of becoming involved in the work of the societies, sitting on committees and even visiting the homes of the poor? This is a question of broad interest to social scientists as well as a matter of specific historical context. Most historians of philanthropy refer to either altruism or self-interest as the motives behind the charitable gift. Indeed, the contest of interpretation between 'altruism' and 'egoism' has long been endemic to discussion of the ethics of social action.[5] In reality, the charity relationship is a remarkably complex and flexible social mechanism which possesses various cultural meanings. For the giver, it draws on deep-rooted impulses of empathy and compassion. It expresses prevalent social norms, such as reciprocity, beneficence and social responsibility (which are profoundly reinforced in western culture by the centrality of charity to the Judaeo-Christian tradition). Moreover, charitable giving also offers an opportunity for self-fulfilment and self-expression, and opens up the possibilities of a public identity.

In fact, there could be a variety of emotions and intentions in play in the actions of the charitable; these could range from sympathy and fellow feeling to the desire to be well thought of, from religious piety to a sense of guilt, from the desire for a well-regulated society to the fear of the mob, from the feeling of having done your duty to a sense of personal gratification at helping others. Reputations for charity work could reinforce the status of the donor, legitimating wealth or even opening the door to political office.[6] The cultural position of the recipient of the charitable gift might be just as complex. For example, the desire of many among the charitable in the nineteenth century to confine the gift to the deserving determined in their minds the characteristics expected of the target of their generosity. This meant that charity was often conditional upon status rather than need. There is evidence to suggest that Victorian supplicants for charitable relief responded to its conditionality by becoming adept at the 'theatre' of charity, acting the parts designated them by the expectations of the donors, appearing at once desperate yet respectable and deserving.[7]

In addition to class, gender was a key factor in the charity relationship. The position of middle-class women in Victorian society was conditioned by the ideal of the 'separate spheres'. In essence, this defined the woman's sphere of influence to be the home and family, whilst to men was allotted the expanding public world of business, politics, culture and all the associated networks of power. This separation of roles was reinforced by a cult of domesticity which revered the sanctity and purity of life in the respectable family home. A woman's place was clear. In the words of the Victorian poet Coventry Patmore, she was the 'Angel in the House'.

The only substantial arena of public activity available to middle-class 'ladies' without prejudicing their respectability was philanthropy. It was more than an avoidance of the boredom of domestic life that projected women into charity work. As Prochaska emphasises, evangelical zeal was central. Women were presumed to possess the 'feminine' virtues of caring and compassion which, it was believed, made them more likely than men to identify with the Jesus of the gospels. Scripture reading informed by evangelical sensibilities had a profound personal impact on many women, setting a model for everyday living and offering the prospect of spiritual redemption and eternal salvation.[8] Furthermore, a cultural precedent had been set for them in the practice of alms giving by the upper-class 'lady bountifuls' in past ages, an image effectively recycled by John Ruskin in the 1860s in his essay *Sesames and Lilies*, as well as the pastoral example of wives and daughters of the clergy who traditionally visited the sick in their homes. Generally, women played an auxiliary role in the running of most charities, forming ladies committees and concentrating on fund raising and home visiting. However, in some areas, such as dealing with children and young women, their presumed qualities ceded them a greater role. Equally, there were a number of women, of whom Louisa Twining and Octavia Hill are only the best known, whose personality and intellect challenged the conventional stereotype, and who were able to carve out philanthropic 'careers'. Women were often innovators in the field of philanthropy – for example, pioneering the employment of paid charity workers and the development of social work practice. Moreover, by the end of the century, experience in philanthropy was leading to career opportunities for women in other areas of public life.

Intellectual Roots

Charitable giving drew upon traditional norms of sympathy, compassion and social responsibility. But the self-help ideology of the nineteenth century, which forged the New Poor Law, also framed the context of philanthropy for most of the century. In this, it securely located the prime responsibility for poverty upon those deemed able to help themselves. Thus most adult, able-bodied persons were rarely considered safe objects for the charitable gift and those less able to help themselves – such as children, the sick and the infirm – were, by contrast, suitable cases for charitable treatment. A root of much nineteenth-century philanthropy was the evangelical revival which began during the later-eighteenth-century. Compared to the optimism about secular human progress common to much Enlightenment thought, the evangelicals were convinced of the power of sin, and the necessity of individual religious conversion and moral regeneration, before there could be any hope of material improvement. Evil was conceived as a palpable and inevitable presence in the world. It brought vice and misery in its wake.

Evangelicalism involved an emphasis upon the 'seriousness' of the Christian life and the importance of a religion derived from personal experience and individual conviction rather than external conformity to doctrine and rules. It lay emphasis upon the centrality of personal religion and placed religious worship at the heart of family values, sanctifying the domestic virtues. The emphasis in evangelical Christianity upon an individual's personal relationship with God, without mediation or intercession, carried with it a clear message of individual responsibility and the virtue of self-reliance. Salvation, in either a religious or material sense, could only result from individual effort. We have already seen the policy implications of evangelicalism in the 'Christian Economics' which contributed to acceptance of the political economy of the New Poor Law, but the influence of evangelicalism was pervasive. It provided the nineteenth century with both its particular blend of Christian values and its general atmosphere of sober respectability and moral earnestness. It made religion central to middle-class culture and, from that base, infiltrated the mentality of many in both the working classes and the aristocracy. It is central to an understanding of voluntary approaches to the problem of poverty.

The evangelical movement was cross-denominational. All the Protestant churches were touched by its teachings and religious style. Although it had its broadest impact upon society through the evangelical wing of the established religion, the Church of England, it characterised the Christianity of many in the nonconformist churches (Methodist, Baptist, Congregationalist). The work of the philanthropic societies was a crucial meeting place for evangelicals from the various Protestant sects. Despite the doctrinal and organisational differences between the churches, the evangelicals shared a common outlook which often brought them together; although this 'pan-evangelicalism' was in decline by the 1830s in the face of increasing sectarian rivalry. None the less, the desire for more conversions and the spread of Christian knowledge propelled many evangelicals into the field of philanthropy. In these circumstances, Christian charity meant working to save individual souls. All Christian teaching stressed the importance of charity, but the evangelicals gave it the greatest emphasis.[9] The evangelical movement gave nineteenth-century charity to the poor its characteristic religious associations. A chief object was the desire to Christianise the poor, to extirpate vice and to encourage the growth of virtue, which was most usually understood to reside in self-proprietorship, sobriety and thrift. It was no coincidence that these were the virtues which the middle-class philanthropists most readily associated with their own lives or those of their ancestors. Such virtues, they presumed, were the path both to material well-being on earth and eternal salvation in heaven. In the light of this view of the world, it would have been as unchristian to have ignored the spiritual needs of the poor as to shut one's ears to the cries of the injured and dying. Evangelical norms made it difficult for Christians to resist the compunction to 'do something' for the distressed; they encouraged a sense of personal responsibility for the care of those suffering from misfortune, distress or oppression. The most celebrated achievement of the evangelical conscience may have been the campaign to abolish slavery. This can be seen as the prime instance of the heightened moral sensibilities of the post-Enlightenment period. The humanitarianism of the late eighteenth century had created a new moral universe which compelled action in the face of human suffering; indeed 'failing to go the aid of a suffering stranger might become an unconscionable act'.[10] However, evangelicals were generally more active on the home front being concerned with the suppression of vice and the stimulation of self-help among the poor.

The theories of the classical political economists added a further dimension. The emphasis of Adam Smith and his followers upon the centrality of the market, the role of technology and the division of labour suggested the need for a hard-working and reliable labour force to ensure the material progress of commerce and manufacture. When linked with the concerns of the evangelicals, this gave a central place to the utility of the moral improvement of the labouring poor. Moreover, the pessimistic warnings of Thomas Malthus about the perils of unhindered population growth reinforced evangelical assumptions about the inevitability of poverty. The particular blend of utilitarian ideas, political economy theorising and evangelical sentiments that characterised nineteenth-century approaches to the problem of poverty found early expression in a series of philanthropic ventures in the 1790s and 1800s. At the end of the eighteenth century, a new view of charity was crystallising which emphasised its potential for social amelioration. In the words of Donna Andrew: 'Elements of evangelicalism, political economy, Malthusianism, and utilitarianism combined to make a powerful platform from which to combat poverty through charity.'[11] However, there were to be persistent tensions within nineteenth-century social thought between its calculating utilitarian dimensions and the evangelical springs of social action. In the history of charity, it can (over?)-simplify matters if we distinguish between the utilitarian emphasis upon the need for discretion, investigation and regulation in the relief of distress (which even in the late eighteenth century was described as 'scientific charity' and in the terminology of the later nineteenth century could be classed as 'charity organisation') and the cultural mediation between the rich and the poor – by which evangelical impulses to 'redeem' the 'lost souls' of the impoverished – extended the hand of sympathy between the classes. Moreover, a distinguishing feature of the evangelical approach to charity was its concern for the spiritual needs of the *donors* of charity. The evangelicals regarded charity as a divine imperative not just because it might save the souls of the poor, but also because heartfelt, personal and spontaneous giving was required of a Christian. Moreover, evangelicalism revived the old idea that wealth was a moral burden and charity was a way of appeasing God's wrath. So for the evangelicals of the early to mid nineteenth century, the act of charity was an act of atonement, having as much to do with saving the souls of the rich as about redeeming the poor.[12] Thus, it would be unwise to assume that political economy and evangelicalism were mutually exclusive theories of the 'true charity'; or to assume that the distinction between 'heart' and 'mind' which they imply can always be easily discerned. Utilitarian calculations and evangelical impulses could reside in the same breast, and were often mutually supportive approaches. Most crucially, whilst evangelical religion enhanced the obligation to respond to distress, this potentially sentimental impulse was accompanied by a prudent determination not to 'demoralise' the poor.

The culture of the discriminating gift may have a longer history than we imagine, but there is little doubt that the half century following 1780 witnessed a plethora of new mechanisms for its realisation.[13] The economic, social and political changes of these years – population growth, industrialisation, urbanisation, agricultural reorganisation and the political insecurity and economic dislocation of the war years and after – all contributed to a collective feeling among the propertied classes of anxiety about social relationships. This anxiety often focused on a perceived loss of personal knowledge about the poor and loss of influence over their behaviour in an increasingly impersonal social order. Thus, the new theory of 'true charity' offered to regain the knowledge of the poor and to restore the control over their lives, twin facets upon which it was assumed charitable giving had traditionally depended. In these aspirations, both utilitarian and evangelical springs of voluntary action were united.

'Self-Help' Charities

The gulf between the classes, entrenched by the spread of urbanism and made more dangerous by political uncertainty, was the central concern of the turn-of-the-century charities. The charitable world view inherited a hierarchical and paternalistic conception of the social order. Despite the rise of market ideology, the centuries' old organicist model of society still held some resonance and distinctions between the social classes were seen as inevitable, indeed, divinely ordained. The poor had obligations rather than rights, and chief amongst these was the duty to be industrious and subservient. In a pre-democratic age, social inequality and the infinite gradations of rank were unquestioned features of the outlook of the propertied classes. Social divisions were seen to require the balm of sympathy and good example from the rich, and social discipline and moral regeneration from the poor. It was the duty of the latter to acquire correct values and of the former to impart them. Thus it was considered vital for charity itself to be carefully dispensed, to reward virtue but not to encourage false expectation. Crucially, it was no longer enough to give money. Indeed the injudicious gift of money could be a most corrupting influence, if unaccompanied by personal influence. This new view of charity required greater personal involvement on the part of the charitable. Evangelical religion demanded action and the charitable society offered the opportunity of personal service. Thus the duty to God and to Man could be satisfied in the work of charity. The role of the charitable volunteer was central.

The central motifs of the new charity were: (1) discrimination in giving; (2) personal contact with the poor; and (3) the fostering of self-help among them. To this end the chief innovations of early nineteenth-century charitable work with the poor were the investigation of applicants' claims, the home visit by the voluntary visitor, and

the systematic gathering of knowledge about the poor. The intention, in the words of the reverend Malthus, was to make 'moral agents'
of the charitable. The best way to achieve this was to practice:

> ... that voluntary and active charity, which makes itself acquainted with the
> objects which it relieves; which seems to feel, and be proud of, the bond
> which unites the rich with the poor; which enters into their houses; informs
> itself not only of their wants, but of their habits and dispositions; checks the
> hopes of clamorous and obtrusive poverty . . .; and encourages with adequate
> relief the silent and retiring sufferer, labouring under unmerited difficul-
> ties.[14]

Spreading the propaganda of self-help was the prime purpose of the
most famous of the turn-of-the-century charities for the poor. The
Society for the Bettering of the Condition and Increasing the Comforts
of the Poor (SBCP) was founded by a distinguished collection of Anglican evangelicals which included William Wilberforce and Shute
Barrington, the Bishop of Durham; its principal promoter was Thomas
Bernard.[15] The underlying premise was that the poor need advice on
how to help themselves and that the educated rich had good advice to
give. The main activity of the SBCP was to gather and disseminate
useful ideas on how to better the condition of the poor, and to recommend the support of those charities which aimed at moral
regeneration. Thus the Society dedicated itself to putting philanthropy
on a more 'scientific' footing. Its *Reports* carried accounts of every
conceivable palliative for poverty; from friendly societies to soup kitchens, from charity schools to dietary reform. It was in this latter field
that most suggestions came. It was blithely assumed that the poor
knew nothing of domestic economy, and even that such ignorance
was a prime cause of their poverty. During the war years, the SBCP
devoted much energy to the food-charity movement and sought to
introduce dietary education to the conventional soup-kitchen format.
Soup was sold only to those deemed worthy, generally selected by the
recommendation of the charitable themselves. The SBCP continued
to provide a forum for the discussion of charity and functioned as a
'clearing house' for information into the 1820s, but it has been claimed
that, by then, it 'had largely been pushed aside as an eccentric vehicle for the promotion of diet substitutes'.[16] Key developments in the
organisation and techniques of charity were taking place elsewhere.
  Prior to the reform of 1834, the Poor Laws were considered by most

in the charitable field to be inferior to voluntary charity. It was widely held that the state system was impersonal and indiscriminate. This was partly because the obligatory character of official relief (through the compulsory payment of the poor rate) was believed to remove the personal element in giving which the evangelicals so prized – not least for its spiritual value for the donor. But also, in an increasingly mobile and urban society, the potential for deception worried the more secular, as well as the evangelical philanthropist. It was increasingly assumed that the voluntary gift possessed the greater potential for linking poor relief to virtue and confining assistance to the deserving. Up to the 1830s, this view had immense implications for the very existence of a state system of welfare provision and, even beyond 1834 (until the later nineteenth century), tended to deprecate any idea of state welfare beyond that of offering a 'safety net' to the destitute. The belief in the superiority of the charity mechanism partly lay in its armoury of investigatory and discriminatory techniques. Most of these were pioneered during the early decades of the century.

The agenda of the new charity involved the investigation of applicants, generally through the visits of charity volunteers to the homes of the poor and the gathering of what we might today term a 'data-base' of information so as to assist charitable decisions and facilitate control of the relief mechanism. The great practical role of evangelical religion was to harness the energies as volunteers of those who (often women) adhered to 'the religion of duty, which placed service above doctrine'.[17] Among the first agencies to develop such techniques were the Strangers' Friend Societies of the late eighteenth century and some of the soup charities of the war years. The Strangers' Friend Societies originated to meet the needs of the 'non-settled' poor, that is, those without a 'settlement' in the parish and not entitled to apply for poor relief other than in their parish of residence. Their work expanded to cover the poor in general.[18]

Strangers' Friend Societies were founded by the Methodists in London and a number of provincial towns, including Liverpool, Manchester, Stockport, Bristol and Dublin during the 1780s and 1790s. Soon they acquired a more general following. As the writer of a local guidebook noted of the Manchester Society: 'The plan met with general approbation, and people of every religious persuasion entered their names on the list of subscribers.'[19] The Strangers' Friend Societies expanded their operations during the war years and some were active into the 1820s. Their *modus operandi* was the home visit.

The full title of the London Society advertised its stated purpose of 'Visiting and Relieving Sick and Distressed Strangers, and Other Poor, at their respective Habitations'; by 1803, the Society was making 10 632 visits to poor families in the metropolis. Visitors in Manchester were entreated 'daily to seek out objects of real woe ... visit their miserable retreats; and ... inquire minutely into the nature of their complaints'. Relief was to be confined to the 'absolutely destitute' and was usually given in kind; gifts of food and clothing, blankets and coal were most typical.[20] Other types of society developed visiting programmes during the first decades of the century. During the wartime slump of 1812-13, the Spitalfields Soup Charity developed 'an exhaustive "data-base" of information on the local needy, continuously updated by "domiciliary visitation" of cases by a rostered panel of investigators and advice givers'.[21] However, it was the anti-begging societies which extended the enquiry methods of charity, combining police and welfare functions in the process.

Giving alms to the beggar is the classic act of personal charity. It is also the one least amenable to regulation. Moreover, since the sixteenth century the act of begging has often been represented as especially open to deception and fraud. The first decades of the nineteenth century, in particular, witnessed an energetic campaign by anti-begging societies in an attempt to redirect the charitable impulses of donors away from the street mendicant, as well as to harry and suppress the act of begging itself.[22] Whether or not to give to the street beggar became a complex moral and intellectual problem under the dual influence of evangelical religion and utilitarian conceptions of appropriate behaviour in a market society. A greater sense of personal responsibility for the suffering of others was tempered by a desire not to 'demoralise' society by being seen to reward the undeserving. Rapid urban growth and more migratory populations significantly reduced the possibility of personal knowledge of supplicants. Economic crises and political insecurity made the problem of mendicancy seem more acute. However, the approach of the community to the vagrant was confused. Although begging was an offence under increasingly repressive vagrancy legislation, the metropolitan authorities were often reluctant to treat beggars as criminals, and thousands of all ages roamed the streets of the capital and the chief provincial towns. Volunteer attempts to control mendicancy provided experiments in some of the key practices of charity investigation.

The first anti-begging voluntary society was formed in Bath in 1805.

Bath was an unsurprising location for such an experiment due its high proportion of rich visitors and popularity as a place of call for seasonal labour migrants. The Bath Society for the Suppression of Common Vagrants and Impostors, Relief of Occasional Distress, and Encouragement of Industry aimed primarily at the eradication of street begging in the town. It operated in conjunction with the magistrates and Poor Law officials, and employed its own police official to patrol the streets and warn off the professional beggar. It was its innovative investigation techniques, however, which reveal its concern to re-educate both the potential charitable donor and the seeker after alms. It sought to replace the giving of money with a relief ticket system whereby the claims of beggars could be investigated and instances of genuine distress relieved. The Bath Society's rationale for this scheme expressed a message which was to be repeated again and again by similar 'charity organisation' societies throughout the century: 'alms given in the street, without investigation, are bounties on idleness and fraud; and ... every shilling so received is a robbery from real distress.'[23] But it would be misleading to suggest that the anti-mendicant societies held to a purely police function. By the 1820s, the Bath Society had broadened its remit beyond the suppression of mendicancy, expanding its welfare role and pioneering practices such as the granting of loans to impoverished small traders and providing relief works for the unemployed. In providing relief, the domiciliary visit and the desire to confine the gift to the deserving remained at the cornerstone of its work.

Similar societies were established in a number of other towns including Edinburgh, Oxford, Colchester and London. The work of the London Mendicity Society, from its foundation in 1818 till its decline in the 1860s, illustrates the combination of punitive and relief strategies pursued by those who sought to organise and rationalise charitable giving. Although the Mendicity Society never saw itself primarily as a law-enforcement agency, it performed a police function especially in the years prior to the formation of the Metropolitan Police in 1829. It appointed its own constables to patrol the streets, apprehend beggars and turn the 'undeserving' over to the magistrates. From the outset, the Mendicity Society's welfare plan had the ambitious aim of co-ordinating the investigation of claims for charitable relief for the whole of the capital. Cases for investigation would arise either from referrals of the Society's constables or from the recommendation of Society subscribers who gave tickets of entitlement to beggars instead of money. These cases were to be investigated by gentlemen volunteers, although the problems of volunteer availability and a lack of uniformity in relief decisions prompted the Society to appoint a full-time salaried official to co-ordinate the work.

However, the relief work of the Society never conformed to the simple neatness of this plan. In its early years it found a number of those turned up in investigation were without access to the Poor Law, either through ignorance or through legal exclusion (see the discussion of the work of the Stranger's Friend Societies above). These were often the sick, the mentally ill, and the elderly. The Mendicity Society acted as relief counsellor in such cases; of those it did not assist directly, some were referred to hospitals and asylums, but the majority were directed to the Poor Law authorities. The essence of investigation was to be discrimination but, like others before and after, the Society found this task daunting. It was tackled by the use of a mechanism that was later to become a stalwart of the Poor Law authorities, the 'labour test'. Able-bodied applicants generally claimed to be out of work, so from 1821, the Society required a three-hour work task as a test of applicants' 'genuineness'. Ultimately such rationalisation was pressed to the point of collapse during successive trade depressions (made worse in the 1840s by the influx of Irish migrants during the Great Famine). In 1819, 1830, 1838 and 1848, the investigation of applicants was abandoned in the face of demand and relief was granted 'indiscriminately'. In 1848, 20 000 Irish poor besieged the Society's relief office and it was forced to suspend operations. Thus, not for the last time in the nineteenth century, prevailing relief practices collapsed in the face of the mass suffering induced by economic depression.

Home Visiting Movement

The mendicity societies were generally at the utilitarian rather than the evangelical end of the charity spectrum. During the second quarter of the century, the district-visiting and home-mission movements were an outlet for the more evangelical springs of social action. Although, as suggested above, it would be unwise to be too watertight about the distinction between these twin impulses of the philanthropic spirit. In particular, the mission to redeem lost souls never excluded the desire to unite the classes or to reward the deserving, and the rhetoric of investigation and discrimination regularly fell from evangelical lips. Particular features of the visiting, provident and home-missionary societies of the 1820s to the 1850s were, first, the extent to which they were a vehicle for the philanthropy of middle-class women – by the mid century the notion of 'social motherhood' was suggesting alternative 'male' and 'female' versions of social action.[24] And second, the incidence of sectarian rivalry between the various societies that threatened attempts at the co-ordination of charitable giving. District visiting had originated as a mechanism of religious reform. What began slowly in the work of the Stranger's Friend, and other visiting societies during the early years of the century, gathered pace into a movement by the 1830s and 1840s: 'Of the many forms of local benevolence that came into prominence in Britain by the mid nineteenth century, none was more important than district visiting.'[25] It brought together the evangelical belief in personal intervention in the lives of the poor as a means of individual spiritual redemption and possible, although by no means essential, material improvement with the more secular concerns of the utilitarian mind for information, investigation and a rationalised 'science' of charity. A key influence was the work of Thomas Chalmers in the poor parish of St John's, Glasgow, between 1819 and 1823. Chalmers divided the parish into 25 districts, each in the care of a church deacon instructed to visit homes and encourage religious faith and self reliance. Unlike the situation in England and Wales, the absence of a formal Poor Law in Scotland left Chalmers's system of voluntary assistance as the only form available. Despite this difference between the two countries, Chalmers was often held up as an example (the same was true later of the similar district scheme operating in the town of Elberfeld in Germany in the 1850s and 1860s).[26]

Domiciliary visiting was to be repeatedly presented as a panacea and organisational plans were generally ambitious. For example, the General Society for Promoting District Visiting, founded by a number of evangelical-sponsored bodies in 1828, planned 'a regular system of domiciliary visitation' whereby 'every poor family might be visited at their habitations ... and their temporal and spiritual condition diligently yet tenderly examined into, and appropriate treatment applied'.[27] This was a federal society, co-ordinating the work of 25 local district visiting societies in London. The parish was the basic unit of organisation for the visiting societies. Thus the Metropolitan Visiting and Relief Association (MVRA), founded in 1843, gathered funds centrally for distribution to individual, parish visiting societies. In the 1840s and 1850s, up to 80 societies with over a thousand visitors, were affiliated to the MVRA. The methods of home-visiting schemes varied but, in general, the intention was to combine religious influence with moral and practical advice, the encouragement of thrift, and the occasional direct relief of distress. Moralising homilies may not have been welcomed in many homes and the charity visitor must have faced the problems of all strangers who seek to gain entry across the doorstep. Thus it was common to conceal the gospel tract inside a basket of consumables. Once inside, advice could be on any subject, but was often related to domestic issues, such as the improved management of the family finances, family health and child care. Direct relief was to be sparingly given and often in the form of food, fuel, clothing and blankets. In fact, it was probably more common to *collect* money from the families visited, as thrift became a central platform of the visiting movement. The MVRA sponsored parochial provident societies in London and numerous provincial societies were formed in part to organise working-class savings. The Liverpool District Provident Visiting Society, founded in 1829, organised its 200 plus volunteers into 21 district committees. Its visitors 'dispensed advice and Bibles, offered material encouragement in the shape of relief and a premium of sixpence on every ten shillings saved'.[28] The visitors of the Manchester and Salford District Provident Society, founded in 1833, made regular weekly collections of the savings of the poor and the Society put much faith in the ability of the domiciliary visit to: 'cultivate a kindly feeling between the rich and the poor, and improve the latter by encouraging cleanly, provident and contented habits'.[29]

By the 1850s, there were literally hundreds of visiting societies operating in metropolitan London and an innumerable number active in towns and cities across the country as a whole. Some were interdenominational, but many were run by particular religious denominations. The MVRA gave grants to London clergy to promote parish-based Church of England home visiting. Virtually every London parish had its visiting society. In fact when Sampson Low conducted his first survey of metropolitan charity in 1850, he found that, of the 250 parish churches in London, only 36 were without a visiting society and these were generally in the richer neighbourhoods.[30] Each denomination developed its own tradition of home visiting. Sectarian rivalry was intense. The evangelicals may have set the ball rolling, but the mission to the poor eventually encompassed all the Protestant denominations, including the Unitarians who were barely considered

Christians by the others, and extended to the Catholic confraternities, such as the Sisters of Mercy, and the various Jewish benevolent and visiting societies. The Catholic and Jewish societies tended not to be proselytising and instead concentrated on their own poor and defending their faiths from outside attack. Most visiting societies targeted specific geographical locations, but others were concerned to reach certain occupations and types of poor person, so there were missions to seamen and miners amongst other employment groups, and missions to lodging houses to contact those who were often without work – the floating population of 'comers and goers' to be found in every big city. The visiting ideal also extended to include a range of societies concerned to visit the sick and infirm in hospital, and at home, including those with specific incapacities. For example, the Indigent Blind Visiting Society, founded in London 1834, pioneered the visiting of those who had lost their sight in later life or were in poor health and unable to work; by 1889, there were 45 such visiting missions to the blind.[31] Workhouse inmates were not neglected by the voluntary visitor. Louisa Twining founded the Workhouse Visiting Society in London in 1858, but soon discovered that the threshold of the workhouse was no easier to cross than that of the poor person's home. The Poor Law Board only reluctantly recognised the Society and guardians did not readily agree to admit its visitors. One problem was the extent to which Miss Twining used the Society to campaign for workhouse reform. However, the practice of visiting the workhouse pauper was encouraged by the example of the Workhouse Visiting Society and related schemes for the welfare and retraining of inmates.[32]

A common feature of the visiting society was its dependence upon volunteers. Unfortunately, these were not always in ready supply and the more grandiose plans of the city-wide societies had often to be tailored to suit a declining volunteer base. The cause of the problem was the exodus of the better off from the city centres in preference for tree-lined suburbs and rural retreats. The experience of the Manchester and Salford District Provident Society was not untypical. Society plans in the 1830s for covering the urban area with a network of district committees and around a thousand volunteer visitors proved to be wildly over-ambitious. The figure of 259 voluntary visitors was reached by 1835, but, as early as 1837, the Society was disturbed by a shortage of volunteers; by the 1860s, the number had fallen to 24. Although district visiting remained an ideal, it became apparent that some alternative would have to be developed, if only to collect the savings of the provident. To this end, from 1845, penny banks were established in the poorer areas of town.[33] Many of the district visiting societies had a similar experience. Smaller or less ambitious societies were more likely to retain their volunteers, but the fact remains that inner districts of the main towns, lacking a resident middle class, were difficult areas in which to recruit charity visitors. This was a persistent problem. Later in the century, the university settlement movement was an attempt to address the issue by setting young university volunteers in residential communities in the East End of London. Another solution was the payment of visitors and the most innovative example of this occurred in the various initiatives of Ellen Ranyard.

The London City Mission had employed paid visitors as early as the 1830s, but they were not allowed to give poor relief, only spiritual advice. The 'Bible women' employed by Ellen Ranyard's Bible and Domestic Female Mission, founded in 1857, were social workers as well as missionaries, and arguably the first of their type. These predominantly working-class women were residents of the districts they visited. Paid around £30 a year (a salary superior to the lower grades of domestic service), they received a three-month initial training in scripture, hygiene and the Poor Law. Their visiting work was done under the watchful eye of lady superintendents. By 1867 there were 234 Bible women in London and the scheme spread rapidly to other cities. The task of the Bible women, as the name suggests, was to sell Bibles to the poor. But along the way, they were trained to offer advice to wives and mothers on the arts of domestic economy: cooking, cleaning and needlework. Moreover, they also ran successful thrift clubs, collecting weekly subscriptions to pay for items of clothing and furniture. This was the classic combination of spiritual welfare and the fostering of self-help. Revealingly, on those occasions when emergency relief was dispensed to the poorest of families, it was a task assigned not to the Bible woman herself, but to the lady superintendents who were 'more conscious of the dangers of indiscriminate relief'.[34]

The Bible women were not the only paid charity visitors in the middle decades of the century. There were other initiatives in other towns. The Manchester and Salford Ladies Sanitary Reform Association may justifiably claim the credit for inventing health visiting. From 1862, working-class women were employed and trained by the Association to teach hygiene to poor women in their homes. In the early days, this consisted chiefly of a demonstration of the power of disinfectant and medicated soap against verminous insects, but gradually the work of the visitors developed and from 1890, six of its 14 visitors were paid by a city council alarmed at Manchester's persistently high infant-mortality rate. The voluntary sector often pioneered activities later taken over by publicly funded bodies. The origins of the paid district nurse can also be traced to the 1860s. Initiatives in Liverpool and London contributed to the development of the profession of home nursing. William Rathbone's District Nursing Society provided a residential training home for nurses in Liverpool. The town was divided into districts in which trained nurses visited the homes of the sick poor, and lady superintendents raised funds and administered the scheme. 'The Lady Superintendent ... was to visit ... all cases under treatment, so as to obtain assurance that the nurse was working faithfully and well ... she was to examine the nurse's register, to consult with her on fresh cases, and to hear her report on old ones'.[35] Rathbone's work in Liverpool was paralleled by another of Ellen Ranyard's London-based initiatives. In the late 1860s, she began to employ working-class women as nursing visitors. Ranyard's Bible nurses were trained in various London hospitals, combined religious exhortation with medical guidance in their home visits, and were once again supervised by lady volunteers. A key purpose was to teach the poor how to care for their own health: 'Mrs Ranyard's agents sought to turn the city's outcast population into respectable, independent citizens through an invigoration of family life.'[36] As in all district visiting, the fostering of self-help was the prime objective.

The Moral Welfare of Children and Young Women

Institutional provision was a hallmark of Victorian society. From prisons to workhouses, from lunatic asylums to industrial schools, the state increasingly dealt with social problems through institutions, on the assumption that it was both possible and desirable to control people's minds, as well as their bodies, in an attempt to reform their behaviour. Charitable funds were similarly devoted to the provision of reformatory institutions. A variety of largely residential homes and refuges were created for the morally deviant and the socially disadvantaged. Numerous protection and rescue societies sought to reform and moralise 'fallen women' and 'girls in moral danger'. Magdalene asylums, training homes and night refuges existed for the rescue and reclamation of the prostitute. Other voluntary organisations tackled the problem of orphaned, abandoned, runaway and otherwise home-less children. From training and industrial schools to holiday homes and emigration schemes, children's rescue societies like Dr Barna-do's coped with and publicised the scandal of child neglect and abuse. It was charitable societies that dealt with these issues and, during the latter years of the century, campaigned for state protection of the child.

By contrast to the case of impoverished adults, the welfare of desti-tute children was not to be left to the encouragement of self-help. The children of the poor were generally seen as a group in need of rescue and reform. The evangelical revival reinforced older attitudes towards the children of the labouring poor. In the seventeenth and eighteenth centuries, the child was regarded as naturally wilful and unruly, in need of strict discipline, training in industrious habits and subject to the inculcation of correct habits and values. Childhood was to be a period of training for adulthood in a pre-ordained social posi-tion. Thus it was the function of the Sunday School movement and the schools of industry that flourished from the end of the eighteenth cen-tury onwards, in the words of Hannah More, a notable advocate of such schools, to 'train up the lower classes to habits of industry and virtue'.[37] Evangelical belief in the inherent sinfulness of humanity re-inforced such assumptions. Equally, however, the Enlightenment thinkers of the eighteenth century had fostered an alternative version of childhood as a time of innocence, possessing its own qualities which were lost as the child became an adult. Best expressed in the lines of Romantic poets such as Wordsworth: 'Heaven lies about us in our infancy ... At length the Man perceives it die away', this notion of childhood as a distinct phase of life encouraged the idea of children's rights, chief of which was the right to a proper childhood. This sus-tained both the campaigners against child labour from Jonas Hanway to Lord Shaftesbury, but also spawned a sentimentalisation of the child as the fount of innocence, which encouraged some contradictory atti-tudes when applied to the children of the poor.[38]

Public concern for the moral as well as physical welfare of poor children came to the fore early in the nineteenth century. The initial focus was on the working conditions of children in factories, mines and in dangerous occupations such as the sweeping of chimneys (the 'climbing boys'). Anxiety was aroused chiefly by official enquiries into working conditions, and the scale of child destitution revealed by the social investigations of journalists and of the statistical societies. Successive Acts of Parliament (1802, 1819, 1833) excluded the child from a select number of employments. However, although the state had intervened to protect a minority of working children, it left a larger number unprotected, notably those engaged in the multifarious occupations of the city streets. Moreover, whilst it was deemed possible in the mid Victorian period to intercede between child and employer outside the home, the relationship between parent and child was considered sacrosanct. John Stuart Mill in his essay on liberty (1859) complained of the 'misapplied notions of liberty' which prevented the state from interfering with a father's 'absolute and exclusive control' over his children.[39]

The early and mid Victorians devoted an enormous amount of emotional and intellectual energy to the problems of childhood. The early novels of Charles Dickens (*Oliver Twist* and *Nicholas Nickleby* which appeared in the 1830s) excited the imaginations of a generation with sharpened sensibilities about the welfare of children. These sensibilities encompassed several concerns ranging from a sentimental idealisation of childhood innocence to acute anxiety about the lifestyle of the street child. At times, this latter concern constituted a 'moral panic' and was linked to the criminality of the 'juvenile delinquent' (almost always male). Everyone who traversed the streets of the major towns and cities would have encountered innumerable impoverished children in ragged and dirty clothes either begging alms or, more likely, occupied in myriad street employments offering services and selling goods, of which the crossing sweeper and the flower seller are only the best known. The phenomenon of children living on the streets, deprived of the benefit of good parents (or subject to the baneful influence of bad ones) horrified enough passersby to generate a spate of philanthropic initiatives to alleviate the problem. What was the problem? It was not purely a question of relieving the destitute. For the immorality and potential criminality of the life of the 'street arabs' was a central concern. Ironically for the moralist who condemned the idleness of the poor, the street child was generally busy at some endeavour or another. It was the realisation that this capitalism of the streets could shade off onto a variety of illegal occupations that spurred many to act. A notable propagandist of preventive action was Mary Carpenter, who divided the children of the destitute into two classes:

... those who have not yet fallen into actual crime, but who are almost certain from their ignorance, destitution, and the circumstances in which they are growing up, to do so, if a helping hand be not extended to raise them; these form the *perishing classes*; and ... those ... who unblushingly acknowledge that they can gain more from the support of themselves and their parents by stealing than by working ... these form the *dangerous classes*.[40]

Mary Carpenter was active in the Sunday-school and ragged-school movements when, in the 1850s, she emerged as the chief advocate of the reform of the destitute child. Her advocacy extended to the founding of reformatories and an industrial school, but her main significance lies in the influence her arguments had on the construction of public opinion on the street child, and the importance of her work in obtaining parliamentary recognition of reformatories in 1854 and industrial schools in 1857. The case she made emphasised the dependent nature of child poverty. There was no argument here for the Smilesian virtues of self-reliance and personal moral responsibility. Moreover, the root of the problem was characterised as less a matter of poverty than a lack of parental love. Thus the solution was to rescue the child from its present circumstances and to reform its morals in the interests of the future happiness of society as a whole, and the eternal happiness of the individual child whose soul was saved.

One of the earliest solutions to the problem of juvenile vagrancy had been emigration. Numerous emigration schemes hoped to 'clear the streets' of destitute children. Between 1834 and 1837, the Children's Friend Society emigrated 1300 London youngsters to agricultural work in the south of Africa. Although there is ample evidence that many of these children were often little better off than transported convicts, emigration remained a common response until the end of the century.[41] It was one of the strategies employed by Lord Shaftesbury and the Ragged School Union.

The ragged schools were devoted to the moral education of the destitute child. Their objectives were essentially evangelical rather than academic and they were inspired by the existing model of the Sunday Schools which, by the mid nineteenth century, were catering for the 'respectable' rather than the 'rough'. In 1844, the Ragged School Union (RSU) was formed from 19 ragged schools, with Shaftesbury as its president. The average attendance in RSU day schools in London rose from 3480 in 1848 to 23 052 in 1870.[42] As the title suggests, the movement classified children according to the condition of their clothes. But the 'ragged' child lacked more than a decent wardrobe. Shaftesbury equated sartorial and family status when he told the House of Commons in 1849 that among a cohort of ragged-school children: '24 had no parents, six had one, three had stepmothers, 20 had no shirts, nine no shoes'.[43] By the 1850s, ragged schools could be found in most towns throughout Britain. Each was independent, although most were members of the RSU. They used volunteer and paid instructors and concentrated on teaching the children to read the Bible. But as well as places of instruction the ragged schools were centres of child care. Most fed their pupils, and several operated thrift clubs and clothing banks. Many undertook specialised work, such as: refuges for the homeless; industrial training schemes; emigration training homes; treats, excursions and holiday camps; and temperance Bands of Hope.[44] The Education Act of 1870, which extended the principle of compulsory education to all children, undermined the work of the ragged schools. Although they were to continue into the twentieth century, direct state intervention in the education of the child redirected charitable energies. The welfare focus narrowed to anxiety over malnourishment and various volunteer societies sprang up for the feeding of board-school children. Finally, the state, seeing the welfare of the child as an investment in the future efficiency and well-being of society, undertook to provide school meals for the poor in 1906. Earlier than this, the state had accepted responsibility for arguably a more sensitive aspect of child care.

The formation of the National Society for the Prevention of Cruelty to Children in 1889, following on from the work of the earlier Societies in Liverpool (1883) and London (1884), aimed at achieving state regulation of what the London society had termed 'Child Slaves'. These were the children sent out at night by poor and unscrupulous parents to beg, to sell or to perform in return for coppers. The inevitable link to child prostitution was an added worry. The NSPCC was an effective lobby and shortly achieved the passage of the 1889 Prevention of Cruelty to Children Act, which prohibited children under ten from such activities and threatened their instigators with fines or imprisonment. Although an inadequate instrument, the 1889 Act was the first statute to limit parental control over offspring, thus meeting Mill's call for a challenge to this 'misapplied notion of liberty'. Subsequent legislation culminated in the comprehensive clauses of the Children's Act of 1908, which touched on every child-related issue from baby farming to child smoking. The work of the NSPCC, however, was not confined to lobbying politicians. It adopted the casework procedures of the social worker to investigate accusations of cruelty to children and either attempt to influence parental behaviour or bring the case to court. However, the Society's 'cruelty men' rarely sought to separate children from their families. Less than 1 per cent of investigations between 1889 and 1903 resulted in a removal from parental custody. In fact, the NSPCC's own statistics suggest that a great majority of cases involved neglected rather than physically abused children, though Society literature continued to focus on acts of parental violence.[45]

Other child welfare agencies in the later nineteenth century sought to undermine the parental rights of neglectful or cruel parents. The rescue and emigration work of Dr Thomas Barnado and others even extended to the forcible removal, or 'philanthropic abduction' as it was called, of a small but significant number of children from homes where they were felt to be in danger. Some were emigrated to Canada without parental consent and Barnado was repeatedly summoned to court in custody cases for this method of pre-emptive rescue. Eventually, the publicity surrounding Barnado's controversial activities culminated in further legislation to protect the child. The Custody of Children Act of 1891 allowed the removal of children from the guardianship of negligent parents.[46] Dr Barnado's Homes was the most famous of the child-rescue societies which emerged during the last quarter of the century. There had been refuges, asylums and orphanages throughout the century, but the work of Barnado and other rescue and reclamation specialists marks a shift to more interventionist strategies than had been adopted by the evangelical world of the ragged schools and mission societies. Most sought to restore some semblance of home life to the 'outcast' children of the cities, hence the emphasis on 'Homes' for the destitute and policies of 'boarding out' children in foster homes, something which Barnado's pioneered. However, the religious character of this work was paramount and although Barnado's was nondenominational, interdenominational rivalry characterised the work of most of the rescue societies. The other prominent bodies in the field were the National Children's Homes, founded by the Weslyan Methodist Thomas Bowman Stephenson, and the Church of England's own institution for destitute children, the Waifs and Strays Society, founded by Edward de Montjoie Rudolf. The Roman Catholic children's rescue societies were organised on a diocesan basis.

Victorian concern for the moral and physical welfare of the young was related to anxiety about the fate of 'girls in moral danger' and the predicament of the 'fallen woman'. There had long been a desire to 'correct' the morally deviant woman and the prostitute was deemed the most extreme example. Asylums and penitentiaries for 'fallen women' dated back to the eighteenth century and perhaps earlier. There were also the Lock Hospitals, dating in many cases from the eighteenth century, dedicated to the treatment of women with venereal disease and whose patients were frequently prostitutes. These traditions continued. But something of a 'moral panic' around the mid century about such morally dark corners of urban life increased public awareness, and propelled a generation and more of charitable women into work with prostitutes.

Unsatisfied that visiting asylums and Lock Hospitals was sufficient, they turned with religious fervour to the very streets and brothels where the prostitute plied her trade. The purpose was to persuade her to purer paths and literally to 'rescue' her from a life of danger and disease. Thus the 'rescue' mentality of much late-century charity extended to the reclamation of the fallen woman. This could be exhausting and perilous work, as lady volunteers faced ridicule and hostility from the women they set out to help, and were threatened or attacked by brothel keepers and drunks. More than any branch of charity this became identified as female activity. It inspired women like Ellice Hopkins, already an accomplished charity volunteer, to visit the vice dens of Brighton in 1866, the beginnings of a prominent career as an activist, writer and campaigner for the rescue of prostitutes, children raised in brothel surroundings, and the 'friendless' girl in 'moral danger'. Thousands of poor women forced into prostitution through poverty and circumstance willingly entered Magdalene Homes in the hope of a better life. However, once inside the regime was generally strict and infused with religious instruction. One prostitute, who eventually returned to the streets, complained: 'I was so miserable always thinking about my sins.'[47] Attempts to treat prostitution as a moral disease were futile. As Frances Finnegan notes of the York refuge: 'Their undoubtedly sincere efforts were bound to fail, since they were attempting to turn individual women from a life of prostitution without attacking the fundamental economic, social and moral issues involved.'[48]

Not all 'fallen women' were necessarily prostitutes, but were often young, female adults either convicted of minor misdemeanours or noted by a figure of authority to be sexually active. In other words, it was less the poverty and more the morality of these young women that drew them to the attention of the rescue movement. In the Magdalene and other rescue homes, the emphasis was upon domestic training and the object of many societies was to turn out girls suitable for employment as domestic servants. For example, the Manchester Ladies Association for the Protection and Reformation of Girls and Women established its own home in the 1880s to provide training for domestic service for 'girls in moral danger'; the girls were generally found work in the houses of the wealthy ladies who ran the Association. Some societies offered a variety of services and facilities for girls and young women, not all of them poor. Thus the Church of England based Girls' Friendly Society, launched in 1874, had a national organisation running lodges, homes, thrift clubs and emigration schemes. It promoted an ideal of womanhood for those it helped. 'The model G. F. S. girl was expected to be devout, kindly, serious-minded, uncomplaining and … relatively uninterested in the opposite sex.'[49]

Rescue work and rescue workers fed into a variety of other campaigns. In particular, moral reform and social purity went hand in hand. Ellice Hopkins devoted much of her energies in later life to her White Cross Army, which traversed the gender boundary to discourage swearing and indecent behaviour amongst men. Such efforts were linked to the campaigns of societies such as the Social Purity Alliance, the National Vigilance Association and the Moral Reform Union. But they also demonstrate the extent to which rescue work raised awareness of the double standard in which women were held morally responsible for sinful acts. This was most clearly expressed in the campaigns against the Contagious Diseases Acts from the late 1860s through to their repeal in 1886. This legislation sought to reduce venereal disease in the armed forces, in ports and garrison towns, by the compulsory inspection, registration and, where necessary, confinement of infected prostitutes against their will for up to nine months in a Lock Hospital. This glaring example of double standards enraged and politicised many involved in rescue work, most prominently Josephine Butler, who spearheaded the campaign of the Ladies National Association for the Repeal of the Contagious Diseases Acts. Related areas of concern were the legal protection of girls living with prostitutes, child prostitution and sexual abuse. Each of these involved campaigns to change the law. In work with women – as with children – voluntary agencies increasingly expected the state to act as the guarantor of legal rights and the protector of the weak and vulnerable.

Care of the Sick and Infirm

The greatest absorbers of nineteenth-century benevolent funds were the medical charities. Financed in much the same way as other charitable societies, the voluntary hospitals were the most visible manifestation of charitable effort. Their existence as institutions devoted to the care of the sick was an eighteenth-century development. Beginning in London with the foundation of the Westminster Infirmary in 1719 and Guy's (unusual in that it was founded by bequest) in 1721, construction spread across the country. The main period of expansion, however, was in the nineteenth century. By 1891, the number of general hospitals had reached 385, plus a proliferation of specialist institutions.[50] As well as the general infirmaries, both large and small, there were several types of specialist institution, such as maternity hospitals, children's hospitals, eye and ear hospitals, dental hospitals, and the Lock hospitals for the treatment of venereal diseases. In addition, charitable gifts supported convalescent homes to aid patient recovery, residential homes for the deaf and for the blind, and for other instances of physical disability. However, it was not always easy for the poor to gain access to treatment. Indeed, it has been argued that the welfare function of the voluntary hospitals may have declined after the eighteenth century as the medical priorities of surgical staff challenged the benevolent purposes of charitable patrons.[51] Nevertheless, the contest for souls remained a significant feature of voluntary medical care in Victorian England.

The voluntary hospitals were places both of medical advance and of charitable dispensation. There was often a conflict of interest between the lay philanthropists, who founded most of the general hospitals, and the medical men, who provided the honorary medical staff of those hospitals. The need for financial stability led most of the charity hospitals to adopt a system whereby subscribers could nominate a number of patients each year. Except in cases of accident and emergency, the prospective patient in England (admissions policy was different in Scotland) could only gain admittance to a voluntary hospital via the recommendation of a subscriber who would certify that he or she was 'a proper object of the Charity'. This was usually meant to exclude 'pauper' cases whose rightful place was thought to be the workhouse.[52] This reliance upon recommendations for hospital admissions granted the subscriber considerable potential for the exercise of patronage. Moreover, generally motivated by compassion or evangelical fervour rather than medical knowledge, the individual subscriber often had non-clinical intentions in recommending patients. They were more likely to refer for treatment the kind of case which might occupy a bed for several weeks, to the exclusion of the acutely sick. Regarding the hospital as a 'reformatory', as well as an 'infirmary', the Christian philanthropist told the hospital patient that the purpose was 'not only to restore your bodily health, but effectually to promote your spiritual Welfare, and eternal Salvation'.[53] Thus a long-stay patient offered ample opportunity for the practice of sick visiting, often by lady visitors, which itself was strong on religious indoctrination.

The association in the minds of the charitable of weak bodies and vulnerable souls is inescapable. The ratio of religious practitioners to medical ones was often high. A survey of the provincial hospitals in 1864 found several examples like that of the Royal Portsmouth Hospital, which was 'used mainly as a refuge for a few chronic invalids who have had the good luck to recommend themselves to some subscriber'.[54] The honorary medical staffs in the hospitals, by contrast, generally wished to admit short-stay acute cases, who could be treated or operated on with quick results. In several London hospitals, they were particularly concerned to admit patients with interesting diseases for teaching purposes. Suitable cases were selected from the crowds of the sick which gathered in the hope of treatment in the outpatient departments of the major infirmaries.

In the larger industrial towns, many of those admitted for treatment were accident cases injured at their place of work. Aware of the financial implications of industrial injury, employers often subscribed to voluntary hospitals so as to secure the right to have their sick employees admitted as patients. This was much cheaper than the provision of adequate safety precautions or of paying the salary for a factory surgeon. Thus half the subscription income of the Huddersfield Infirmary in the mid nineteenth century was derived from the town's industrialists.[55] Considering the restrictions upon entry, what social class of patient was admitted? The evidence is varied. Patients in a small provincial general hospital like the Salop Infirmary in 1845–46 covered a wide range of employments, from agricultural labourer to prostitutes, from clerks to quarry workers. However, it is unlikely that many of the very poor found their way into one of the voluntary hospitals. Of the teaching hospital patients classified by occupation in the census of 1861, the vast majority were wage earners employed in industry, domestic service or agriculture. A tiny proportion were in middle-class occupations.[56]

Dispensaries may have been of more direct importance in the treatment of the sick poor, although they have rarely been a subject of historical research.[57] Beginning later than the voluntary hospitals (in the 1770s), by 1820, around 60 were operating in London and the provinces. They were run on similar lines to the hospitals, except that they concentrated on outpatients and home visits by dispensary physicians. However, dispensaries were generally of lower professional status than the hospitals and were commonly staffed by younger medical men starting out in their careers. None the less, it has been claimed that their contribution to public health was greater and that their physicians became expert in the natural history and treatment of epidemic fever.[58] Dispensaries dealt most directly with the poor, but they experienced a crisis of funding from the 1830s as the ideology of self-help and the rise of the Poor Law medical service developed. From the mid century, provident dispensaries became more common, based upon weekly contributions, they represented a shift away from paternalism and towards self-help.

The variety of voluntary medical provision had as much to do with the professionalisation of 'doctoring' in the nineteenth century and the need for medical men to make their way in the 'market for medicine' as it did with the needs of the sick poor. However, not all doctors were 'on the make'. There was a tradition of general practitioners doing a certain amount of unpaid work among the poor. Some even set aside a few hours a week when they would attend the poor without fee (although medicines were probably still charged for). In 1825, the Huddersfield Medical Society drew up a scale of fees according to the incomes of patients, recommending that those 'occupying houses at a rent under fifteen pounds per annum shall be charged for visits or not according to the discretion of the practitioner'.[59] However, as the medical profession became more competitive during the century and as attitudes towards the poor hardened under the impetus of the New Poor Law, the doctor who did not charge or was indifferent to the size of his fee was often viewed with hostility by his colleagues.[60] The degree of professional resentment of free treatment was exacerbated by the experience of many practitioners on low-paid contracts with Poor Law unions or on the doctors panels of the friendly societies.

Whilst the voluntary health services of the eighteenth and the first half of the nineteenth centuries were the product of a combination of philanthropic contributions and professional medical interests, the contributory funds of working people themselves became more important as the century progressed. Although the pace of change should not be exaggerated, this trend to contributory schemes pointed to the future in voluntary hospital finance. From the mid century, local workplace-collection schemes had helped to fund particular hospitals. The Hospital Saturday Fund, founded in the 1870s, was designed to organise such contributions on a grander scale. When the Saturday Fund established a penny-a-week scheme in the 1890s, its collections took on a 'quasi-insurance' character which alarmed some in the medical profession. Working men were starting to claim a right to treatment rather than relying on the 'gift' of a subscribers' recommendation. By 1900, Hospital Saturday and other contributory schemes provided over 17 per cent of the ordinary income of provincial hospitals in England and Wales. The trend to contributory schemes continued into the interwar period and by the 1930s, they provided 30 per cent of hospital income, easily exceeding income from charitable sources. The other major source of revenue by this time was patients' fees. These twin sources sponsored an expansion in private hospital provision, which continued till the formation of the National Health Service in 1948. However, such later developments should not be anticipated. In 1900, charitable income (subscriptions, donations and voluntary collections) still provided over half of ordinary income, and paying patients contributed a mere 2 per cent. The voluntary medical services were still charitable as well as private.[61]

Later Victorian Charity

Although the later decades of the century witnessed an increasingly less equitable economic or ideological climate for voluntarism, it would be misleading to defer to hindsight in hastening the demise of charity, which remained central to welfare provision into the early twentieth century. However, the utilitarian and evangelical impulses of Victorian philanthropy hardened into more clearly separate strategies. In particular, the Charity Organisation Society, formed after the poor-relief crisis of the 1860s, sought to reserve the charitable gift for the 'deserving' and condemned the spread of charity to areas such as the relief of the unemployed. By the 1890s, voluntarism in all its varieties was facing the prospect of closer relationships with the state which went beyond the lobbying of the child welfare societies. This convergence of philanthropy and the 'public sector' heralded a partnership which, in the twentieth century, was to see a subordination of voluntarism to the more pro-active welfare policies of central government. The evangelical drive which had generated so much charitable endeavour since the 1780s stimulated new charities throughout the second half of the nineteenth century. But the pan-evangelicalism of the early nineteenth century had largely disappeared. The Anglican resurgence of the second quarter of the century and the religious revivals which periodically swept communities of church and chapel from the 1850s until the first decade of the twentieth century contributed to denominational rivalry. A practical stimulus was the alarm generated by the religious census of 1851 which revealed very low church attendance in poorer neighbourhoods. However, revivals had only short-term implications for congregational growth.[62] The more enduring, if homespun and unsung, strategies for sustaining church and chapel membership among the working classes were the various voluntary activities located in church halls in the evenings and on Sunday afternoons. Chief amongst these parochial institutions was the mothers' meeting. An extension of the district visiting movement, the mothers' meeting gathered together working-class women in an environment of domestic culture (chiefly needlework) and religious exhortation. If numbers are anything to go by, it was a great success. Prochaska estimates that upwards of a million women and their children attended weekly meetings by the turn of the century. Supervised by lady volunteers and in meetings of up to 50 or 60, the mothers' meeting became a ubiquitous feature of charitable provision in the second half of the century. It was arguably the greatest philanthropic experiment in bringing the social classes together.

By the 1880s, most parishes, and many charities aimed at the poor, organised mother's meetings. According to their historian, these gatherings embodied maternal culture, were centres of female comradeship and, by the close of the century, had become a source of advice on infant welfare and family health.[63] The mother's meeting was only the most common example of the parochial voluntarism encouraged by religious revivalism and denominational rivalry. Bible classes, youth groups, choral societies, temperance organisations, such as the Band of Hope, and a host of other ventures epitomise the association of philanthropy with spiritual regeneration and the desire to consolidate church communities.

The foundation of so many charitable agencies in the mid-century period, at a time when the issues of poverty and unrest were less at the forefront of the public's attention than they had been during the 1830s and 1840s, is witness to the power of the evangelical movement. This trend continued and as many as two thirds of the charities set up in the second half of the century were evangelical in inspiration. Barnado's and the Salvation Army are perhaps the most famous examples. The evangelical springs of social action could be more impulsive and inclusive than the more utilitarian priorities of some charity intellectuals. As we have seen, these twin roots of welfare charity need not necessarily be seen in opposition. But the evangelical mind was less likely to turn away the undeserving applicant on the grounds that *all* were capable of being saved. Spiritual redemption was the ultimate evangelical purpose: self-help was only a means to that end. Few of the organisers of charity saw it that way.

Charity Organisation Society

The charitable impulse was a complicated phenomenon and since the later eighteenth century, there had been those who sought to organise the charitable and the charitable gift so as to restrain and redirect philanthropic energies. Thus some societies existed to influence the giving of others rather than to fulfil a philanthropic purpose themselves. The Charity Organisation Society (COS) was founded in London in the wake of the poor-relief crises of the 1860s, and in the context of fears about the demoralisation of the working classes and the spectre of the 'residuum'. It began life in April 1869 as the Society for Organising Charitable Relief and Repressing Mendicity, but rapidly became known by its shorter title. In the later nineteenth century, the Charity Organisation Society in London and other similar or branch agencies across the country attempted to restrain and control the charitable gift; to reduce the total amount of charitable giving and to direct the remainder only to those they considered deserving. The *bette noir* of the charity organiser was the indiscriminate gift: that is, charitable giving without knowledge of, or enquiry into, the circumstances or character of the recipient. Instead, the COS argued, charity should be discretionary. It was not a right to be claimed but, literally, a *gift* at the discretion of the donor. As such it carried moral implications for both giver and receiver alike.

Thus it was held that charity must be conditional upon 'good habits'; that is, it must sustain and not undermine the best efforts of the deserving to remain thrifty and self-reliant. It must help the poor to help themselves and must not have the effect of making them dependent upon external support. As it was, those who joined the COS deplored the huge amounts devoted to charity. These funds, it was felt, were actually fuelling the fires of destitution rather than relieving the distress that so agitated the philanthropic conscience. The spectre of a return to the dependency culture of pre-1834 times haunted the would-be charity organisers. C. S. Loch, the Society's secretary from 1875 to 1913, denounced indiscriminate alms giving as a 'voluntary ... insufficient ... wasteful ... self-imposed tax on the rich'. Another of the Society's leaders, Octavia Hill was horrified by what 'impatient charity is doing to the poor of London'. To Edward Denison: ' ... [t]he gigantic subscription lists which are vaunted as signs of our benevolence are monuments of our indifference.'[64]

Before considering the work of the COS, it should be recalled that they were not the originators of charity organisation, although they gave it this particular name. As we have seen, the concern for a 'scientific charity' – which co-ordinated giving, acted as a storehouse of information, aimed to educate the giving class, and organised district visiting of the poor in their homes – can be found as early as the 1790s in the activities of the SBCP and others, was stimulated by the example of Chalmers's work in the Glasgow of the early 1820s, and found expression in a number of societies in the early and mid century. The foundation of the COS in 1869 was the culmination of the charity organisation movement not its genesis. That being said, the proliferation of charities, and the perceived unevenness and overlapping of provision since the middle of the century, made the organisation of charity seem more necessary than ever. No other Victorian charitable society has been given as much attention by historians as the COS, but opinion on its character and importance is mixed.[65] The Charity Organisation Society should be studied both as a voluntary society – with its own philosophy, organisation and practices – and also as a platform for a number of influential intellectuals convinced of the efficacy of voluntary solutions to social problems who were, by the turn of the century, fighting a rearguard action against the threat of centralised state-welfare programmes, which they felt undermined the principles of self-help and social progress. The fact that the COS has been judged by some to have failed in its practical endeavours should not serve to obscure the impact its leaders had at the highest level on the welfare debates of the time.

The COS had three key aims which came to define the significant areas of its work. Firstly, it set out to co-operate with the Poor Law authorities at a local level in order to establish a more effective line of demarcation between the responsibilities of the boards of guardians and of the voluntary charities; this involved the ideal of a deterrent Poor Law acting as a safety net for the destitute and as a sanction against the 'undeserving', whilst a better organised charitable sphere could eradicate the indiscriminate gift and reserve charity for the 'deserving' case only. Rather than relieving distress, it was argued, 'misplaced charity' actually encouraged pauperism because it offered something for nothing, thus demoralising the deserving poor. The issue of the Goschen Minute endorsing its strategy showed that the Society had official support at the highest level (see Chapter 2).

Secondly, alarmed at the proliferation of often competing societies, and appalled at the overlapping in provision and apparent lack of discrimination between applicants, the Society saw its function as the 'organisation' of other charities so as to better co-ordinate charitable effort, and facilitate the exchange of reliable information for those whose donations supported the societies. To this end, it published lists of approved charities and advice and guidance literature for charity workers, and undertook to influence public opinion in the direction of a more judicious and, as it regarded it, 'scientific' approach to the charitable gift. Once more the indiscriminate gift was the enemy; and the supposedly 'sentimental' charity of the evangelical societies was a prime target. Finally, the Society's chief organisational mechanism was that of casework; the visiting and investigation of all applicants for relief, not so as to act as a relief-giving agency, but as a mechanism of moral improvement in the individual. More prosaically, this involved casework as a means of vetting applicants for both charitable assistance and, as many COS activists hoped, for official poor relief as well. By the 1880s, investigation and casework had become the chief preoccupation of the COS and its main *raison d'être*. It developed its own 'casepaper' practice, focusing upon poor families and for each case recording details such as employment history, patterns of income and expenditure, evidence of thrift (e.g., friendly society or savings club memberships) or conversely, of the receipt of poor relief. Its rigorous and intrusive methods and the fact that it turned down most applicants as undeserving earned it few friends amongst either the poor or, indeed, amongst other charities. The COS managed to alienate many within the charitable community, especially those evangelical charities of which it was most critical. Furthermore, it was largely unsuccessful in its attempt to redirect the efforts of the charitable or to reduce charitable expenditure. Moreover, it is a mistake to think of the COS as a national society at all. Despite claims to the contrary, although COS branches or similar societies were founded in a numbers of provincial towns and cities, they never functioned as a national network of charity organisation societies. Even within London, its federal structure gave individual COS branches great leeway in their approach to charitable relief. Bob Humphrey's study of the charity-organisation movement in the provinces has concluded that, although the provincial societies professed commitment to the principles of the London COS, in reality, they displayed a wide variety of practices. For example, the Central Relief Society in Liverpool, although it affiliated to the London COS, continued to act as an agency of direct relief and the District Provident Society in Manchester, whilst professing to be a charity organisation society, made little attempt to organise other charities. The COS ambition of co-ordinating relief was rarely realised in practice and there are few examples of successful co-operation with local Poor Law guardians, even in London. The intention of the home visit to bring the rich and poor together generally foundered upon the old problem of a shortage of volunteers, and it became common to employ paid investigators.[66]

The COS was not a monolithic body nor was it an unchanging one. The view that the Society consistently expressed 'a sternly individualist philosophy'[67] has been undermined by those who point to the views of certain of its key intellectuals (chiefly Bernard Bosanquet and C. S. Loch) who, whilst espousing individual responsibility as the cause of poverty, linked charity to a theory of citizenship and notions of an ethical community.[68] There is certainly much evidence to suggest that, for some, the social work of the COS offered an alternative form of social advance that did not require centralised state welfare, but equally did not hark back to the certainties of the earlier political economists. However, 'harder and dryer' views generally prevailed in the Society. For example, the idea of 'friendly visiting', by which the home visit was meant to forge a relationship of mutual obligation and trust, and which Jane Lewis argues was 'significantly different from the older nineteenth-century concept of district visiting', may, in the event, have involved little more than the old aim of getting the poor family to see the virtues of middle-class values and culture.[69] Nevertheless, the COS has often been credited as the originator of modern social work. The Society itself claimed descendance from Thomas Chalmers's work in 1820s' Glasgow and the Elberfeld experiment in mid-century Germany. But it is also to the long-standing English example of home visiting and rudimentary casework that we should just as readily look for the roots of charity visiting, which acquired its new name of 'social work' in the era of the COS. It was in the professionalisation of social work that the real innovations of the COS lay, especially the detailed elaboration of casework practice and in the idea of training social workers. The Society in 1897 began training courses in co-operation with the Women's University Settlement and established its own, short-lived, School of Sociology in 1903 (absorbed by the London School of Economics in 1912). However, the focus in much writing about the COS on its contribution to the history of social work, and its relation to modern welfare practices, should be accompanied by more attention to the nineteenth-century world of voluntary visiting of which it was a part.

If there was a diversity of ideas within the COS, there is little doubt that its intellectuals had the ear of the powerful and well placed. The COS enjoyed an influence on official thinking out of all proportion to its impact upon the activities of the charitable. It was regularly represented on official enquiries into social problems, and its intellectuals were regarded as 'experts' on poverty and social welfare. This was in part due to Loch's effectiveness as the Society's long-standing secretary, but also was a consequence of the Society's desire to maintain its influence on all kinds of welfare policy. This latter point is illustrated by the extent to which the COS was willing to adapt to both the growth of the labour movement and to the emergence of state relief outside the Poor Law. For example, Jose Harris has noted the Society's toleration of relief funds and public works for the unemployed, as long as COS members could keep control of the administrative strings.[70] As the years went by, a new generation of COS activists were more willing to adapt to a changing ideological climate. When the Conservative government of Arthur Balfour decided to appoint a Royal Commission on the Poor Laws and the Relief of Distress in 1905, the 18 commissioners included 11 members of the COS. The Majority Report of the Royal Commission, published in 1909, was largely written by Helen Bosanquet of the COS and was signed by all the COS commissioners. As McBriar argues, this Report's recommendation of the abolition of the boards of guardians, abandonment of the aim of abolishing out-relief, and proposal of semi-official status for voluntary investigation is indicative of the extent to which a 'younger guard' within the COS had moved towards a public-private partnership in the relief of the poor.[71]

Several of the COS 'younger guard' had been influenced by Samuel Barnett, a founder member of the COS, who became convinced that it did not understand the needs of the poor. Instead of casework with individual families, Barnett pioneered social work in the community via the Settlement House Movement. Toynbee Hall, the Universities residential settlement in East London, opened in 1884 with Barnett as its first warden. The idea was to place young university men (and later women) in the midst of the poor in order to unite the classes in common experiences and shared community. The objective was very different from that of the evangelicals anxious for conversions. Barnett was at pains to stress that the relationship was to be reciprocal, the poor were not to be preached at or patronised. The solution was intentionally radical. In Barnett's eyes, the answer to poverty and demoralisation was 'the abolition of the space which divides the rich and poor .... Not until the habits of the rich are changed, and they are again content to breathe the same air and walk the same streets as the poor, will East London be saved.'[72] Not for the first time – nor, indeed, would it be the last – the antidote to poverty was conceived in terms of personal relationships, between rich and poor, in a shared humanity. Before the century had closed, there were 30 settlement houses on the Toynbee Hall model across London and in provincial cities.

Housing and Unemployment

The COS was active during an era of crisis in which the problems of poverty, housing and unemployment were at the heart of the social problem. In the 1880s and 1890s, perception of poverty shifted towards a focus on the inner city: the housing crisis, the unemployed and casual poor, the fear of unrest in the mid 1880s subsiding into a bleak, but less dangerous image of 'mean streets' and 'grey lives' in the 1890s. Moreover, these were decades of debate in which confidence in the post-1834 strategy of a harsh Poor Law and discriminating charity was waning. How did charities react to the issues of housing and unemployment in an uncertain ideological climate? In the first place, the problems of the homeless and the inadequate provision of housing stock for the poor were areas for charitable effort which sometimes trod on the toes of the property owner. In an age when, of all civil rights, the right of property ownership appeared to receive most respect, it proved impossible for any agency to devise satisfactory arrangements which combined slum clearance with the provision of cheap housing. Only at the very end of the century did the (local) state, in the shape of a handful of municipal councils, start to get involved in the provision of public or subsidised housing. Whilst slums were often condemned as 'unfit for human habitation' or cleared for the purposes of road widening or major building projects, such as occurred in the West End of London, those evicted from the demolished properties were not rehoused, but simply squeezed into increasingly overcrowded and inadequate housing elsewhere.

The housing crisis of the later nineteenth century propelled charities into the provision of subsidised and model accommodation, chiefly lodging houses and blocks of flats. The most notable ventures into philanthropic housing were run on semi-commercial grounds, the famous 'philanthropy plus 5 per cent'. Model dwelling tenements were constructed on this principle in the big cities from the 1860s onwards. The Peabody Trust, the Improved Industrial Dwellings Company and others had built in over 50 locations by the mid 1880s, but the requirement for a profit meant that the rents they charged were generally beyond the reach of the poorest families. Although thousands were rehoused by the model dwellings movement, and this may have freed up accommodation for those lower down the social scale, historians generally conclude that 'philanthropic capitalism' of this sort was of limited significance in either the housing crisis of the later nineteenth century or the broader problems of poverty. Moreover, all the experiments were urban and there was little philanthropic interest in providing rural housing. Similarly, company housing, although sometimes architecturally and socially innovative, as at Port Sunlight built by W. H. Lever or the garden suburb constructed by George Cadbury at Bournville, was of marginal significance to the national picture and generally benefited the better-off working families rather than the poor.[73]

The best-known charitable attempt to provide housing for the families of the poor, rather than of the artisan, was the work of Octavia Hill and her followers in London and other cities. A granddaughter of the sanitary reformer Southwood Smith, and co-founder of both the COS and the National Trust (the latter in 1895), Hill was a major figure in the world of philanthropy from the 1870s to the early twentieth century. Her housing experiments offered cheap accommodation for poor families, combined with close supervision to ensure that tenants maintained clean and moral habits, those who did not come up to scratch were evicted. This reflected Hill's assumption that bad housing was the consequence both of neglectful landlords and the character of some tenants. Her landladies (for they were generally women) were to be social workers as well as house managers and rent collectors. As in much Victorian charity the solution to social problems was sought through personal relationships between individuals. Hill vigorously opposed municipal housing for the poor, arguing that state responsibility should halt at slum clearance, regulating building standards and enforcing sanitary laws. The mere threat of municipal action, she maintained, stifled voluntary effort.[74] By 1900, in London there were already several council estates and an acceptance of the role of municipal housing. However, it was not until the Housing Act of 1919 that the role of the state as a major provider of working-class housing was clear. Prior to 1914, the case remained strong, even among members of the newly formed Labour Party, that council housing would create a dependent and demoralised population, and that the true role of the state was not to house people, but to ensure that people could satisfactorily house themselves.[75]

In the last 20 years of the century, the problem of urban unemployment loomed larger – even than housing – on the agenda of many charities. Throughout the century, the vagrant had been occasionally offered an alternative to the workhouse casual ward via the night asylum and strangers' friend refuges, which were always intended for the genuine workmen on the tramp in search of employment rather than the permanent vagrant or the temporarily homeless. The problem of unemployment and homelessness in the later century produced periodic 'sleeping out' crises, in which the streets of the larger cities were crowded with out of work men and women. There had been charitable societies specifically for the relief of the unemployed ever since the eighteenth century. They were usually local and small scale. A common criticism throughout the period was that they attracted mendicants to the neighbourhood.[76] The COS opposed such societies as agencies of indiscriminate relief. But the COS approach through casework was of limited value even to that small proportion of the unemployed whom they were willing to help. Between 1886 and 1896, an average of fewer than 800 cases a year were 'assisted to find employment' by the London COS.[77]

In the event, the COS was prepared to tolerate limited public relief works during years of high unemployment and also to co-operate with other local agencies (guardians and municipal authorities) in the organisation of relief funds, chiefly since it hoped to bring its influence to bear to prevent indiscriminate giving. The most notable instance of this had been the Mansion House Fund of 1886, which had dispensed nearly £100 000 in a panic spate of giving in response to the serious unemployed riots in the West End.[78] Subsequently, the Lord Mayor convened a Mansion House Committee that administered relief funds in the Capital between 1886 and 1894. In this forum, representatives of public and voluntary bodies and the churches debated how best to deal with the seemingly intractable problem of unemployment. Generally, the COS would co-operate only with minor public work schemes. This pattern was repeated across the country, where the major agency involved in such work creation was the local municipal authority. Other voluntary charities, however, were less circumspect in dealing with the unemployed.

Home colonisation, settling unemployed men to work on vacant agricultural land, was a major strategy in the treatment of unemployment in the closing years of the century. It was also a strategy which attracted charitable funds. These so-called labour or farm colonies were organised by local authorities, Poor Law guardians and voluntary charities. Some were punitive and disciplinary, while others were worthy, if largely futile, exercises in retraining. The first practicable experiment in the field was organised by the London Congregational Union in 1886, when it arranged for the employment of 150 London unemployed by a Lincolnshire farmer. Other charitable ventures included that of the English Land Colonisation Society affiliated to the interdenominational Christian Social Service Union. But the largest, and most controversial, scheme of home colonisation was that of the Salvation Army, based on General William Booth's *In Darkest England and the Way Out* (1890). This was an effective exposé of social conditions, in which Booth compared the lives of the poorest in England to the lot of the African native. Booth's was a radical agenda. Although he acknowledged the extent to which 'misery' of the poor 'arises from their own habits', he also condemned: 'Those firms which reduce sweating to a fine art, who systematically and deliberately defraud the workman of his pay, who grind the faces of the poor, and who rob the widow and the orphan, and who for a pretence make great professions of public-spirit and philanthropy'.[79]

The founder of the Salvation Army set out to offer the nation a plan of social and spiritual redemption based on agricultural colonies at home and emigration overseas. Booth's programme epitomised the extent to which the evangelical charities undermined the desire of the charity organisers to drive a wedge between the Poor Law and charity, reserving the latter for the deserving or, as the COS were beginning to call them in the 1890s, the 'helpable'. Booth could not have been more explicit in his rejection of this line of demarcation. The inclusive approach of the evangelical meant that it was precisely the poorest who were to be saved first. The 'denizens in Darkest England', for whom Booth appealed, were:

> those who, having no capital or income of their own, would in a month be dead from sheer starvation were they exclusively dependent upon the money earned by their own work; and those who by their utmost exertions are unable to attain the regulation allowance of food which the law prescribes as indispensable even for the worst criminals in our gaols.'[80]

In Darkest England challenged the adequacy of self-help and, indeed, of charity itself as a remedy for poverty and unemployment.

The 'social salvation' scheme of the Salvation Army was followed through with all seriousness during the 1890s and into the new century. It enshrined the notion that only if the environment of the poor was radically altered could their character be reformed. It was to social reform not self-help that Booth looked, and the Army acted as a pressure group for greater state responsibility for the unemployed. But this should not suggest an abandonment of voluntary action, quite the reverse. The Salvation Army sought to secure official sanction for its own work with the unemployed. In the event, its network of workshops, labour bureau, labour colonies and emigration policy that it built up in the 1890s was never officially adopted. However, the fact that the 'Darkest England' scheme was considered at all as a means of dealing with the residuum – either by the state delegating responsibility to the Salvation Army or by incorporating its 'social wing' as a branch of public administration – suggests that voluntary solutions to social problems were considered relevant by those in public office and supports Finlayson's idea that, by the later nineteenth century, the welfare path being trod was that of 'convergence' rather than confrontation between the respective spheres of voluntarism and the State.[81] As Jose Harris observes: 'The Army's colony and workshop were frequently inspected by politicians and social reformers as evidence of what could and could not be done to rehabilitate the unemployed.'[82]

Into the Twentieth Century

The central state only slowly assumed direct welfare responsibility beyond the relief of destitution and, before 1900, government ministers still displayed a willingness to seek informal, decentralised and voluntary solutions to welfare problems. The Salvation Army scheme is witness to the continued vitality and imagination of the voluntary sector at the close of the nineteenth century, and of its increasing desire to pursue a partnership with the state. The extent to which children's charities in the 1880s and 1890s were looking to the state for a legal framework of child protection is further indication of a convergence of voluntarism and the state. The path of convergence had even been followed by the COS in its desire to co-operate with the Poor Law and was to be further pursued when the Society sought a semi-official status for its casework practices in the Majority Report of the Poor Law Commission in 1909.

The voluntary charities had exhibited a wide range of responses to the social problems of the later Victorian years. They were to be equally divided over the spread of state responsibility after 1900. MacBriar's identification of a 'younger guard' within the COS by the time of the Royal Commission on the Poor Laws between 1905 and 1909, which was more positive towards public bodies and which acknowledged environmental causes of poverty, is indicative of changes pointing towards the so-called 'New Philanthropy'. The clearest expression of this before 1914 came in the Guild of Help movement.[83] Unlike the COS, this was a decentralised movement which sprang from the civic consciousness of provincial cities like Bradford and Halifax. The Guild of Help has been seen as marking the transition from charity to social work and ending the notion of philanthropy as something done to the poor by a privileged class.[84] However, the extent to which the 'New Philanthropy' broke with the traditions of self-help and moral exhortation before 1914 was limited. In the founding city of Bradford: 'thrift, sobriety and hard work were the cardinal virtues preached by the Guild.'[85] Like the COS it concentrated on home visits and casework. Although its visitors were called 'helpers', they were not allowed to give material assistance, only moral guidance and practical advice. Helpers were reminded that: 'always the best gifts to the poor are self-respect and provident habits, and one of the worst gifts that can be inflicted on them is the habit of depending upon alms.'[86] This is where we came in. Despite adjustment to a changing climate of ideas the rationale of the self-help charities remained remarkably consistent.

It was the survival of a moral dimension to the social reform ideology of the early twentieth century that in part explains the degree of convergence, rather than conflict, between public and voluntary agencies in the extension of state responsibility for social welfare before 1914. Arguably, the real transition to a 'new philanthropy' came during and after the First World War, when charity found itself more clearly subordinated to rather than a partner of the state. This encouraged a coming together of the disparate parts of an emerging 'voluntary sector' in the National Council of Social Service in 1919, the predecessor of today's National Council for Voluntary Organisations. As the twentieth century progressed, the process of convergence between voluntarism and the state increasingly became a relationship of dependence in which the voluntary sector worked to supplement expanding state provision. By the mid twentieth century, the emergence of the 'social welfare state' marked the culmination of the transition from the nineteenth-century pattern, when 'active citizens' had sought welfare solutions outside the state, to a new one in which an 'active state' took upon itself to bestow welfare entitlements upon its citizens.[87] Before 1900, however, the transition to the 'active state' was largely in the future, its precise contours and character undetermined, and the future role of the voluntary sector yet to be established.

4

THE WORKING CLASS, SELF-HELP AND MUTUAL AID

For those in poverty, the presence or absence of state welfare provision is a major issue. In the late twentieth century, the forms and interviews, the officials and regulations of the welfare bureaucracy are an everyday fact of life for the poor. By contrast, the impact of the state in the nineteenth century, although real, was much more distant. The contraction of taxed-based redistributive policies from the 1830s and the concurrent outpouring of charitable funds might suggest a voluntary redistribution to replace the decline in state provision. However, voluntary income was variable, and the causes supported more often reflected the enthusiasms and anxieties of the charitable than the practical needs of the poor. Whilst the contribution of both the voluntary sector and the state to the provision of care and welfare in the nineteenth century should not be underestimated, in the prevailing climate of individualism and self-help, much was left to the resources of the individual. Those in poverty, and those in fear of poverty, were most dependent upon their own resources and those of their family, their neighbours and their class.

'Self-help' invokes the ideology of individualism encapsulated most famously in the book of the same name published by Samuel Smiles in 1859. The mutualist character of much of 'private' welfare provision instead invites the term 'mutual aid'. For example, the collective character of social insurance through the friendly society found expression in the conviviality of its proceedings, and the sharing networks which sustained many a poor family through hard times depended on reciprocal understandings between neighbours. There are, of course, cases

109

of private provision that appear more individualist than these examples: for instance, the depositor in a savings bank or the purchaser of a commercial insurance policy does little to participate in the mutual principle, at least in those actions. However, although different individuals might be seeking either to maximise their own self-interest or to participate in a collective exercise of mutual aid, in terms of welfare provision, the outcome was the same. Through formal or informal means the working class were providing for their own welfare rather than (or as well as) acting as supplicants to external agencies, whether Poor Law officials or charity committees.

It seems ironic that moralists and charity reformers spent so much time preaching 'self-help' to the masses in the face of overwhelming evidence of self-reliance and mutual assistance arising from within the working class itself. Despite the repeated and routine condemnations of working-class fecklessness and improvidence throughout the century, there is ample indication of self-help and mutual aid amongst the poor, although it was often in forms which the propertied classes did not understand or suspected of being subversive. In times of hardship, unemployment, sickness, childhood, old age and death, a majority of the working class drew on their own resources or the support of their relatives and neighbours before they considered asking for poor relief or charity. In large part, the self-help and mutual-aid strategies discussed below arose from the experience of life during an era of rapid social and economic change, facilitated for some by rising living standards, but also reinforced by the restrictions placed upon public relief after 1834 and the stigma associated with the status of being a pauper.

It is common to speak of the 'victims of poverty'. Such words are meant to convey the powerlessness of individuals in the face of events beyond their control, but which none the less have a great impact upon their lives. However, such language obscures the various ways in which people endeavoured to 'make ends meet' in the struggles of everyday life, supported others in similar circumstances and, when possible, made plans to prevent poverty which were both individual and collective. In all this, individuals, families and groups, who possessed comparatively little power within society, can be portrayed as dynamic rather than passive; active agents in the shaping of their own histories rather than the victims of poverty or dependants on welfare. Thus the savings clubs and friendly societies, the credit and pawn economy, and the 'neighbourliness' of poor districts were strategies designed to prevent or to survive the incidence of poverty. Although the same individuals and families might deploy several of these, it is helpful to consider them as separate institutions. Consequently, this chapter deals first with the mechanisms for accumulating personal savings in preparation for times of need and insuring collectively with others against identifiable risks, such as sickness and unemployment (chiefly the friendly society, trade union, co-operative society and savings bank). Secondly, I turn to the importance of regular credit in the working-class economy, from retailer, pawnbroker and money lender, plus the more informal support networks and survival strategies between neighbours and kin which sustained individuals, families and communities through periods of poverty. Partly because of relative neglect by historians of the working class, initial attention is given to the friendly societies, numerically the largest working-class movement in the nineteenth century and which originated the principle of contributory social insurance so prominent in Britain's welfare tradition.

Friendly Societies

The friendly society movement was the oldest and most successful example of working-class mutual aid.[1] Through the pooling of member's weekly contributions, they enabled working people collectively to afford welfare benefits which they would never have been able to pay for as individuals. Chiefly these benefits included sick pay, the possibility of medical attendance during illness, and the payment of funeral expenses so as to avoid a pauper burial in an unmarked grave. In the later nineteenth century, doctors were often hired on contract and in the larger societies joined a 'panel' from whom members could choose. Unpopular practitioners could be removed from the panel. The cost of benefits such as these would vary, but generally fell between sixpence and one shilling a week depending upon age of entry to the society. The goal of social security would require regular payments over a number of years. Consequently several of the successful societies imposed a minimum wage clause or excluded certain more irregular trades. Equally, persons admitted normally would have to be of sound health, and to be deemed of regular habits and good moral character. It was also common to require the payment of an entrance fee. These restrictions upon membership were necessary on actuarial grounds.

The survival of each friendly society depended on its calculation of the risks insured against and no society wanted to elect to membership someone regarded as a 'bad risk' either on grounds of health or income. The payments of the members were the funds of the society, there were no charitable contributions to fall back on (although the small number of 'county societies' were charitable in origin). For those able to enjoy society membership, the returns were more than financial and gave them a taste of the personal security only available to those who could afford to plan their lives.

Friendly societies had their origins in the seventeenth century, but it was during the later eighteenth century and the early nineteenth century that they began to flourish. The reason for this is partly tied up with the growth of industrial occupations, but also related to changes in the organisation of work, especially the migration of labour associated with the rapid pace of urbanisation. One of the repercussions was an increase in economic insecurity for the majority of working people. It was not so much a question of advancing levels of poverty; indeed wage rates and real incomes were generally higher in the towns than in the countryside. Rather, it was a matter of declining levels of social security. Although the agricultural labourers of the eighteenth century possessed less in the way of disposable income than their nineteenth-century urban counterparts, generally they had enjoyed a greater degree of job security and most had the benefit of a more inclusive welfare system under the Old Poor Law. Friendly society membership was higher in those regions whose populations were expanding fastest as a result of inward migration, chiefly the Midlands and the North West, and lower in the more completely agricultural counties of the South and East.

Although there are no entirely reliable figures, returns for 1815 and 1831 suggest a situation in which Lancashire had by far the largest number of members of local societies and, at 17 per cent, the highest proportion of population who had joined a society. Other counties with 10 per cent or more of their population in local friendly societies in 1831 included Cornwall, Devon, Leicestershire, Monmouthshire, Nottinghamshire, Shropshire, Staffordshire and Warwickshire. Counties in which 3 per cent or fewer were members of local societies were Berkshire, Herefordshire, Sussex and Westmoreland; Cambridgeshire, Kent, Norfolk and Lincolnshire all had fewer than 5 per cent of their population in societies. Membership was concentrated in regions attracting migrant labour. The link between friendly society growth and urbanisation in the early nineteenth century has been particularly emphasised by Martin Gorsky, who argues that the societies acted as a kind of 'fictive kin' for migrants workers, providing: 'social networks, conviviality, and personal and financial support at times of life crisis'.[2]

The classic organisational form at this early stage was the local sick club, with meetings held in the local inn or public house. Sometimes societies were organised in a particular trade. In either case, meetings were regular and attendance was often a condition of membership. Committees were usually appointed to administer sick relief according to the rules drawn up at the society's formation. Society funds would be kept in a safe place, often a heavily padlocked chest with different keys held by separate members of the committee. Members might also be contributors to a slate clothing club or boot and shoe club, or any other of the innumerable examples of working-class thrift. The friendly societies were later to take on a national importance which was reflected in their organisation. However, in this early period many societies were short-lived. The most ephemeral were the dividing societies which paid sick relief, but regularly divided up their funds and distributed them to members before reforming as a new club. Dividing societies were by their nature confined to a particular locality. These dividing clubs or tontines provided only limited cover against sickness and funeral costs and no medical attendance. They could not offer their members the interest from an accumulating fund, but if they had to close down, only one year's contributions would be lost.

The period after 1830 saw a significant change in the organisation and size of the friendly society movement. Whilst the earlier societies had been local and independent, the friendly society movement of the middle and later nineteenth century came to be dominated by the 'affiliated orders'. These were societies with a central body to which individual societies could affiliate, becoming branches or lodges of the larger affiliated order. The advantages of the new affiliated orders lay in the benefits of scale involved. It was possible to spread the risks and the costs across several branches and so provide benefits over a wider geographical area, particularly important for those travelling in search of work who could obtain a tramping allowance from different lodges whilst on their journey.[3] This new method of organisation had its origins in the early nineteenth century when particular societies took the initiative in opening other 'lodges' in the same area. This is how the Manchester Unity of Oddfellows started in about 1810.

Around three years later in Leeds, the other major affiliated society began life as the Royal Order of Foresters; but a secessionist movement in Lancashire in the 1830s led to the establishment of the Ancient Order of Foresters. The Manchester Unity and the Ancient Order were to become the largest affiliated orders and the only ones with national coverage, having around half a million members each by the 1870s. These affiliated orders experienced a period of very rapid growth during the 1830s and 1840s. Of the 3074 English lodges of the Manchester Unity of Oddfellows still active in 1875, 1470 or 47 per cent had been founded in the ten years between 1835 and 1845 alone. (Number of lodges founded: 1825–35: 455; 1835–45: 1470; 1845–55: 297; 1855–65: 358; 1865–75: 354.[4]) The most remarkable increases were in the northern and midland counties of Lancashire, Yorkshire, Staffordshire, Cheshire, Derbyshire and Warwickshire. Why did the attractions of 'oddfellowship' appear so strong at this time? Was it a reflection of rising real wages? Over the longer term, this was undoubtedly a feature in the continued growth of friendly societies throughout the century, but the evidence suggests that the late 1830s and the early 1840s, far from being a period of rising living standards, were instead characterised by trade depression and unemployment. The industrial districts of Lancashire and the West Riding of Yorkshire were especially badly hit by the downswing of the trade cycle between 1837 and 1842. Yet it was precisely in these regions that friendly society growth was most marked. It is more profitable to look to a political rather than an economic explanation for the sudden surge in affiliated-order membership. It can be no coincidence that the period of most rapid growth followed the passage of the Poor Law Amendment Act of 1834. This was as much in anticipation of the new relief system as experience of it, since it took several years for the New Poor Law to be introduced in the industrial districts. However, it was widely believed that parish relief would be entirely removed from the able-bodied, and the spectre of the workhouse (the dreaded 'bastille') hung over the textile regions causing great anxiety and a rush to join friendly societies in the hope that this would insure members against recourse to a reformed and restricted Poor Law.

Hostility to the New Poor Law remained strong within the friendly societies throughout the mid Victorian period. The intensity of feeling aroused gives the lie to notions that the friendly society movement was merely a mouthpiece for liberal values. To many it must have seemed as if the avoidance of the workhouse had become the whole *raison d'être* of the movement. In a history of the Oddfellows published in 1845, J. Burn complained that thanks to the 'cold and heartless nostrums' of political economy: 'The face of the country has been covered with barracks for lodging paupers, by which means the working man has been taught to look upon himself as a *thing* depending upon others, rather than as a being whose labour and industrious habits added dignity to his position in society.' Comparing provision in the workhouse unfavourably with that in the country's prisons, the head of the Ancient Order of Foresters complained that: 'were it not that there is a fearful hereafter, it were far better to be a highwayman and a murderer than to be driven to the parish for relief.'[5]

It had been an intention of the New Poor Law to encourage the self-help institutions, as well as discourage relief applications. The Poor Law Report had expressed the belief that more strictly regulated poor relief would stimulate benefit-society membership. The annual reports of the Poor Law Commission in the years following 1834 suggest that the authorities believed fear of the workhouse was driving men into friendly societies. John Tidd Pratt, the barrister charged with approving friendly society rules (and later the first Registrar of Friendly Societies), conveyed the welcome news that there had been a large increase in the number of new societies seeking registration after 1834.[6] Official interest in friendly societies extended further than the operation of the Poor Law. Initial suspicion that all combinations of working men were subversive or that thrift would be better organised by the higher social classes soon gave way to a more positive attitude. The state's role was to become that of an 'enabler'. The main principles guiding legislation on the friendly societies was the offer of certain benefits (most importantly exemption from rates and legal protection of funds) in return for voluntary registration. By 1846, the chief instrument of government policy was the office of the Registrar of Friendly Societies. The main function of the Registrar was to issue certificates of approval to societies which applied for them. It was also possible for building societies, co-operatives and savings banks to register, and the report of the Royal Commission on Friendly Societies of 1874 referred to the Registrar, John Tidd Pratt, as the 'minister of self-help to the whole of the industrious classes'. Under Pratt's idiosyncratic guidance the work of the Registrar's office expanded considerably.[7] However, it was the insurance element of friendly society practice rather than its mutual conviviality of which Pratt most approved.

The weekly or monthly meetings of friendly society lodges were occasions for conviviality and fellowship. Thus the attractions of membership included the sense of belonging to a brotherhood and the feelings of camaraderie that 'club nights' and regular 'feasts' could arouse. The public-house locale for many of these occasions provided an atmosphere at once gregarious and agreeable. The lack of temperance implied was only one of the aspects which worried the moral reformer (although the societies were at pains to emphasise the 'temperate conviviality' of their gatherings and those preferring to abstain from 'intoxicating liquors' could join the Independent Order of Rechabites founded in Salford in 1835). Other causes of concern were the lack of external regulation involved and the integration into working-class culture that the 'club nights' symbolised. The lodge encouraged an atmosphere of social cohesion and solidarity, which went beyond the simple employment of the insurance principle and alarmed the middle-class moralist. It must be remembered that the 'true' friendly societies (those which were genuinely self-governing rather than the centrally administered 'ordinary' societies or the so-called 'county societies' sponsored by the propertied classes) were fraternal associations rather than insurance companies. Thus they were a mixture of self-help and mutual aid. An expression of this was the willingness of some larger societies to sustain long-term payments to the elderly to keep them out of the workhouse. Additionally, it was sometimes the case that lodge members would accept the exaction of a levy or contribute to a special collection either to continue support to certain members who had exhausted their entitlements or to actually keep societies afloat when funds were exhausted (a not uncommon occurrence in the early days of actuarial science). The lodge structure and club rituals were further expressions of a fraternalism which could transcend the principle of sickness insurance.

An important part of the club night was the elaborate ceremonial involved. This was most marked in the lodges of the affiliated orders. The Oddfellows and the Foresters developed ritualised procedures and intricate sets of rules. Officials rejoiced in extravagant titles with a Grand Deacon opening lodge meetings and every district under the guidance of a Grand Master. The sub-Masonic character of these practices served to bind lodge members together, giving the proceedings and the individuals involved an air of significance generally lacking in their everyday lives. Moreover, it should be borne in mind that the 'club' character of the 'true' friendly society, although fraternal in principle, could mitigate against too socially inclusive a membership. Lodge rules were often concerned with the behaviour and character of members, as well as the payment of dues. The award of medals and certificates for excellence was paralleled by the imposing of penalties for breaches of the regulations. Fines were levied on recalcitrant members, especially those who were seen to abuse the sick-pay regulations. Issues of respectability, moral probity and personal decorum were covered in many friendly society rule books. These were more than a matter of form and tradition. It was a question of social proximity, a matter of whom societies had in mind as members; with whom they wished to associate. The question of membership may chiefly be an issue of cost but in the convivial culture of the club meeting, it was also a matter of the acceptable boundaries of social interaction, indicative of the role of social distinction as well as class solidarity. Equally, however, it was the very conviviality of the lodge meeting that repelled many among status conscious lower-middle-class groups, like clerical workers, and in part explains their preference for the non-convivial sickness insurance of the Hearts of Oak and other so called 'ordinary' societies.

The insurance element was strongest and the mutuality principle least developed in what the Royal Commission of 1874 referred to as the 'ordinary' (or general) friendly societies. These were centrally run, sometimes nationally organised, offering life and sickness insurance, but lacking the lodge organisation of the affiliated orders and many of the local societies. The ordinary societies grew rapidly in the second half of the century. The largest was the Hearts of Oak, founded in 1842. Its membership of 10 571 in 1865 multiplied to 64 421 within ten years and stood at almost a quarter of a million by the end of the century. Contributions were sent and benefits received through the post or they were collected and distributed by agents paid on a commission basis. The lack of any semblance of local organisation meant that there was no social bond between members. The management of the ordinary societies was in the hands of a committee reporting to an annual general meeting. These were insurance businesses rather than 'friendly' clubs. Members were reported to 'dislike the nonsense and mixed company of the club nights, and look for an investment of their savings on purely business principles'.[8] This impersonal form of society approximated to the commercial insurance companies, which themselves were successfully extending operations into the homes of the working classes over the same period.

Burial Insurance

Overlap in provision between the friendly societies and the commercial sector was most marked in the area of death or burial insurance, what became known officially as 'industrial life assurance'. It was quite normal to cover the costs of a 'respectable' funeral along with regular friendly society contributions for sickness benefit. But for those who could not afford the expense, the cheaper alternative was the burial club. With the costs of between one halfpenny and three pence a week, this was the most basic form of 'contingency insurance', and the most widespread and earnestly maintained form of saving. Why was this particular form of saving and insurance so popular? The answer lies partly in the fear of a pauper burial, but also in an increasing emphasis on the ritual observances of the 'respectable funeral'. The way one was buried was an emblem of social position. The expanding middle classes emulated the pomp and ceremony traditionally associated with the aristocratic burial and the profession of undertaker grew to meet the demand. The horse-drawn funeral carriage rich in plumes, attended by black-attired heralds and pallbearers; the graveside rituals accompanied by the tolling bell and the careful lowering of the lead-lined coffin into a (soon to be) ornately marked grave were, together, hallmarks of social status and familial respect. Moreover, the manner of interment had deeply rooted religious implications regarding the resurrection of the body and expected reunion with relatives in an afterlife. Such imperatives enhanced the need for the integrity of the corpse. Equally, a marked grave is a place to return to, both as a sign of respect and as a means of remaining close to lost loved ones. The 'decent funeral' desired by the working classes involved at least some elements of the individuality of such a 'send off ', even if the cost and grandeur would be on a reduced scale. However, the greatest fear was of an anonymous pauper funeral.

By contrast to the respectable funeral, the family of the person buried 'on the parish' would experience a ritual of a quite different order and status. There is evidence of a decline in the care and dignity of the pauper funeral under the New Poor Law as the principle of 'less eligibility' was imposed. Official regulations set out to stigmatise the pauper funeral as an event to avoid. Since they were not paying, relatives were not involved in the funeral arrangements, which were in any case perfunctory, nor could they be sure of a place at the graveside. The use of palls or bell-ringers was forbidden, and economy urged in all expenditure to ensure a ritual lacking in dignity or individuality. The materials employed were to be of the cheapest kind. The bodies of the dead, often wrapped in paper shrouds, were enclosed in flimsy wooden coffins. Interment was in a mass grave, dug to accommodate as many as 20 coffins, and quicklime was liberally used to facilitate repeated use of the same opening. The place of burial was unmarked, save for the wooden or stone markers bearing an official number that were the only evidence that generations of the poor had been laid to rest in that particular spot. Apart from this, there was no individual burial place for relatives to return to and no respect for the integrity of the bodies of the dead. Add to this the impact of the Anatomy Act of 1832, which allowed the use of pauper corpses for dissection by anatomists (thus dispensing with even the pauper funeral), and it is not hard to understand the terror inspired by the prospect of 'ending up on the parish'. The dead pauper was truly of no consequence. As the poet, Thomas Noel observed: 'Rattle his bones over the stones/ he's only a pauper whom nobody owns.'[9]

Avoidance of a pauper funeral explains why the practice of paying into a burial fund reached so far down the social scale. It was the outlay which families were most anxious to maintain. Maud Pember Reeves noted that the usual amount paid out in Edwardian London was a penny a week for each child, twopence for the wife and three-pence for the husband. Those whose children died uninsured would scurry between neighbours and relatives in a desperate attempt to se-cure the cheapest non-pauperising funeral. Ten shillings was the lowest reported charge an undertaker would make and funerals could not be obtained on credit. The average cost could be much higher.[10] In an age of high infant mortality rates, it was prudent parents who prepared for the likely eventuality of burying some of their own children. The simplest of burial clubs maintained a basic fund to cover the funeral costs of members and their families, which was topped up by a levy each time a funeral was paid for.

Local burial clubs were often short-lived since funds were generally less secure than in the sick clubs. However, as the century progressed, the business of the burial societies expanded and some of them be-came national in scope. The two largest were based in Liverpool, the Royal Liver and the Liverpool Victoria. In 1875 the Royal Liver had around 600 000 members and the Liverpool Victoria, about 200 000. In organisational terms these were centrally run collecting societies with contributions collected week by week, door by door. The friendly collecting societies functioned as insurance companies in all but name. In theory they were controlled by the members, but in practice were in the hands of managers and agents. The experience of membership was little different from the payment of premiums on a life insurance policy purchased from one of the agents of an industrial assurance company, such as the Prudential. Aggressive canvassing by the commercial companies in the later nineteenth century took business away from the more ephemeral and unreliable of the burial clubs, although the major collecting societies retained a large share of the burial insurance business into the twentieth century.

The Size of the Friendly Society Movement

It might be reasonable to assume that most working-class families would take out various kinds of insurance whenever they could afford to do so: a key problem being that not all who did so could keep up the payments as regularly as they might like. But how many were in the position to purchase a degree of social security in this way? The evidence is hard to come by and what data we do have has to be handled with some care. The friendly societies were the key agency of social insurance in the nineteenth century. But we have no clear information on the proportion of the population who were members, since registration was always voluntary. However, some of the estimates are remarkably high. On the basis of evidence before it, the Royal Commission on the Friendly Societies of 1874 concluded that there were around four million members of friendly societies and about eight million interested in them as beneficiaries. Members were to be found in 32 000 societies of all descriptions, both registered and unregistered, possessing a total of almost £12 million in funds.[11] If accurate, these are very impressive figures.

On the basis that the vast majority of friendly society members were male and over the age of 20 (for female members see below), they imply that some 60 per cent of adult males in England and Wales belonged to a friendly society of some description. However, the Royal Commission's calculation was based on a case study of Lancashire, an atypical county, and included burial clubs and collecting societies. In doing so they were counting those whose contributions were intended to cover funeral costs alone. For many, this was their only form of saving and it is stretching the evidence to accept the four million figure, as F. M. L. Thompson does, as a measure of the 'provident population'.[12] A more appropriate guide to the proportion of the population in a position to cater for their own welfare would be to ask: how many were providing by voluntary means for security in times of sickness, unemployment and old age? At a time when the state took such limited responsibility for social welfare, it is a key question.

The figure of four million members from the fourth report of the Royal Commission on the Friendly Societies may exaggerate the size of the working-class self-help community, but by how much? Would a more legitimate assessment lie somewhere between the Royal Commission estimate and the known membership figure of almost 1.9 million for those friendly societies making a return to the Registrar General of Friendly Societies in 1872? Even this lower figure comprised around 25 per cent of the adult male population of all social classes. But this is a known *under*-estimate of membership. In the first instance, there was the notorious reluctance of many societies to submit their rules to the Registrar. This non-registration was particularly marked among the smaller local societies. Furthermore, there is the problem of the non-return of data from those societies that actually did register. In 1872, a higher than average number of societies responded to the request for details of membership, and yet it was little over half of registered societies which provided such a return. This data still included burial society members, but must provide the very lowest assessment of the extent of welfare provision by self-help and mutual aid.

It is likely that the self-help community was larger than the 25 per cent of males over the age of 20 implied by the returns for 1872. Local studies can provide some useful indications. Geoffrey Crossick has calculated that in the region of 35–40 per cent of occupied adult males in 'Kentish London' (Deptford, Greenwich and Woolwich) in the 1860s and 1870s were members of 'true' friendly societies (excluding burial clubs).[13] In a detailed study of friendly societies in Glamorgan, Dot Jones puts the figure even higher, claiming that: 'at least half the adult male population ... contributed to friendly societies through the whole period 1800–1910.'[14] National assessments are fraught with all the difficulties of finding reliable evidence. However, Paul Johnson has made an estimate for the turn-of-the-century in broad agreement with the results of local research in London and Wales. He calculates the proportion of sickness benefit members of friendly societies in 1901 at 41 per cent of the total adult male population.[15]

On the basis of the returns for 1872 plus the calculations of historians, it is safe to conclude that, by the second half of the nineteenth century, at the very least one in four, but most probably more than one in three, adult males were making private provision for their own and their family's welfare through membership of a friendly society.[16] Either figure would constitute a significant community of interest in Victorian society. Such a self-help community dwarfs the proportion receiving state welfare through the Poor Law and overshadows the numbers aided by voluntary effort through charities. Moreover, friendly society membership outstrips all other working-class institutions in size. Estimates of trade union membership in the 1860s varied from 500 000 to 800 000. (Although, as we shall see, trade unions were also providers of social insurance.) Membership of the co-operative movement stood at around half a million in the 1870s. The evidence suggests that friendly society membership continued to rise through to the end of the century and beyond.

The Social Composition of Friendly Societies

What do we know about the social composition of the membership of the friendly societies? The evidence is even more sparse and anecdotal than that for membership totals. Contemporary impressions are sometimes misleading since commentators often failed to distinguish between health insurance and burial insurance. In general, however, most observers support the idea of a hierarchy of thrift in which sickness insurance was the preserve of the artisan class and above. For example, according to Sir George Young, 'members of the affiliated orders are for the most part handicraftsmen .... With few exceptions the lodges of a society like the Manchester Unity are practically closed against agricultural and other unskilled labourers.' Young was of the opinion that the unskilled were 'generally unwilling or unable' to afford sick pay contributions on top of the cost of burial insurance.[17] Historians have generally confirmed this impression. If we exclude the burial and collecting societies from the equation and confine ourselves to those who could afford the regular payments necessary to insure against loss of earnings during sickness, then most historians report a concentration of members in the higher paid, higher skilled occupations. Before questioning this assumption, let us review some of the historical literature. There is a paucity of direct evidence and most of this relates to the affiliated orders.

Gosden's analysis of occupational data – gathered by the Corresponding Secretary of the Manchester Unity of Oddfellows between 1846 and 1848 – revealed a membership characterised by the better paid trades: particularly those in textiles, mining, printing and building. Artisans of all sorts were well represented. For example, whilst carpenters and joiners constituted only 2.68 per cent of occupied males in England and Wales according to the Census of 1851, 6.0 per cent of MUOF members were in that occupation. The high representation of occupations in wool and cotton manufacture may have reflected the strength of the Manchester Unity in the north of England, but also the relatively high wages customary in those industries (both points I will return to later). Equally, the strikingly poor showing of agricultural occupations (masked by the categories used in the survey) was indicative of the relatively low rates of pay on the land.[18] Moreover, as suggested above, the affiliated orders catered especially for the needs of those industrial occupations in which 'tramping' was common. This was the case for carpenters, shoemakers, blacksmiths and tailors, prominent occupations among the Manchester Unity membership.

Other studies of the affiliated orders tend to reinforce Gosden's conclusions that the friendly societies drew heavily on skilled labour for support. For example, Robbie Gray's analysis of the membership of a single lodge of the Oddfellows in Edinburgh between the 1850s and the 1870s found that the majority (over 70 per cent) came from the skilled trades, with the rest made up in almost equal proportions from business/white-collar and unskilled occupations. Crossick's evidence for the Woolwich Foresters over a similar time span confirms this impression, albeit with a higher representation for unskilled trades (an average of 30 per cent of new members over the 1845–76 period).[19] However, studies of the Oddfellows and the Foresters may be unrepresentative, due to the higher than average contributions and benefits in the affiliated orders. The evidence is hard to come by, but the unskilled might have been represented in larger numbers in the local sickness benefit clubs. There were unskilled members in the towns and cities but what of the countryside? Despite the comments of Sir George Young quoted above, there is evidence of agricultural-labourer membership of the affiliated orders, as well as of the smaller sick clubs. But the numbers varied from county to county and regional distribution was uneven. In some counties with predominantly rural occupations, such as Wiltshire, membership was high in the 1870s, and the Royal Commission on the Poor Laws of 1905–9 heard evidence that the Ancient Order of Foresters was well established in agricultural counties such as Norfolk.[20]

This is all rather anecdotal, but it does serve to undermine the blanket assumption of a uniformly skilled membership. It is certainly probable that the social status of members varied according to the type of society. The dividing societies and slate clubs, with their generally lower subscriptions, would have been the most accessible to the unskilled and lower paid. At the other end of the spectrum, it was the ordinary societies like the Hearts of Oak which had the highest contributions of all, and research suggests the social rank of members was correspondingly superior. For example, clerks constituted over 11 per cent of membership in the Royal Standard Benefit Society in the late 1870s compared with under 3 per cent in the Oddfellows and the Foresters.[21] We have no real certainty about the social composition of the rank-and-file membership of friendly societies beyond these examples and generalisations. And the picture is more inconclusive than some historians pretend, due to the shortage of direct evidence.

Historians rarely relate information about the membership of friendly societies to evidence on employment patterns. To do so might assist us is assessing the extent to which friendly society membership extended below the ranks of the skilled worker. However, it is not possible to 'read off' occupational structures, let alone internal class divisions, from the nineteenth-century census reports. These were cultural constructions, just like any other text, representing the intellectual concerns, policy priorities and status hierarchies of the time.[22] Moreover, there are serious practical difficulties involved in such an exercise, notably the problem of separating manual from non-manual occupations.[23] However, attempts have been made, and J. A. Banks postulates occupational figures for the adult male population for 1841 (excluding 'professional' and 'intermediate' occupations) of 20 per cent skilled, 44 per cent semiskilled and only 14 per cent unskilled. This relative distribution changes remarkably little over the rest of the century. The figures for 1881 being 21 per cent, 36 per cent and 18 per cent respectively.[24]

Others have turned to contemporary accounts for their models of occupational structure. In doing so, they have been able to get clearer, although not necessarily more accurate, estimates of employment patterns within the working class. Dudley Baxter's *National Income of the United Kingdom* (1867) has long been a popular choice.[25] G. D. H. Cole's adaptation of Baxter's evidence suggested a division of the manual working class in 1867 into the 'highly skilled' (14.4 per cent), the 'lower skilled' (33.3 per cent) and the 'unskilled and agricultural' (52.3 per cent). In a similar fashion, Francois Bedarida has estimated the proportions at 15 per cent for 'highly skilled workers', 45 per cent for the 'unskilled' and 40 per cent for 'intermediate zones' (the semiskilled and above).[26] Occupational figures are only indirect evidence, and conclusions drawn from analysis of the census data differs from the views of contemporaries like Baxter, but either set of figures suggest that, on a numerical basis alone, it is unwise to presume that friendly society membership was confined to a 'labour aristocracy' of the highly skilled. Assuming a strata of the highly skilled existed, it is unlikely to have constituted more than 20 per cent of the male workforce. Therefore even the lowest estimates of friendly society membership must have included workers from outside the ranks of the 'better-off artisan' of legend. It may be reasonable to conclude that sickness insurance extended deep into the social structure of the male working class.

There is some evidence from Lancashire, the home of the friendly society movement, which supports this contention. Indeed the strength of the whole self-help movement in Lancashire (including the co-operative retail society) should give us the clue for, in this industrial heartland, the typical worker was not an artisan but a factory operative. The Poor Law Commissioners' Report on Stockport in 1842 included an occupational breakdown of members of the Stockport district of the Manchester Unity of Oddfellows. This revealed a membership dominated by textile employment. Spinners and weavers together accounted for 36 per cent, whilst lowly labourers and cardroom workers outnumbered craft groups like tailors, carpenters and joiners, and smiths. On the basis of this evidence, Neville Kirk has observed: 'It would ... be wrong to conclude that the affiliated orders were essentially "aristocratic" in composition. Rather their appeal was to the broad mass of regularly employed and relatively well-paid operatives.'[27] Quite clearly, there were regional variations in friendly society membership patterns and other factors, such as local tradition and custom, may be important. However, the ability to sustain regular payments was the crucial factor rather than the status of the trade.

Trade Unions

From the earliest days, some trade unions had offered the 'friendly' benefits of sick, accident and unemployment pay. Although this welfare function may have partly originated in a desire to mask trade union activities at a time of illegality (from 1799 to 1824 under the Combination Acts) and official hostility (extending into the 1830s and symbolised by the transportation of the 'Tolpuddle Martyrs'), it remained an important feature of trade unionism throughout the century. Trade unionists may well have found that the benefits of membership lay as much in the prospect of a degree of social security as in the hope of industrial solidarity in a trade dispute. The distinctive feature of these trade-union 'friendly' benefits was unemployment pay. Not available through a friendly society, it apparently acted as a serious inducement for the craft apprentice to join his union.[28] However, the benefit most commonly provided by trade unions was the funeral grant. Unlike sick pay, this could not conceivably be regarded as protecting the industrial rights of the worker, and instead should be classified as part of the extensive life-insurance arrangements of the working class.

The friendly benefits of union membership have been neglected in histories of the labour movement, which have tended to concentrate on industrial relations, the policies of the leaderships, and the politics of labour.[29] In fact, the welfare functions of trade unionism expanded considerably in mid-century craft unions, such as the Amalgamated Society of Engineers (ASE) and the Amalgamated Society of Carpenters and Joiners. The Webbs noted how the craft unions in the engineering trades had originated as local benefit clubs. For example, the Journeymen Steam-Engine and Machine Makers' Friendly Society, formed in 1838, provided members with unemployment benefit, a travelling allowance, a funeral grant and a lump sum in case of accident. In 1846, it added a small sickness allowance and, shortly afterwards, an old age pension to superannuated members.[30] By 1851, the Journeymen Steam Engine Makers had evolved into the Amalgamated Society of Engineers with 11 000 members. It was the high subscriptions of this craft union which sustained its welfare as well as its trade purposes. The friendly benefits of the craft unions may have been exceptional. The lower subscriptions of the unskilled unions formed in the 1880s and after meant there was less available for welfare benefits. At present, the evidence is too slight to be able to say much more about the welfare function of trade unions. But we can reasonably assume that the 'friendly benefits' enjoyed by many members of craft unions consolidated the social-insurance community among male workers.

Female Friendly Societies

Consideration of the social composition of the friendly societies is fundamentally a question of the social class of the male who joined. The friendly society movement was male dominated. But we should ask why this was so. The barring of certain occupations from membership should (but rarely does) lead on to the consideration of another absence, the relative exclusion of females. Indeed, there *were* female Foresters, female Oddfellows and the like, but they were always in a minority. However, there were also women-only societies catering specifically for the needs of the female population. Their existence suggests a concern amongst women for mutualism, self-protection and independence paralleling that of the men. There had been female societies since the early days of the movement. Most offered comparable mutual benefits to their male-dominated counterparts, sometimes with the distinctive addition of a specific childbirth allowance. In addition regular meetings gave members the same opportunities for association outside the family circle as the men. They were strongest when women's wages were higher than average and there were stable employment opportunities for men. Without the latter, the married woman's wage would be absorbed to cover male loss of earnings.

Female friendly society membership, and separate women's societies, endured longest in the textile districts of the North and the Midlands. For example, in Stockport, one friendly society member in ten belonged to a female society in 1803, and there were 37 female societies in existence at some time between 1794 and 1823, constituting about one third of the total. In Cheshire as a whole, female friendly societies made up 27 per cent of total membership in the returns of 1824. The figure for Lancashire was 18 per cent. Where women's economic position was more marginal, female societies were correspondingly weaker. This was the case in London, where female friendly societies declined from 15 per cent of the total in 1794 to only 3 per cent by 1837.[31]

There has been very little research on female societies.[32] However, the 'Dorcas' Female Friendly Society at Tregaron in Cardiganshire has been the subject of a detailed study. Active in the 1840s, it was aimed at women between the ages of 12 and 40 most of whom were in domestic service. There was little difference between the experience of membership of this female society and that of a typical male-dominated friendly society. The costs were lower than in the affiliated orders. An entrance fee of one shilling was followed by regular contributions of sixpence a month. Two years' contributions were necessary to qualify for benefits. These consisted chiefly of sickness and funeral benefits. Attendance at members' funerals was considered obligatory. Regular monthly meetings were held at the local inn, and an annual feast day included a church service and celebration tea. The Society printed its own rule book, which was given to new members on the payment of their admission fee. Members were expected to take their turn in running the Society, by acting as stewards at meetings and visiting sick members.[33]

Low levels of female literacy often meant that it was male clerks who recorded the proceedings at meetings. Female societies were as much concerned with respectability as male societies, although, by meeting in pubs without their children, they displayed a different notion of respectable womanhood from that which confined middle-class ladies to the domestic sphere. Moreover, they acknowledged the ambiguity of women's labour by taking the performance of household chores into account when granting sick pay. All friendly societies took steps to ensure that claimants were genuinely sick and not secretly at work on their trade. In women's societies, however, it was found necessary to rule out unpaid housework as well as waged work if sick benefit was to be paid only to the genuinely ill. This could mean withdrawing benefit when a wife was found to be doing the housework, cooking, cleaning and the like.[34]

Female societies tended to be small in terms of the number of members per society, and in 1874, according to the fourth report of the Royal Commission on Friendly Societies, they comprised only 22 691 of the registered membership of 1.8 million. But this was after a period of decline. Female participation in the friendly society movement continued to fall during the second half of the century, and became less independent in that local societies run by and for women became rare. This was in direct contrast to the pattern of expansion among male workers as chiefly represented in the growth of the affiliated orders. Dot Jones's work on the Welsh friendly societies suggests a peak for female membership in the 1840s and 1850s, when as many as one in ten of the adult female population of Wales subscribed to registered and unregistered societies. By contrast, whilst male membership was at its height in the 1870s, female participation had fallen to one in 25 of the adult population of women. By 1919, it had plummeted to less than one in a hundred. By then, the surviving female friendly societies were mainly situated in rural areas corresponding to the greater participation of women in the workforce.[35] This gives the clue to the decline in female memberships. Whilst the nineteenth century witnessed a permeation downwards of the ideology of the separate spheres which encouraged the notion that woman's place was in the home, there was a parallel exclusion of women from many employments in factories and mines. The persistence of female employment in the cotton mills of Lancashire and Cheshire goes a long way towards explaining the numbers of women in those counties' affiliated lodges, although there was no female representation amongst the leadership.

Whilst men's wages rose during the second half of the nineteenth century, women experienced no comparable improvement in their incomes. Increasing male incomes assumed the nature of a 'family wage', thus excluding the wife from independent financial status. Adult single women, especially widows, were the most vulnerable in this situation. The Royal Commission of 1874 recommended that the proper provision for a working-class woman was through the man's club and even considered the prohibition of female societies meeting in public houses. Equally, the affiliated orders considered it most appropriate to deal with women's needs through male members, with special widows' and orphans' schemes. This was accompanied by the advice to young working girls that their best bet was to invest in a savings bank until they married.[36] It will be no surprise to discover, as we shall below, that women provided the largest group of savers in the trustee savings banks that flowered during the second half of the century.

Savings Banks

Savings banks and building societies were primarily agencies of cash accumulation rather than poverty avoidance and, in the hierarchy of thrift, came above the 'necessities' of the burial club and sickness insurance. They were certainly not mutual-aid associations, and are classifiable as examples of self-help in terms of the motives of individual investors rather than the principle of collective organisation. Of the two, the building societies of the nineteenth century had the least to do with working-class finances and need not detain us here.[37] The savings banks had a broader base of appeal and a more mixed class of depositor.[38] However, in their origins they were the most paternalistic of all the self-help strategies. Many were founded from the later eighteenth century onwards on a semi-philanthropic basis, the idea being that the regular deposit of small savings would encourage providential habits. The groups most commonly targeted by such provident institutions were domestic servants (especially females), apprentices and journeymen. By the 1820s, savings banks were being founded on the trustee principle. This enabled them to evolve from provident institutions to become self-supporting banks, paying interest on the deposits of investors.

The state soon became interested in the savings banks and the advocacy of MPs like George Rose, who had first-hand experience of the management of a savings bank in Southampton, led to protective legislation in 1817 and 1828. These acts marked the beginnings of an official interest which was to culminate in Gladstone's establishment of the Post Office Savings Bank in 1861. Part of the concern of the legislators was to maintain a preferential return for depositors (allowing the trustees of savings banks to invest bank funds with the National Debt Commissioners), whilst putting a ceiling on the size of the deposit so as to deter the propertied classes. Despite this government 'sponsorship', the trustee savings banks were of limited use to those at immediate risk of falling into poverty, applying for charity or entering the workhouse. They were of most value to the small saver who had cash to spare. Savings bank balances were generally tiny and most commonly entered in the names of domestic servants, women and children. In 1860, Arthur Scratchley, an authority on working-class thrift, concluded that less than a third of savings bank depositors could be described as working men; over half being women and children. Historical research has tended to confirm this impression, the most identifiable occupation being domestic servant.[39]

An attempt to reach the poorer classes was the penny bank. Savings banks would not usually accept deposits of less than one shilling. Beginning in Glasgow in the 1840s, the penny bank movement was an attempt to foster thrifty habits as a bulwark against pauperism. Initially the intention was to provide 'feeders' to existing savings banks, funds being transferred once they had reached a guinea. They proliferated in the middle decades of the century, often based in churches, chapels, mechanics institutes, factories and schools. Generally founded by philanthropists, like the Huddersfield banker Charles Sikes (the leading advocate of a Post Office Savings Bank) and Colonel Edward Ackroyd of Halifax (who started the Yorkshire Penny Savings Bank in 1859), the penny banks are perhaps more a story of charity than self-help. Whilst they offered a home for the smallest savings, their security often depended upon the sponsorship of the 'monied classes'. The penny banks and the trustee savings banks received considerable competition after 1861 from the advent of the Post Office Savings Bank (POSB). This was the state's most direct intervention to encourage working-class thrift. It paid a similar rate of interest to that offered by the trustee savings banks, a standard 2.5 per cent on every £1 deposited. The business of the POSB grew rapidly, outstripping the membership numbers and funds of the trustee savings banks by the 1880s. This was partly due to its more accessible opening hours, but also to the transfer by many savings bank of their business to the Post Office. The POSB was responsible for a massive expansion in the number of savings accounts. Whereas in 1870 the POSB and the trustee savings banks had a total of 1.2 million and 1.4 million accounts respectively, by 1899 the figures had risen to 8 million for the POSB and 1.6 million for the trustee savings banks.[40]

What does this tell us about working-class investment in the savings bank movement? The POSB depositor had, on average, about half the amount held by account holders in trustee savings banks. This was taken by contemporaries to imply that the POSB carried 'providential habits into a lower stratum of society than that reached by the ordinary savings banks'.[41] The average balances in POSB accounts in 1899 stood at just over £4 and 83 per cent of accounts were under £25. Many accounts were of limited duration (less than a year) or dormant containing only small amounts, suggesting that much saving was short term, perhaps related to specific projects. What evidence we do have of the depositors confirms Scratchley's assessment of 1860 about the trustee savings banks, that is, that over half were women and children. For three months in 1896, the POSB recorded the employment of new depositors in an attempt to discover the social status of its clients.[42] Analysis is not helped by the fact that the classifications were aggregated in such a way as to exaggerate the extent of working-class depositors. They are not a precise guide, but reveal enough to show that less than

20 per cent were manual workers (artisans and mechanics, labourers, miners) and that the other main groups were 'professional, official, commercial and independent' at 7.5 per cent; domestic servants (mostly female) at 9 per cent; lower middle class (chiefly clerks, shopkeepers and their assistants) at 11 per cent; 'children and scholars' at 21 per cent; with the largest group being formed by those entered simply as women (married, spinsters and widowed) at 26.5 per cent.

The high proportion of children's accounts reflects the drive to foster thrifty habits in the schools. The POSB seemed the obvious vehicle for such savings. The social class of these scholars remains unknown. The predominance of female-held accounts is also difficult to interpret. Many working-class women may have taken the responsibility for saving over the Post Office counter. However, the large number of spinsters suggests women of independent means. Thus it would be unsafe to conclude that the POSB was characterised by the working-class depositor. However, whilst manual workers and their families did not own the bulk of POSB accounts, the number of depositors involved was not inconsiderable. Although the POSB survey was for new depositors in 1896, if it can be taken as a typical distribution pattern, then it suggests that about 20 per cent of the POSB's 6.8 million depositors that year, that is, 1.3 million, were manual workers. To this should be added an unknown figure for children's and women's accounts from working-class families.

Co-operative Societies

As with the 'friendly' functions of trade unions, there has been surprisingly little research on co-operative retailing.[43] Most interest has been shown in the 'heroic' phase of Owenite co-operation before the 1840s. But the numbers involved at this communitarian stage were small compared to the size of the later, retail co-operative movement which, having stood at about 20 000 in 1850, topped one and a half million by 1901.[44] It was this latter movement which arguably had most impact on peoples lives, and is most representative of their values and aspirations. In terms of social composition, historians in general have concluded that co-operation became 'a movement of the better off and thriftier sections of the working class'.[45] However, as with the friendly societies, the picture might be one of regional variation. Whilst Crossick's analysis of the membership of the Royal Arsenal Co-operative

Society in south London (the capital's largest co-op) points to a predominance of skilled workers, and a very low proportion of semiskilled and unskilled,[46] according to Kirk, the situation was different in the textile North West. As with the latter region's friendly societies, whilst the founders and leaders were generally from the craft occupations, the rank-and-file membership drew heavily on the operative classes.

The serious impact of the Cotton Famine of the 1860s on the retail societies of Lancashire and Cheshire is evidence of the large number of factory workers helping to sustain the co-operative movement in the North West. At the height of the Cotton Famine, membership of the Stalybridge Co-operative Society plummeted from 1800 in 1862 to 672 in 1863, and the membership of the Stockport Society fell from 1020 to 720 in the three months between June and September 1862.[47] Martin Purvis's suggestion that, in exceptional centres of co-operation, such as Rochdale, as many as 20 per cent of the total population were co-operative society members by 1901 supports Kirk's view. Purvis claims that in Rochdale 'most families must have had co-operative links'.[48] Moreover, in the textile districts, with their relatively high levels of female employment and numerous opportunities for young workers in the cotton mills, many less well-off families were able to pool their incomes in order to shop at the co-operative store. As with the friendly societies, it was less the rank or class of occupation and more the regularity and size of the household income which determined membership.

What was the attraction of co-operative retailing to the working-class family? Analysis of its practices suggests that, to most members, it was the prospect of purchases leading to regular dividends which was the most appealing feature and the one most likely to explain the spread of the co-operative movement. The 'divi' enabled families to save whilst benefiting from the supply of unadulterated, although not always cheap, food and groceries in the co-operative stores. Members were 'share' holders benefiting from the regular distribution of profits. If withdrawn, the quarterly dividend allowed for a degree of financial planning and was most commonly used to subsidise the payment of rent. In other words, although for some it was a question of cash accumulation (the interest on share capital being allowed to build up with the dividend undrawn), for many more less well-placed families, it was a matter of making ends meet. This is further reflected in an aspect of co-operation which most leading co-operators had enormous difficulty accepting, that is, the extent to which co-operative societies extended credit to members.

The ideal of co-operative retailing was to wean the consumer off the credit regularly given at commercially-run shops (allowing 'tick' was an ideal way of 'hooking' a customer and ensuring their loyalty) and at the 'truck shops' sponsored by some employers. The idea was to replace such habits with a system of cash payments only – at the co-operative store. Cash-only trading had been one of the principles of the Rochdale Pioneers of 1844 and it remained central to the philosophy of the co-operative retailing movement. The giving of credit to working-class consumers was regarded as an evil, firstly because it was associated with the exploitation of the working-class customer through the charging of high prices for poor quality produce, and secondly, because it was believed to encourage extravagance and undermine thrift. It smacked of bad management and lack of financial planning in the working-class home. Unlike the situation today, in the nineteenth century the extension of credit was most commonly represented in negative terms, as the accumulation of debt. The leaders of the co-operative movement wasted no time in condemning it roundly. As one of the local figures in London co-operation observed in the 1870s: 'We have, through the agency of the store, learned the value of thrift – learned to live and thrive on the ready-money system. Not one pennyworth of goods is taken without payment.'[49]

It was part of the mythology of the co-operative movement that several early societies had failed because they had too readily granted credit to their members. This added to abhorrence of the practice expressed by the co-operative leadership during and after the mid-Victorian period. But despite the rhetoric, in reality, there were always co-operative stores which sold goods on credit in certain circumstances, especially during downturns in trade. However, it appears that this practice became more widespread during the later nineteenth century. By 1886, over half of the 946 registered industrial and provident societies in England admitted to granting credit. The drift to credit continued, with over 80 per cent of registered societies giving credit by 1911. In a survey by the Co-operative Union in 1891, societies granting credit said they did so in times of sickness or temporary distress, when wages were paid at too great an interval to permit cash payments, when customers lived at a distance from the store, and in order to compete with local shopkeepers.[50] It seemed that credit was so essential to the working-class economy that even the co-operative movement had to adapt to provide it. Why was this? To answer this question will take us beyond the territory of poverty prevention and into that of poverty survival.

Self-Help and Poverty

Does the existence of friendly societies, co-operative societies, savings banks and trade unions giving welfare benefits betoken a sense of social security among sections of the working population? Was poverty something that touched only a minority? Or should it remind us that, for all but the most well-paid and securely employed, friendly societies and co-operative stores could not remove, but only ameliorate the insecurities of working-class life? It was the relative absence of state provision beyond a safety net for the poorest, plus the social stigmas attached to those who fell into it, that stimulated (rather than originated) the growth of such voluntary welfare. Moreover, this particular 'self-help community' within the working class (there were others, witness the self-help strategies of women's neighbourhood networks discussed below) was not a homogenous grouping. It encompassed, at one end, the upwardly mobile upper-working-class family whose sons and daughters were entering lower-middle-class jobs as clerks and shop assistants, and at the other, the prudent labouring family whose joint income allowed for the payment of club subscriptions. In between stood a multitude of circumstances, and a variety of semiskilled and skilled occupations. Thus, since memberships were likely to have been more socially complex than the misleading 'artisan equals friendly society' equation, they should not be classed as separate in experience or aspiration from those who were not thus protected. The friendly society could not offer immunity from poverty.

Indeed the prevalence of credit facilities at most co-op stores by the end of the century implies that there were strategies which were common across all sections. The need to make small purchases and the unreliability of income which required some form of credit were recurrent features of life for those on all but the highest wages. The use of the pawnbroker was widespread, although not a strategy open to the poorest, who had nothing to pawn. The non-institutional mutual-aid networks of kin and neighbour, and the informal welfare practices (without which no society could manage) of such things as child minding or sick nursing were important elements in the lives of all working-class families, but loomed largest in those with the least resources. With the highly skilled earning approximately twice the wages of the unskilled, the gap in experience and culture within the working classes between those on the highest and those on the lowest incomes could be immense. But it would be unwise to replicate the rhetorical flourishes of the time which too readily distinguished between the 'respectable' and the 'rough', and which constructed notions of a 'labour aristocracy' as justification for the harsher treatment of an unrepentant 'residuum'. Such a simple division was undermined by the development towards the end of the century (in the work of Charles Booth and of Seebohm Rowntree) of a theory of life-cycle poverty and its impact, especially on the family of the unskilled labourer.

The 'poor' were not a permanent category and the insecurities of working-class life left few untouched by poverty at some time in their lives. Even in Textile Lancashire, the heartland of the friendly societies and retail co-operatives, only a small minority of working-class families got through life without some experience of poverty. Of Oldham in the 1840s, Foster reported that, although the incidence of poverty hit labourers' families disproportionately harder than those of craft workers or skilled factory operatives, only around 15 per cent of all working families escaped entirely. Although individual circumstances were different and family size could be crucial, in his comparison of Oldham, South Shields and Northampton, Foster concluded that: 'poverty was not so much the special experience of a particular group within the labour force as a regular feature of the life of almost all working families at certain stages in their development, especially in old age or before young children could start earning.' Crossick's analysis of admissions to Greenwich workhouse in South London during the 1860s and 1870s found a quarter to be skilled men. Even the most secure of artisans faced the risk of poverty and disgrace.[51]

How helpful were the benefits of friendly society membership anyway? Before considering the non-institutional and 'informal' means whereby people coped with poverty, it is worth asking questions about the availability of friendly society membership and the extent of the benefit entitlements for those who qualified. Friendly society benefits were of undoubted importance in the lives of many families, who might otherwise have been left destitute through illness and, in some cases, the provision of reduced benefits kept the elderly out of the workhouse. However, whilst valuable, the degree of security provided should not be exaggerated. To begin with, making regular contributions to a friendly society over a number of years did not guarantee protection against the costs of being ill. Much depended upon the financial stability of the society to which the payments were made. In the first half of the century, actuarial calculations were often unreliable and many benefit societies, especially the smaller local clubs, became insolvent. This might be down to a lack of skill within the administration of the society or, more likely, the use of unreliable measurements of the incidence of sickness and mortality. It was not until the middle years of the century that sufficient statistical data concerning sickness and mortality were available with which to calculate reliable tables of contribution and benefit.[52]

When a benefit club failed, the members, including those who had paid regular contributions over a long time, were left in the lurch. This would be especially hard on someone who had paid into a sick fund as a young adult only to find the club breaking up in his middle age, just when he was most likely to need the sickness benefit for which he had contributed. Contributions were not transferable to another club and, moreover, many benefit societies were reluctant to admit men over the age of 40 or would only do so on the payment of a large initiation fee. The situation improved during the second half of the century, and the problem of financial insolvency lessened greatly as the affiliated orders came to dominate the movement and actuarial skills were more dependable. Nevertheless, when a benefit club failed it must have been particularly galling for members who discovered that their accumulated contributions now counted for nothing; even more so if they were forced for this reason to apply for assistance to the Poor Law guardians or the relief committee of some charity. The other main cause of a loss of entitlement was the failure to keep up regular payments. The club member who did not pay his (or her) dues lost the rights of membership. Since the friendly societies did not insure their members against unemployment, the maintenance of contributions whilst out of work was essential. The loss of membership rights was a blow which might lead to the workhouse for the individuals concerned. In 1881, there were 11 304 adult male indoor paupers who had been friendly society members, including 7391 who had failed to keep up their subscriptions, while the societies of the remainder had failed.[53]

For those fortunate enough to be insured at the time of sickness, what benefits could be drawn? The entitlements of members in most societies were quite specific, and confined chiefly to sickness benefit and a funeral grant. A few female friendly societies gave a childbirth allowance as well as sick pay, but only a tiny minority of women (and their children) enjoyed such benefits in their own right. They relied on those doctors who charged low (or no) fees, the outpatient departments of the voluntary hospitals, and medical relief from the Poor Law. For the insured male, the amount of sick pay varied from society to society, generally in proportion to the size of contributions required (although in the early years of the century, societies sometimes failed because they set too high a level of benefits). Generally, sickness benefit was in the region of seven to fourteen shillings per week, that is from one third to one half of the average wage. However, there were time limits on this, which became a problem in prolonged illnesses. The full rate was usually given for a six-week period only, to be followed by a reduced rate, normally half the full amount. The right to free medical attendance was additional, but only became widespread during the second half of the century. Although it often extended to the cost of medicines prescribed by the doctor, it did not cover specialist treatment or surgery. A doctor's certificate came to be required by most societies as proof of incapacity to work and as a check against malingering. It should be remembered that sick pay and medical attendance were available only for the insured member and not for any other member of his (or her) family. Only a tiny minority of members paid extra contributions to a (commercially run) medical-aid association, thus securing the services of a local practitioner for the whole of the family. This was chiefly a development of the last quarter of the century.

The burial grant was sufficient to cover the costs of a respectable funeral. As we have seen, the avoidance of a pauper funeral was the most fundamental impulse behind regular saving. Despite widespread abhorrence of poor relief, the workhouse and the stigma of pauperism, it was not the deterrent features of the New Poor Law alone which reduced relief rolls. Burial clubs, friendly societies and trade unions helped to keep many from the Poor Law. Their benefits did much to both alleviate suffering and provide a degree of protection. But this was an incomplete shield against the exigencies of life. Most notably, the friendly societies provided only limited assistance to the elderly. As we have seen, there was very little take up of the old-age annuities offered by some larger societies and, more commonly, the help given was that of reduced sick payments to the infirm. Old age was the time at which the threat of the workhouse loomed largest. Up to a third of the elderly ended up in some form of pauperism. There are reliable indicators which point to an overall pattern of rising average real wages from the 1820s onwards; a process that accelerated in the later nineteenth century.[54] Although generalisations such as this must be immediately qualified by reference to regional, occupational and gender differences, it none the less paints a picture of overall improvement which helps to explain the increasing membership totals of friendly societies and co-operative societies as the century progressed. Of course, statistics of average real wages on their own are not a measure of well being. Amongst the other factors which need to be considered are the impact of working conditions, unemployment, health, and patterns of leisure and consumption. Moreover, the issue should be set against a backdrop of rising inequalities both between and within the social classes.[55] For the purposes of the present discussion, it is enough to note the general insecurity of working-class life in the nineteenth century. Few amongst the better paid or highly skilled enjoyed job security. A downturn in the trade cycle or a business failure could lead to unemployment, regardless of the degree of skill or the rate of pay. Dismissal was often immediate and without notice. In these circumstances, friendly society membership was of no advantage and only a few trade unions provided unemployment benefit. Faced with the rent to pay, food and fuel to buy, and club or insurance payments to be maintained, families would soon be forced into debt.

It was the ever present threat of poverty which heightened fear of the workhouse and the labour test in the homes of even the skilled working man. Of course some occupations were more secure than others. Carpenters, engineers, compositors and cotton spinners benefited from good wages and transferable skills. These should have been the true 'aristocrats of labour'. But even here unemployment was a problem. Among the compositors in the London print trade in the 1830s, more than 20 per cent were out of work at least once in any one year. This was a particularly overstocked occupation and, in 1837, apprentices made up 40 per cent of the labour force.[56] Under-employment was an increasing problem highlighted by surveys and reports at the end of the century, but present throughout. Under-employment or casualisation was most marked in the employment patterns on the docks and in the building industry, hitting the labourer hardest, but also touching many skilled occupations. As the Webbs noted: '"To go in" for one half-a-day, one day, two, three, four or five days out of the five and a half is common to bootmaking, coopering, galvanising, tank-making, oil pressing, sugar boiling, piano-making, as it is to dock labouring, stevedoring, crane lifting, building.'[57] The vagaries of the weather and seasonal fluctuations in demand influenced several trades. For example, skilled jobs in the building industry were as much hit by bad weather conditions as were those of unskilled labourers. Carpenters, masons, painters, glaziers, plumbers, slaters and bricklayers were regularly laid off during the markedly severe winters of the mid to late nineteenth century. Casual labour was a feature of particular trades. For example, bricklayers in London could not be certain of more than seven months' work during the year, and the workforce in the more lowly trade of journeyman painter doubled during the busy months as seasonal workers joined those more regularly engaged. The seasonal patterns of the rich – country seat in the winter, London for the 'Season', seaside resort or spa for the summer months – determined the employment levels in innumerable London trades from tailors and milliners to saddlers and farriers.[58] Outside London, the seasonal rhythms of the rich had most impact on the economies of county town, spa towns and seaside resorts. The clothing trades were highly seasonal and subject to short-time working; hatting, shoemaking and tailoring were all affected. In the middle of the century, Henry Mayhew noticed how a ready supply of labour was depressing wages and causing unemployment in a numbers of traditional trades, including tailoring. A few years earlier, Thomas Carter, a Colchester tailor, had written of the profound insecurity which had come to characterise his occupation: 'The tenure by which journeymen tailors hold their employment is more than ordinarily slight. No workman of this craft can be sure of remaining in his present master's service after he has finished the garment he has in hand.'[59] By the latter part of the century, tailoring had become notoriously casualised and the term 'sweatshop' had entered the language.

The difficulties which could face even the educated artisan are illustrated in the life of Joseph Gutteridge, a silk-ribbon weaver of Coventry, who published his autobiography, *Lights and Shadows in the Life of an Artisan* in 1893. Although the freethinking and fiercely independent Gutteridge was in several ways exceptional, the hardships he and his family experienced and the means by which they survived were typical of many others. Newly married with young children, he was laid off after completing his apprenticeship in the depression of the 1840s. For a time, they made their way through 'odd jobs' whilst lodging with his wife's mother, but when she died the family were forced to move to a new district, where they were unknown. Before they could put down sufficient roots to be able to draw upon the help of their neighbours, poverty forced a further move into 'a very low neighbourhood'. For a time, prospects improved after Gutteridge compromised his ambition to be self-employed and accepted factory work as a journeyman. After three months the firm folded and the family faced another bout of hardship. Recently purchased furniture was pawned to pay the rent and buy food, some was broken up and burned in the fire to provide warmth for a sick child. Since Gutteridge 'would rather have died from sheer starvation' than apply to the guardians, the family went two days without food in bitterly cold winter weather. Finally, it was the help of neighbours and friends that brought them through the crisis.

By the 1850s, times were better for the Gutteridge family and Joseph was able to draw ten shillings a week from the Manchester Unity of Oddfellows during a bout of illness. However, during a strike and lockout in the ribbon trade in 1860, his trade union gave him no strike money. His savings prevented him from destitution and, he believed, this earned him 'the neglect of the trades union officials'. The friendly society and trade union member in a skilled trade had, none the less, experienced much that others who survived poverty would recognise. The impact of unemployment, the extra hardship when there were young mouths to feed, lodging with relatives and moves to cheaper accommodation, trips to the pawnbrokers, the support of neighbours and friends. Even the proud and self-reliant Gutteridge concluded in his old age that in being 'too independent to ask favours', he had not realised 'the fact that no one can be independent, but that all are reciprocally dependent upon each other'. He had learned the limits of self-help and one of the lessons of surviving poverty.[60]

Surviving Poverty: Wives and Mothers

The concept of the male 'breadwinner' was central to nineteenth-century approaches to the labour market. Ideally, the 'breadwinner' was to earn a 'family wage', that is, one sufficient to keep his spouse and children housed, fed and clothed. This notion was not only behind much of the thinking of the New Poor Law (to Nassau Senior it was better that the poor man did not marry at all than that he should be unable to act as the 'breadwinner' to a family), it was also reflected in many of the attitudes and assumptions of male-dominated working-class movements of the middle to late nineteenth century, such as the affiliated friendly societies (which only provided separately for women as widows) and the skilled trade unions (which viewed the employment of married women as undermining male wage levels). The 'domestic ideology' sustained the ideal of a gendered division of labour within marriage, in which paid employment was the prerogative of the husband and the unpaid management of the household was the responsibility of the wife. This ideal of the 'separate spheres' of public (male) and private (female) constrained the position of middle-class women. Equally, the ideal was conveyed repeatedly by the charity workers, health visitors, medical officers and other 'experts' who pronounced on the running of the working-class home. By the later nineteenth century, it formed a central element in all the education and (domestic) training offered to working-class women. The strong message was that married women did not go out to work. Their place was in the home.

The ideal was inevitably linked to motherhood and the advice was always the same: the good mother stays at home to care for her children. Moreover, the key presumption behind official policy on the protection and care of children (e.g., the Prevention of Cruelty and Protection of Children Act, 1889) was of parental responsibility not only for child care, but also for the economic maintenance of children. Thus, as the century wore on, not allowing your children to work came to be regarded as an aspect of child care. Since the good running of the household was a female preserve, child care was officially presumed to be predominantly the woman's responsibility. She must be constantly at home, providing the supervision and care her children require. By the turn of the century, an infant-welfare movement had emerged which sought to reorganise the mother-child relationship toward this direction. Through the operation of official policies and the efforts of an army of volunteers, such ideas did not just 'trickle down' to the poor they were 'laid down with a sledgehammer'.[61]

Helen Bosanquet of the COS, writing in the 1890s, caught the characteristically strident tone. The loss of the breadwinner's wage in 'emergencies', such as unemployment, illness, death or desertion, might force married women to seek some form of employment: 'But we will all agree that for the woman to have work is an unmitigated evil where there are children.'[62] If child care was the woman's responsibility, so was the financial management of the home. However, the

bourgeois ideal of the 'Angel in the House' was more prosaically trans-
lated in a plebeian setting. Whilst married men were to work in factory,
workshop and mine as 'breadwinners' to their families, married wom-
en were to aspire to be 'good managers' at home. This latter role carried
responsibility for the family budget; spending and saving were wom-
en's work as much as cooking, cleaning and child care. There is oral
history evidence that the rightness of this role had been fully absorbed
by working-class women by the beginning of the twentieth century. Elizabeth Roberts reports that most of her female respondents 'saw little
distinction between their own good and that of their families'.[63]

This ideal of family relationships and responsibilities should be set
against an economic model which had sought, initially through the
New Poor Law, to create a fluid labour market, whilst preserving the
family as a key institution in the stability of society and the state. In the
long run, the ideal was to be challenged during the late twentieth
century under a combination of practical pressures and ideological
change. Meanwhile, in the nineteenth and early to mid twentieth centuries, the social identity of the 'good' wife and mother became
intrinsically linked to this ideal, and also to the related goals of respectability and social advance. The socially aspirant family would
perforce need to ensure that the wife neither went out to work nor
'took in' work to sustain the family economy. The ability to 'keep' a
wife became one of the measures of working-class respectability. It was
also regarded as vital to social progress. A report to the National Association for the Promotion of Social Science in 1861 complained that:
'the wife and mother going abroad for work is a fine example of a
waste of time, a waste of property, a waste of morals and a waste of
health and life and ought in every way to be prevented.'[64] Thirty years
later, Helen Bosanquet welcomed evidence that fewer married women
were working:

> One of the most hopeful signs of social improvement is the extent to which
> married women are withdrawing from the labour market; that the working
> classes should recognise the importance of the women's home duties is a
> sign of their higher intellectual standard, and that they should be able to
> set them free to so large an extent from outside work is a proof of their
> improved material condition.[65]

The domestic ideal may have become more realisable for working-
class families with the rising real wages of male workers in the later

nineteenth century and again in the interwar years of the first half of the twentieth century. (Although employers may have simply been more successful in using the 'marriage bar'.) However, for most of the nineteenth century, whilst the domestic ideal was a powerful cultural construct, it was in conflict with the everyday experience of life for many working-class households. In the poverty surveys of Charles Booth and Seebohm Rowntree towards the end of the century, the line of poverty was drawn in relation to a so-called 'moderate' family dependent upon the earnings of a male 'breadwinner'. Rowntree estimated the subsistence wage for such a family at 21s. 8d. a week. The introduction of the concept of the breadwinner at the heart of calculation should not surprise us, but to contemporaries it demonstrated, as the better informed had known for a long time, that low wages were a major cause of poverty. Put another way, a considerable proportion of working men did not earn enough on their own account to prevent their wife and children from becoming destitute. Many married women worked, sometimes full time, more often part time; much of this work was home based and often involved other family members, especially children.

The common insufficiency of the husband's wages alone to maintain the household and keep the family together could create much tension, anxiety and discord within the home, particularly since the social and economic context of this projected division of labour was cut along gender lines. The notion of 'manliness' was linked to the concept of the 'breadwinner' – the 'real' man was one who could provide for his family and exercise authority in his household. In this light, it is easy to understand how sensitivities could be ruffled and stereotypes undermined in the distribution of resources within the family budget. This may explain why so many wives were anxious to keep their management strategies, especially their credit dealings, secret from their spouses. If to low pay we add under-employment and the consequent irregularity of income it involved, and the 'emergencies' of sickness and infirmity in the homes of the uninsured, then we begin to comprehend the impact of poverty in the lives of working people. We can also more readily understand the pressure that was placed on the wives – whose duty it was to manage the family finances – and appreciate the strategies with which they tried to ward off the spectre of poverty.

Just as there were distinct regional as well as occupational differences in earnings so were there in the means of supplementing them.

Although credit was as common a strategy in rural districts as in the towns, and it was common to run up debts until harvest time when the extra income from the whole family working in the fields might be used to pay off debts, the opportunities for credit were generally fewer and, in particular, there were few village pawnbrokers. To offset this, in country districts labourers could grow their own food, mostly those which were easily cultivated and required little attention; cabbages and root vegetables were common. However, many agricultural labourers had no garden and allotments were much rarer after the enclosures of the early nineteenth century. They were to be found in only one third of parishes by 1833 and were often advocated as a means to ease rural poverty, becoming a major political issue in the 1880s.[66]

However, there was also food in the hedgerows and wild places. One elderly Norfolk woman interviewed in the 1970s recalled that, in her childhood home, they took advantage of 'all the food that was for free; watercress from running streams, rabbits, pigeons, wild raspberries, wild plums and blackberries, crab apples, hazel nuts, chestnuts, walnuts. No squirrel hoarded these more carefully than we did.'[67] Of course not all such acquisitions were legal. Although some farmers allowed their labourers to catch rabbits, others did not, and the penalties for all involved could be harsh. Poaching was a frequent means of supplementing a poor diet in hard times. It was often the only way to procure fresh meat. Joseph Arch, writing of his childhood in the Warwickshire of the 1830s, could not blame those who resorted to this crime: 'It is my deliberate opinion that these men were to some extent justified in their actions; they had by hook or by crook to obtain food somewhere, in order to enable themselves, their wives and their children to live at all, to keep the breath in their bodies. Necessity knows no law but its own.'[68] It was not exclusively a male crime. At a sitting of the Oxford Quarter Sessions in 1868, two women were sentenced for offences connected with the theft of food; one to three months imprisonment with hard labour for receiving five stolen rabbits; another to 14 days with hard labour for stealing a peck of beans from a farmer.[69]

We know far more about the social history of working-class women than we did a generation ago. There has been particular interest in the study of working-class women in the later nineteenth and early twentieth centuries, especially their patterns of employment, marriage and motherhood.[70] The responsibilities placed upon them put women, especially wives, at the heart of family life. This meant they

were allotted a variety of tasks and needed a range of skills. As well as
the domestic chores of cleaning, cooking, washing and mending, there
was the chief responsibility for the care and upbringing of the children; the management of the weekly budget in the face of scarce
resources and unpredictable incomes; often the use of their labour
power to contribute to the family income; and finally, their role as
unpaid carers in the often unrecognised provision of 'informal welfare', notably through the nursing of the sick and the care of the
elderly. Of these, it was the woman's budgetary skills which determined whether she would earn the accolade of being a 'good manager'.
And it was this responsibility which put married women in the front
line in the fight against poverty.

For most of the nineteenth century (until the Married Women's Property Act of 1882), married women were forbidden by law from the
ownership of property in their own right. It is therefore somewhat ironic that although legally subject to her husband and subordinated to
him by custom and tradition, married women, in practice, were the
guardians of the family purse. This made them responsible for every-
thing from the payment of the rent and purchase of food and fuel to a
whole range of credit arrangements. It was wives who dealt with the
'tallyman', paid the burial-insurance agent when he called, visited the
pawnbroker, and occasionally borrowed from the backstreet moneylender. All this she might keep secret from her spouse. As Melanie
Tebbutt has noted: 'A woman's management of the family budget was
a world entirely separate from that of her husband.'[71] It was even
customary in many areas for the man's wage to be 'tipped up' to the
wife each pay day in return for his 'spends'. In such practices, the
husband explicitly avoided the burdens of domestic economy. Where
this was not the custom, the wife was still held responsible for household management, even though she might be quite unaware of the
totality of her husband's income. Moreover, this was the common experience in most working-class families, regardless of occupational
status. As Elizabeth Roberts has observed, whilst there might be differences in the household finances of the skilled and unskilled:

> It would be misleading to make too clear a division between the wives of
> labourers and those of the skilled men. The latter were still obliged to keep
> a tight control of their spending, and if a skilled man was unemployed, or
> ill or, indeed, if he died then his wife, like her poorer sisters, was obliged to
> adopt various other strategies in order to survive.[72]

What were those strategies? Going out to work was the most obvious answer, however, women generally took paid employment of necessity, in the interests of their families not for personal gain. Work was rarely a path to liberation for working-class women anywhere in Europe in the nineteenth century.[73] There may even have been an inverse relationship between the size of the family income and the quantity of women's earnings, in which the latter rose as the former fell. However, we have an inadequate picture of the statistics of female employment. Women's work was poorly recorded in the nineteenth-century census. Moreover, aggregated tables of the percentage of married women in work were not given in the census volumes until 1901. What the evidence does show is much regional and occupational variety, with the most significant concentrations of married women in full-time work outside the home in the textile and pottery industries. In the census of 1911, 13.7 per cent of married women in England and Wales were recorded as being in full-time work, (a figure not much different from the estimate in 1857 that one seventh of married women worked) although in weaving towns like Blackburn and Burnley, the figure of wives and widows in paid work was as high as 42 per cent.[74]

Paid part-time work was more widespread, but so diverse that it is impossible to quantify with any certainty. Agricultural sub-employments had been reduced by the spread of enclosure and the consequent disappearance of the wastes and commons. This tended to increase rural dependence upon the male wage, although it did not entirely remove opportunities for women and children.[75] The most common urban occupation away from home was domestic work, especially 'charring'. More married women were homeworkers, working on materials supplied by an employer. Rates of pay were notoriously low. In the East End of the 1890s, Arthur Harding's mother made matchboxes for Bryant and May at twopence farthing a gross. However, it was the cheap-clothing trade which provided the most common source of home work in London. In the 1850s, Mayhew found wives working in the 'slop' (cheap) end of the tailoring trade for whom '7d. a day (less by the expense of thread, candle, etc.), is considered good earnings'.

There were a variety of employment patterns across the country, according to the industrial character of the locality. Nottingham women made lace and hosiery at home, whilst those in Northampton made boots and shoes.[76] It is even more difficult to quantify the innumerable varieties of self-employed women, the so-called 'penny capitalists', whose activities (e.g., taking in washing or sewing, childminding, letting to lodgers, selling home-made goods from the backstep) were defensive strategies against poverty rather than money-making ventures in their own right.[77] The income from taking in washing was low and the widows and wives of men on low incomes were often washerwomen. Such work required an initial capital outlay – typically the purchase of a mangle – sometimes bought for the recently bereaved by a beneficent employer or via a neighbourhood collection.

Credit and the Pawnbroker

Credit was more relevant than saving to the everyday family budgeting of most working-class wives, especially those in families where the husband was in casual or seasonal employment or the household income from all sources was low. In such circumstances, the uncertainty of the weekly income made forward planning difficult. Moreover, it must have seemed unwise to commit the much-needed pennies of the moment to some unknown future event. The burial club was an exception to this since the higher death rates of the nineteenth century, and in particular the incidence of infant mortality, made funeral costs something which all would want to save for if they could. The hand-to-mouth character of poor people's finances meant that small sums of ready money were essential to survival. Credit at the local shop was a crucial element in this. The shopkeeper who sold goods 'on tick' or ran a 'slate' for reliable customers was a feature of most poor neighbourhoods. In a survey of four working-class districts of Manchester in 1840, 420 of the 651 provision dealers were selling on credit.[78] Prices might be higher for the small quantities purchased, but repayment would often be in instalments. Critics often maintained that this revealed a lack of thrift. Why not save during the good times? In fact, in view of the fragile basis of family income, in a majority of working-class households the availability of credit was crucial to survival and did at least as much as regular saving to keep down the levels of pauperism, especially in the second half of the century. Apart from shop credit, the most usual means of making ends meet was the pawnbroker.

'Of the numerous receptacles for misery and distress with which the streets of London unhappily abound there are, perhaps, none which present such striking scenes as the pawnbrokers' shops.' Thus, in an essay published in 1836, Charles Dickens described 'a low, dirty-looking, dusty shop' at the corner of a court off Drury Lane. Outside, the pawnbroker's sign of the three balls and a shop window containing numerous unredeemed pledges of low value: cheap plate and trinkets, beds and bedding, carpenter's tools, and 'wearing apparel of every description'. Inside, the customers, mostly women, offer the items they have brought to pawn. They present a moral hierarchy from the poor to the abandoned, to the dying. An old woman haggles over the value of a child's frock and a silk handkerchief; 'a young delicate girl of twenty', watched by her mother, seeks to pledge a 'Forget-me-not' ring; a prostitute with 'attire, miserably poor, but extremely gaudy'; and 'the lowest of the low', a drunken woman, 'dirty, unbonneted ... and slovenly' with only 'the hospital and the grave' to look forward to, make up the quartet.[79] Dickens's concentration on the female customers in his Drury Lane shop is characteristic of the way in which the pawnshop epitomised the economic dependence of women. It was also largely an urban phenomenon, with the heaviest concentration of pledge shops in London and in industrial Lancashire.

Pledging goods was not confined to the poor nor even to the working class. There was a hierarchy within the pawnbroking trade. At the top were the high-street, or 'city', pawnbrokers whose dealings were chiefly in more valuable items, such as plate and jewellery. Then there were the so-called 'industrial' traders whose custom was in the 'soft goods' (clothing, bedding and household items) regularly pledged by their working-class clientele. The elegant glass partitions and the individual cubicles of the 'city' pawnbroker, in which the pledger could be assured a degree of privacy and discretion, bore little relation to the more public and often frenetic atmosphere of the backstreet pledge shops. There were innumerable gradations in this hierarchy between the highest and the lowest class of pawnbroker, and the artisan or clerk trying to 'keep up appearances' might be found frequenting various levels of establishment. At the lowest level of the trade were the unlicensed 'dollyshops' operating illegally and dealing in the most inconsiderable items. Often corner provisions shops would take goods in return for food, although this was a prosecutable offence. Sometimes, all household goods were pawned till nothing was left, as in the case of Joseph Gutteridge referred to above.

But pledging was not merely the last resort in an emergency, for many it was a normal way of funding routine expenditure. It has been calculated that, on average, every working-class family in Britain made at least one pledge a fortnight, or something over 30 each year, and dealers in the 'low' trade could take as many as 10 000 pledges a month.

In one month, April 1840, the total value of property pledged by 10 000 poor families in Manchester was judged to amount to as much as £28 000.[80] Hence the pawnbroker was often referred to as the 'poor man's banker' (despite the fact that the majority of clients were women). However, such a term validated a relationship that was a consequence of factors beyond the control of the poor, namely the structure of employment, the inadequacy of wages, and the large families which resulted from the non-availability of effective birth control methods.

The pawnbroking relationship was both integral to and parasitic upon the working-class economy. The rates of interest on low-value pledges made the relationship very expensive, especially for regular clients pledging small items. Pawnbrokers were licensed and interest rates (and other aspects of the trade) were regulated by acts of parliament (notably those of 1800 and 1872). A rate of one halfpenny per month could be charged for every 2s. 6d. (2s. 0d. after 1872) loaned. In reality, on loans of less than 2s. 6d. and for under one month in duration, the rate remained the same. Thus the smaller the loan the higher the interest charged. Despite this, pledge shops thrived in the poorer districts where most goods pawned were of low value. Surveys among pawnbrokers operating in Liverpool during the 1860s suggested that the vast majority of pledges were under 10s. in value and around half were less than 2s. 6d. Moreover, at the lower end of the trade, 66 per cent of pledges were redeemed within the week.[81] The inadequacy of the money available to the women who generally managed domestic finances and the variety of weekly outgoings they faced gave the 'pop' shop or 'uncle' a key role in the survival strategies of the poor. The rapid decline of pawnbroking in the second half of the twentieth century suggests that, for the poor at least, it was a mechanism of necessity not of choice.

A regular weekly 'pledge cycle' operated almost universally in working-class neighbourhoods, in rhythm with the hand-to-mouth, cash-based economy of innumerable working households. The busiest day was Monday when the best clothing, worn only at the weekend (the 'Sunday best'), was returned to pawn. On Tuesday, it was common for Monday's washing, now dried, to be pledged to raise more cash. Wednesday was quieter, but Thursday and Friday's trade might be brisk as money ran out towards the end of the week. The rush to redeem pledges came after wages were paid to those in regular work; by the second half of the century in factory districts, this was most commonly on a Saturday afternoon. Most pawned goods were of low value, but some bought items for their pledge value rather than anything else. Small but valuable possessions such as watches, rings and brooches could be a ready source of credit and were pawned several times. Married women were often forced to pawn their wedding rings on a Friday in the expectation of returning the pawn ticket to redeem this valuable item once more on Saturday night. Such pledges smack of desperation and illustrate that it was the need for ready money which most commonly brought people to the 'popshop'. To those households which were losing the battle against 'hard times', the pawnshop itself could become an agent in the family's decline once all pledgeable goods were gone.

The pawnbroker's profit came from a combination of the interest charged on redeemed goods, and the sale of those items which had not been redeemed by repayment of capital loaned plus interest within the legal period of twelve months and seven days. Thus pledging could seem an initially attractive option to a family strapped for cash, but raising the money to redeem pledges could be a more formidable operation. In any case, it was not a strategy open to the poorest since they could offer the broker the least security. Whilst some regularly pawned the same bag of rags, others were refused due to the low chance of being able to redeem their worthless bundles. The poorest families of all were those which existed below the pledging classes, and their decline in a spiral of debt would be accelerated when it became apparent to neighbours that they could no longer be regarded as credit worthy. As Robert Roberts remarked: 'News of domestic distress soon got round. Inability to redeem basic goods was a sure sign of a family's approaching destitution, and credit dried up fast in local tick shops.'[82] An investigation in Manchester in the early 1840s had uncovered several cases facing destitution, with possessions converted into pawn tickets:

J. G., a poor widow, aged 79, residing in Silk Street, Ancoats. Her employment was 'odd jobs'; had a female lodger, who worked in a neighbouring mill. Here we found 27 pawn tickets, amounting to £1. 10s. 3d., some of which had 'run out'.
C. L., wife, and three children under five years old. Hand-loom weaver, in a cellar; has eight tickets, amounting to 17s. 9d., 'I burnt all that were out.'
D. D., hand-loom weaver, in a cellar; partially employed; wages from 4s. to 5s. per week. Twelve tickets, amounting to £1. 1s. 8d. …. Not a chair in the place, and nearly destitute.

> T. M.; a widow; one daughter, aged seventeen; has not received any money for six weeks, but 2s. from a lodger. Seventeen tickets, amounting to £3. 3s. 3d., ... has been better off; seemed a very decent person; said – 'Had good clothes, obliged to pawn them to keep from starving.'[83]

Beyond the credit from the shopkeeper (or even the co-operative store) and the pawnbroker, there lay that of the moneylender. Very often the backstreet loan shark was a woman. Loaning at interest was itself sometimes a strategy for avoiding poverty for the lender. Interest rates could be phenomenal, although many who loaned did not regard their profit as interest. Relationships with your neighbours could be more equal. Indeed, one of the most interesting aspects of recent research on poverty has been the development of the concept of social networking.

Neighbourhood Networks

During the nineteenth century, increasing residential segregation created an urban structure fractured along class lines. The growth and complexity of the suburbs was paralleled by the springing-up of working-class districts in or near places of work. It would be wrong to either simplify this process or the patterns of social interaction which it implied. But on the whole, contacts between the social classes were reduced as patterns of residence became more socially homogenous than they had been prior to the massive urbanisation of the nineteenth century.[84] There was less residential differentiation within the working class. Although there were always poorer neighbourhoods than others (the slums) and, in the smaller factory communities, there would be a high degree of occupational uniformity, the evidence suggests a degree of social mixing in many working-class districts in which only the best paid artisans could afford the higher rents in the better parts of town.[85] Most working-class districts accommodated households across a range of incomes and grades. Though few could have ever felt secure from the threat of poverty at some stage in their lives and at such times many relied on a community of interest with their neighbours and kin.

In the crowded working-class neighbourhoods of Victorian cities it was almost impossible not to have close knowledge of others, their problems and their personalities. The social networks which arose within the poorer neighbourhoods were based on a common need for sharing and support. Along these 'mean streets' with their cramped houses, tenements and courts in which large families shared passageways, washhouses and toilets, the historian's conventional division between public and private spheres appears less relevant. Domestic life regularly spilled over into the public space of the narrow, traffic-free street. In such overcrowded districts, it was difficult, and not necessarily wise, to 'keep one's self to one's self'. Almost nothing escaped notice and everyone's behaviour was subject to public scrutiny. Privacy was at a premium and the need to live so close to others encouraged the growth of community standards of normative behaviour, covering such things as relations between neighbours, the behaviour of children (viewed as a common responsibility), and those domestic tensions which became public knowledge. It was women, and more specifically married women, who formed these networks and it was their 'street talk' or gossip which provided the necessary exchange of information.[86] In an environment in which everyone shared the same 'economy of makeshifts', such networks were supportive as well as regulative. A family's ability to cope with poverty was influenced by its standing in the community. In this, much depended upon the wife's reputation: was she a good manager, did she repay her debts, could she be relied upon to support others in need? All these were ultimately questions of reciprocity. It was the reciprocal nature of community relations within working-class neighbourhoods, and within the extended families of the poor, that was essential to the shared endeavour to 'make ends meet'.

What sort of support was offered? According to Ellen Ross poor women shared 'extensively and unsentimentally'.[87] Gifts of small sums of money, like a penny for the gas, or of domestic necessities, such as linen or cooking utensils, might be exchanged. Chores might be done or errands fetched during illness or confinement. There might even be loans of pawnable goods or even communal collections at times of crisis or tragedy so that a cash starved family might get by. Although their social superiors often declared it the 'charity of the poor to the poor' it was not like receiving alms because there was a cultural expectation of some similar service being returned at a future date. This is not to imply that all such 'giving behaviour' between neighbours and within families consisted of calculated acts of mutual exchange as Anderson has argued, nor to accept that such generosity was always disinterested altruism, rather that the common experience of making ends meet in the face of limited outside help created an interdependence vital to survival, which found expression in normative values of generosity and reciprocity.[88] Shared social knowledge and prevalent norms engendered a generalised anticipation that a favour would be returned. Within families it becomes enmeshed with notions of duty and love. In mutual-aid networks outside the family, such reciprocity need not be immediate or between the same individuals, it could be deferred or mediated, but always integral to the gift was the obligation to reciprocate. Help might be given because others had once helped you in a similar situation, or an obligation might pass from one generation to another; for example, a daughter might reap the reward of having had a neighbourly mother. Equally, such 'social credit' could be used up if neighbourly generosity was abused and the obligation to reciprocate was repeatedly ignored. The responsibilities of women for the domestic economy and child welfare created networks of interdependence centred on the home and quite separate from the reciprocity of adult male life focused as it was on workplace and leisure time.[89]

These norms could operate even in cases where the pattern of everyday friendship had broken down. Agnes Hunt, a Queen's Jubilee District Nurse in Hammersmith, London, in the 1890s, told the story of next-door neighbours, the wives of casual labourers, who never got on; 'their only conversation had been unprintable abuse from their respective back doors.' Yet the moment one of these neighbours heard that the other was dying of heart disease, 'she, who in the day earned her living at the washtub, made of her poor tired body a human pillow for her lifelong enemy to rest upon, as the invalid could not breath unless she was practically sitting up, and no other pillows were available.'[90] It is precisely this sort of unnoticed and unpaid care within the community and inside the family which most welfare systems, including our own, take for granted. 'Sitting up' with the sick and dying, providing long-term care for the elderly and the handicapped, and looking out for neglected or needy children are examples of what one might reasonably call 'informal welfare'. The Poor Law authorities and the charity organisers worked on the expectation that women within the family would act as carers in such cases.[91] Despite improved institutional care after the 1870s for the sick, the elderly, the insane and for orphans, in the face of only limited state welfare provision outside the workhouse and the uncertain distribution of charitable resources, it was the neighbourhood and the family which provided most support and care in times of hardship, illness, incapacity and old age.

The support networks of neighbourhood and kin were especially important in the lives of those on the lowest incomes, those below the level of benefit-club membership. The insecurity of life could not be removed nor the threat of destitution eliminated, but at least there was a 'buffer' of support as families traversed crucial points in the life cycle and, for those facing the crisis of unemployment, family breakdown, loss of housing and so on. But how extensive were these support networks? The evidence is not clear, but it seems fairly certain that the more stable and well established the neighbourhood, the greater the degree of mutual trust and interdependence. Yet the nineteenth century was an era of population movement, urbanisation and social change. As the migration from rural to urban which characterised the century progressed, is it reasonable to assume the existence of stable neighbourhoods at all?

In the suburbanised and private world of modern urban life in the Western industrialised nations of the present, 'neighbouring' is no longer an essential part of everyday life. The historical evolution of more private, home-centred lifestyles in which social interaction with neighbours is limited or regarded as 'interference' has been a long-drawn out and rather uneven process. Beginning in the early modern period and accelerating in the two and a half centuries since 1750, it has been very much associated with both the separation of home and work, and the social and residential segregation characteristic of urban modernity. This 'privatisation process' has not destroyed the need for networks, but its culmination has been the replacement of the neighbourhood as the chief locus for them. Beginning with the higher social classes, it is often assumed that industrialisation, and the drift to towns in the nineteenth century, undermined the vitality of neighbourhood life amongst an increasingly mobile and fractured urban working class. The disrupted structures of labouring life would take some generations to re-establish. Put another way, it takes time for a new district to become an established neighbourhood.

We can no longer study the neighbourhood networks of the nineteenth century at first hand, but a study in the 1950s of Bethnal Green, in the East End of London, concluded that the close-knit pattern of community life (based largely on kinship networks) was the result of several generations' development.[92] Given that most of the urban working-class districts of the nineteenth century were new creations, it might be assumed that the social complexities of neighbourhood life would not emerge immediately. Much of the evidence on the support networks of poor neighbourhoods comes from the work of oral historians interviewing the elderly in the 1960s and after. This confirms the existence of such networking at the end of the nineteenth century.[93]

To what extent did such neighbourhood networks exist earlier in the period? Migrants to the growing cities of the early and mid nineteenth century were drawn chiefly from the surrounding countryside, whilst a significant proportion came from Ireland. Michael Anderson's important study of census data for the Lancashire textile town of Preston for the years 1841 to 1861 suggests the significance of kinship networks at that time of high population mobility. He found that 70 per cent of his sample for 1851 had been born outside Preston. In the absence of official sources of information and advice, new migrants faced especial difficulties in finding work and housing and 'adapting ... in hundreds of other ways to the new community.'[94] Anderson concluded that newcomers relied greatly upon the support of kin already living in the town. The continuing demand of the cotton mills for labour led to chain migration and the creation of residential clusters, in which relatives settled close to one another or shared the same accommodation in 'extended families'. He did not deny that neighbours provided help, but maintained that only kin provided 'a structured basis of reciprocation in a heterogeneous and mobile society'.[95] To what extent should we generalise Anderson's findings about Preston to the rest of the country and the century?

Standish Meacham concluded that if Anderson was describing the early period of neighbourhood formation, by the end of the century, what Meacham called the 'classic' pattern of neighbourhood life had emerged. This was because it was not until the era of intensive urban growth and high rates of population mobility had passed, and residential stability was established, that neighbourhood ties could mature into a system of reciprocal attachments on the basis of mutual trust. Similarly, Carl Chinn, reflecting on Anderson's work on mid-century Preston, points to the 'relatively stable urban culture' prevailing at the end of the century, as identified by Ellen Ross in her studies of the East End and by Robert Roberts in his Salford autobiography, *The Classic Slum*.[96] Newly arrived migrants would be the least likely to have the support of community networks and therefore would be the most likely to become dependent upon poor relief. This was probably the case in Manchester in the 1840s, where evidence suggests that the non-settled poor, that is, those least able to have earned the necessary 'social capital' with their neighbours, were 'almost six times more likely' to apply for poor relief at times of distress than the resident population. To what extent they could rely instead upon the help of kin is not clear.[97] There is a suggestion, from a study of Bethnal Green in London's East End in the 1850s, that, in certain circumstances, a high degree of population change could actually obstruct the formation of family networks.[98] The picture is not clear. This has caused some to conclude that the 'function of the neighbourhood as a source of informal support could not be taken over on a large scale by family networks *until* a considerable part of the urban population was more or less settled.'[99]

In the long run, the demographic, social and cultural changes of the industrial era did not of necessity lead to the disintegration of informal social networks, but rather to their transformation. Where kinship could provide the basis of support, this reduced the need for reciprocity between neighbours, but equally it might work the other way round. Moreover, as Anderson's own researches showed, movement within Preston was generally only over short distances. Almost 40 per cent of males who moved house between the 1851 census and the 1861 census had relocated within 200 yards of their previous address, and up to 60 per cent were living within less than half a mile. Thus, whilst most changed their address, few changed their neighbourhood.[100] This short-distance mobility within towns is a well-known phenomenon and was particularly marked among those in less-skilled and casualised occupations.

In many neighbourhoods, extended families might spread across a number of households in the same or nearby streets, and relationships of proximity and interdependency often involved a mixture of kin and community. Moreover, many took in lodgers (or became lodgers) not as a business proposition – lodging houses were found in every town – but as a survival strategy. For example, in his study of a working-class district in mid century Manchester, Peter Rushton found a tenth of families taking in lodgers to supplement the household income. This was most common at the stage in the family life-cycle when children were too young to work and economic resources might be few. Rushton found a third of couples in this category in 1851 sharing their often cramped housing with lodgers. Taking in lodgers was a regular feature in the domestic economy of the poor right through the period and beyond. It was an arrangement which offered crucial support to new migrants (often beyond kinship connections) and provided cheap accommodation for others, such as young married couples, single parent families and widows.[101]

There is much that we need to know about neighbourhood activity in the earlier parts of the nineteenth century, but given the exigencies of everyday life in the uncertain economic climate of Victorian towns and cities, and the financial needs of families on insecure and low incomes, it is likely that some degree of community identity would soon grow up: 'the tenacity and adaptability of neighbourhood communities were much greater than one might think'.[102] Certainly, Boot's researches on the Manchester of the 1840s suggest that those with roots in a neighbourhood showed considerable reluctance to apply for poor relief. He found an average time lag of six weeks between becoming unemployed and receiving relief, and concluded that this: 'attests to the depth of private and communal resources they could resort to in times of distress, their hostility to the Poor Law, and the depth of poverty reached before they obtained relief from the Poor Law authorities.'[103]

It seems that, wherever possible, poor people would prefer anything to an application for poor relief. This is a commonly expressed view in historical accounts and is linked to the ideas of respectability and popular abhorrence of the workhouse and the labour test.[104] However, it may be a result of an over-concentration on the unemployed male, who certainly found it more difficult to get relief, especially after 1870.[105] Equally, it would be less applicable to those unintegrated into any form of kin or neighbourly networking. As we saw in Chapter 2, reluctance to resort to poor relief was much less marked among more marginal groups, such as the casually employed and female heads of families (widows with children and so on). One of the reasons for the 'crusade against out-relief' after 1870 was the desire to deter such groups from applying. Thus the common assumption that the able-bodied substantially rejected the Poor Law since it was stigmatising, actually disenfranchised them and offered out-relief at less than subsistence level is only partly true. Much would depend upon how desperate the circumstances were and how willing people were to accept poor relief, along with what could be got from charities as another part of the 'economy of makeshifts'.[106] Even the families of the skilled could be reduced to accept public relief. Gillian Wagner recounts the case of the wife of a boilermaker in the 1880s, whose husband's will had been broken by the loss of his job. The sole responsibility for family maintenance fell upon her shoulders. Although there were savings of 2s. 6d.

and she had her earnings selling shellfish, she also received poor relief in cash and kind of two shillings, plus a couple of loaves of bread. Unfortunately, this was not enough to keep the family together and, in the end, she had to let her 11-year-old son go to one of Dr Barnado's homes.[107]

5

POVERTY AND WELFARE IN HISTORICAL PERSPECTIVE

During the first two decades of the twentieth century, the liberal conception of rights and responsibilities, which had underwritten the political and social system of the Victorian era, began to disintegrate as central governments increasingly intervened in domains, such as social welfare and industrial relations, formerly confined to the 'private sphere'. The intellectual roots of this chiefly lay in the New Liberal redefinition of liberty in the late nineteenth century, in which negative determinations of liberal basic rights were superseded by the 'positive' rights of opportunity and social 'justice' to be realised through the actions of the state.[1] International trade and imperialistic rivalries encouraged the process, culminating in the experience of the First World War, which did considerable damage to 'liberal' values. Ultimately, the 'liberal state' was transformed into the post-1945 'social-welfare state' in which central government stood committed to the social rights of citizens.

The extent to which the liberal state had begun to dissolve prior to 1900 was limited. It is true that, towards the end of the nineteenth century, central governments began to look beyond the relatively narrow confines of the Poor Law. The treatment of the elderly and of the unemployed were the main areas in which legislative proposals came forward. But, although there were Royal Commissions on the Aged Poor (1895) and Old Age Pensions (1896, 1899), it was the case of unemployment relief where action was taken as early as 1886 (see Chapter 2). But this was a fitful and inconclusive process, largely inspired by the desire to discriminate on moral grounds between relief applicants,

160

and operating through the auspices of local rather than central government. By the 1900s, the central state was more ready to intervene in the fields of social welfare and industrial organisation. It is not the purpose of this chapter to provide a detailed account of the origins of the Liberal welfare reforms of 1906–11, still less to consider the subsequent development of a 'social-welfare state'. These are hardly neglected issues. Too often the balance of welfare in the nineteenth century, with its leaning towards voluntarism and mutual aid, has been subordinated to narratives of the later development of state responsibility in which the origins of the Liberal welfare reforms figure prominently. The focus of this study on the welfare system before 1900 has been an attempt to bring non-state agencies back into the picture and to emphasise how comparatively limited were the obligations of the liberal state to the poor.

Arguably the most significant breaches of the liberal state's defences before 1900 came in areas which only indirectly affected the position of the poor. However, even after 1900, most of this legislation was administered through existing or newly created local state authorities, and much of it merely continued the Victorian practice of acting to control abuses and set minimum standards. Thus the state extended its responsibilities in the areas of public health and housing. Water supply and sewerage had become exclusively public areas of competence by the end of the 1840s. Legislation in the 1870s established a national network of district sanitary authorities, each with a medical officer of health possessing powers of inspection, although it was not until the 1890s that municipal authorities acquired powers to enforce minimum standards of sanitation in new housing. Housing acts in 1885 and 1890 granted local government borrowing rights to build public housing, although outside London only a small number of council-housing projects were under way by the early 1900s. None the less the opportunity was there for some notable experiments in 'municipal socialism', at a time when solutions were still being sought through a combination of the local state and voluntarism. Local rather than central state competence was also preferred as elementary schooling up to the age of ten became a responsibility of elected school boards under the Education Act of 1870, then was made compulsory in 1880 and free of charge in 1891.

Central as opposed to local state responsibility was clearest in the field of industrial safety. As with sanitation, this involved the extension of existing commitments. The pioneer factory acts up to the 1840s

had applied only to the textile industries and the hours and conditions of labour of women and children, not men. Such minimum
standards were only slowly extended to include other industries and
workshops as well as the factories, and the retail trade was not touched
until the 1886 Shops Act. Despite government inspection, enforce-
ment remained a problem. The Factory Act of 1901 further
consolidated standards on working conditions and safety for women,
but it was not until the Coal Mines Act of 1908 that adult male hours
of labour were restricted. However, under trade union pressure, employer liability for accidents at work in most occupations was
established by the Workmen's Compensation Act of 1897.

In the twentieth century, the responsibilities of the state in providing social security and relieving poverty have expanded enormously.
Much has been gained in terms of rising living standards and social
expectations. In the process, however, the balance within the 'mixed
economy of welfare' shifted towards state bureaucracies and away from
voluntary organisations and institutions of self-help. Government became the 'bearer of the social order', with degrees of responsibility
and authority which would have been anathema to the nineteenth century liberal. Along with the growth of state welfare bureaucracies came
universalist ideologies of provision and the rise of health and welfare
professions, the most notable of which is the medical profession. The
latter found its powers enhanced through the National Insurance Act
of 1911, and doctors obtained significant powers in the National
Health Service introduced in the 1940s. In particular, the lowly general practitioner has been a major beneficiary of the NHS, enjoying
considerably more status and control over conditions of service than
the Poor Law or friendly society serving medical men of the last century.

The self-help institutions have fared least well as a result of their
'partnership' with the state. Initial friendly society opposition to state
pensions was overcome before the Old Age Pensions Act of 1908. Its
non-contributory nature made it more palatable. But the societies lost
much of their independent and self-governing role when they were
absorbed into the national insurance schemes of 1911. These were to
be administered through 'approved bodies', including the commercial collecting and industrial insurance societies, as well as the friendly
societies. The National Insurance Act established compulsory insurance against sickness, disablement and maternity, but not death (thus
leaving the business of the commercial collecting societies intact). It
is significant that the state's first venture into social insurance was

conceived as a partnership between government, voluntarism and the market. The desire to reward self-help and individual responsibility remained central to the welfare philosophy of New Liberalism. Undoubtedly, the intention was to expand the self-help community, but the state was to do more than 'enable' – it was to supervise the process. In doing so, it undermined the viability of the very institutions which had provided the social insurance model on which legislation was based.[2]

The self-help institutions have withered during the twentieth century. Their fraternal culture has become a thing of the past, and their functions have been superseded by a combination of state provision and commercial insurance. Friendly society memberships declined markedly during the interwar period, largely as a result of the existence of state insurance schemes for sickness and unemployment benefit. They also lost ground to the market, especially to insurance companies that sold endowments to top up the old-age pension. The sociability, promise of economic security and social esteem, which the Victorian friendly societies had embodied, did not seem so attractive to the generation which came to maturity between the wars. It was the fraternal lodge-based societies which declined most rapidly, while by contrast, centrally-run collecting societies, like the Hearts of Oak, continued to expand. Indeed, rather than a decline of self-help, the interwar years witnessed an expansion of savings, but it went into hospital contributory schemes, life insurance, endowment policies, and the newly introduced National Savings Certificates bought over the Post Office counter rather than the friendly societies.

However, this is further disproof of the oft-repeated Victorian contention that the 'hand to mouth' economy of the working classes, and their apparent improvidence, reflected their low moral character rather than their inadequate earnings. The major constraint on working-class saving was that of low pay. The impossibility of ever saving enough to provide for such eventualities as old age was a psychological, as well as material barrier which the introduction of a state pension did much to remove. Rather than undermining individual thrift as opponents argued, the extension of state welfare may have actually stimulated it.[3] In more recent times, governments have been as concerned to see an extension of credit and share ownership as to sustain the culture of thrift. Moreover, in contrast to the decline of the friendly societies, the provision of social security and cash accumulation through the market has expanded in the twentieth century.

So much so that discussion of the future of social welfare in the 1980s and 1990s has often centred on competing claims of the state and the market.[4]

Equally, the role of charity has been transformed by its 'partnership' with the state. The process of statutory welfare services replacing voluntary ones, which had begun at a local level before 1914 (as in the case of health visitors for example), continued apace. After the welfare state reforms of 1945–51, the voluntary bodies were more often working (often at a local level) to provide personal social services alongside statutory agencies. They became more secular in outlook and less ambitious in social goals, reflecting the changed ideological climate of the post-1945 era. Their partnership with the state became less equal, and their role supplementary to and dependent upon that of government.

But the political priorities of the Thatcher years – and, in particular, the rhetoric of a return to 'Victorian values' – sought a revival of self-reliance and a renewed welfare role for voluntary charity. During the high unemployment of the 1980s, voluntary agencies working with poor families reported an increased demand for their services for the first time in a generation and official policy drew in charitable resources alongside state benefit to the poorest. This attempt to redefine the boundary between state and voluntary sector and to return to an older version of the public/private partnership has produced few tangible results. However, the belief remains strong in many quarters that an active voluntary sector is an essential element in civil society. Moreover, in the face of rising social-security budgets and a continuing political commitment to low taxation, the impulse to 'reform the welfare state' remains. In this, there may well be government pressure on voluntary organisations to expand their welfare provision. Indeed, the state may call the tune. The dependent status of the voluntary sector extends to financial support and it has been estimated that at least one third of its income in Britain in the 1990s is derived from public sources.[5]

Despite advances in living standards during the twentieth century and evolving notions of citizenship in the discussion of social rights, poverty persists in the era of the welfare state. And – as if to illustrate that such concepts are culturally specific – the definition, measurement and nature of 'poverty' remain subjects of debate and calculation.[6] Our welfare system is equally a cultural construct. It is not merely a response to physical need, but arises out of the balance of social, political and ideological forces at a particular time. However, the ideas and values it embodies in turn have an impact on the politics and social values of the day.

As we venture into the twenty-first century, the welfare state can seem permanently in crisis. The future balance of forces between the state, the market and the voluntary sector is unclear. Governments once more are under pressure to restrain costs and the apparent certainties of the post-war consensus have evaporated. Any reform of the welfare system is more likely to involve a contraction than an expansion of state responsibilities. This may not mean the removal of benefits and entitlements, but the pegging of their value. For example, the current inadequacy of the state old-age pension raises serious doubts over its likely worth when today's young adults retire. This concern has generated a 'pensions industry' providing what the nineteenth century would have termed 'deferred annuities' against a poverty stricken old age. However, although with more disposable income and longer life expectations this is a more attractive proposition than in the nineteenth century, it will still not cover all. Nor will everyone be prudent enough or financially able to make such provision. The future holds the prospect of residual state support at 'pauper' levels for those without a private pension. The problem of the aged poor is once more at the centre of the welfare debate.

The chief trend in the 'mixed economy of welfare' is once more away from state responsibility and towards the individual and the family. In the 1980s and 1990s, governments rediscovered individual obligation in such areas as child support, setting up the Child Support Agency to seek out absent fathers. The family is also at the centre of concern at the highest levels about young women who are single parents. The spectre of a dependency culture, in which recipients of benefit get cut off from the disciplines and sociability of the market, has returned to be one of the central issues on the welfare-reform agenda. If the responsibilities of the individual are once more at the heart of the welfare debate, so is the 'informal welfare' that springs from the ties of kinship, friendship and community. Residential care of the infirm and elderly has been shifted away from the NHS to become a local authority and private institutional burden. Along with this has come a commitment to support the informal carer in the home as more and more people, who in the 1950s and 1960s would have received residential health care, are now cared for by kin, with a dwindling level of domiciliary-based support from health service workers.

In a number of welfare areas, central government is once again talking the language of the 'enabler' rather than the provider.

Instead of searching the past for the origins of the present as if it were a final settlement, our current inclination should be to study former welfare systems in their historical context. Rather than a culmination of welfare history, the post-war welfare state may be seen in the future as an experiment, which governments felt unable to sustain in the face of demographic and social change, escalating financial costs and a political climate which favours low taxation. For what has been given can be taken away. More now than at any time since the coming of the welfare state, we can expect change and even a Labour government is prepared to 'think the unthinkable' about social welfare.

APPENDIX

Table A1   Poor Relief Expenditure in England and Wales, 1696–1930

year	total (£000s)	average expenditure per head of population (shillings & pence)	year	total (£000s)	average expenditure per head of population (shillings & pence)
1696	400	1s. 5d.	1856	6 004	6s. 4d.
1748–50	690	2s. 3d.	1857	5 899	6s. 2d.
1776	1 529	4s. 4d.	1858	5 879	6s. 1d.
			1859	5 559	5s. 8d.
1802–3	4 078	8s. 11d.	1860	5 455	5s. 6d.
1813	6 676	12s. 9d.	1861	5 779	5s. 9d.
1814	6 295	11s. 10d.	1862	6 078	6s. 0d.
1815	5 419	10s. 0d.	1863	6 527	6s. 5d.
1816	5 725	9s. 10d.	1864	6 423	6s. 3d.
1817	6 918	12s. 4d.	1865	6 265	6s. 0d.
1818	7 890	12s. 1d.	1866	6 440	6s. 1d.
1819	7 532	13s. 0d.	1867	6 960	6s. 6d.
1820	7 330	12s. 6d.	1868	7 498	6s. 11d.
1821	6 959	11s. 8d.	1869	7 673	7s. 0d.
1822	6 359	10s. 6d.	1870	7 644	6s. 10d.
1823	5 773	9s. 5d.	1871	7 887	7s. 0d.
1824	5 734	9s. 2d.	1872	8 007	7s. 0d.
1825	5 787	9s. 1d.	1873	7 692	6s. 8d.
1826	5 929	9s. 2d.	1874	7 665	6s. 6d.
1827	6 441	9s. 10d.	1875	7 488	6s. 4d.
1828	6 298	9s. 4d.	1876	7 336	6s. 1d.
1829	6 332	9s. 5d.	1877	7 400	6s. 1d.
1830	6 829	10s. 0d.	1878	7 689	6s. 3d.
1831	6 799	9s. 10d.	1879	7 830	6s. 3d.
1832	7 037	10s. 1d.	1880	8 015	6s. 4d.
1833	6 791	9s. 7d.	1881	8 102	6s. 3d.
1834	6 317	8s. 10d.	1882	8 232	6s. 4d.
1835	5 526	7s. 7d.	1883	8 353	6s. 4d.
1836	4 718	6s. 5d.	1884	8 403	6s. 4d.
1837	4 045	5s. 5d.	1885	8 492	6s. 4d.
1838	4 124	5s. 5d.	1886	8 296	6s. 1d.
1839	4 407	5s. 9d.	1887	8 177	5s. 11d.
1840	4 577	5s. 10d.	1888	8 441	6s. 1d.
1841	4 761	6s. 0d.	1889	8 366	5s. 11d.
1842	4 911	6s. 2d.	1890	8 434	5s. 11d.
1843	5 208	6s. 5d.	1891	8 643	6s. 0d.
1844	4 976	6s. 1d.	1892	8 848	6s. 1d.
1845	5 040	6s. 1d.	1893	9 218	6s. 3d.
1846	4 954	5s. 11d.	1894	9 674	6s. 6d.
1847	5 299	6s. 3d.	1895	9 867	6s. 7d.
1848	6 181	7s. 2d.	1896	10 216	6s. 9d.
1849	5 793	6s. 8d.	1897	10 432	6s. 9d.
1850	5 395	6s. 2d.	1898	10 828	7s. 0d.
1851	4 963	5s. 7d.	1899	11 287	7s. 2d.
1852	4 898	5s. 5d.	1900	11 568	7s. 3d.
1853	4 939	5s. 5d.	1910	14 850	8s. 4d.
1854	5 283	5s. 9d.	1920	23 501	12s. 6d.
1855	5 890	6s. 4d.	1930	40 631	20s. 6d.

Sources: P. F. Aschrott, *The English Poor Law System* (2nd edn, 1902) Table VII; M.Blaug, 'The myth of the Old Poor Law and the making of the New', *Journal of Economic History*, 23 (1963), App. B; K. Williams, *From Pauperism to Poverty* (1981), Tables 4.1 and 4.6;. P. Slack, *The English Poor Law, 1531–1782* (1990),Table 1.

Table A2   Poor Relief Totals in England and Wales, 1849–1900

year	mean number total paupers	ratio per 100 population	mean number indoor paupers	mean number outdoor paupers
1849	1 088 659	6.3	133 513	955 146
1850	1 008 700	5.7	123 004	885 696
1851	941 315	5.3	114 367	826 948
1852	915 675	5.1	111 323	804 352
1853	886 362	4.9	110 148	776 214
1854	864 617	4.7	111 635	752 982
1855	897 686	4.8	121 400	776 286
1856	917 084	4.9	124 879	792 205
1857	885 010	4.6	122 845	762 165
1858	908 886	4.7	122 613	786 273
1859	865 446	4.4	121 232	744 214
1860	844 633	4.3	113 507	731 126
1861	883 921	4.4	125 866	758 055
1862	917 142	4.6	132 326	784 906
1863	1 079 382	5.3	136 907	942 475
1864	1 014 978	4.9	133 761	881 217
1865	951 899	4.6	131 312	820 586
1866	916 152	4.3	132 776	783 376
1867	931 546	4.3	137 310	794 236
1868	992 640	4.6	150 040	842 600
1869	1 018 140	4.6	157 740	860 400
1870	1 032 800	4.6	156 800	876 000
1871	1 037 360	4.6	156 430	880 930
1872	977 200	4.3	149 200	828 000
1873	883 688	3.8	144 338	739 350
1874	827 446	3.5	143 707	683 739
1875	800 914	3.4	146 800	654 114
1876	749 476	3.1	143 084	606 392
1877	719 949	2.9	149 611	570 338
1878	729 089	2.9	159 219	569 870
1879	765 455	3.0	166 852	598 603
1880	808 030	3.2	180 817	627 213
1881	790 937	3.1	183 872	607 065
1882	788 289	3.0	183 374	604 915
1883	782 422	3.0	182 932	599 490
1884	765 914	2.8	180 846	585 068
1885	768 938	2.8	183 820	585 118
1886	780 712	2.8	186 190	594 522
1887	796 036	2.8	188 414	607 622
1888	800 484	2.8	192 084	608 400
1889	795 617	2.8	192 105	603 512
1890	775 217	2.7	187 921	587 296
1891	759 730	2.6	185 838	573 892
1892	744 757	2.5	186 607	558 150
1893	758 776	2.5	192 512	566 264
1894	787 933	2.6	205 338	582 595
1895	796 913	2.6	208 746	588 167
1896	816 019	2.7	213 776	602 243
1897	814 887	2.7	214 382	600 505
1898	813 986	2.6	216 200	597 786
1899	831 938	2.6	219 041	612 897
1900	792 367	2.5	215 377	577 122

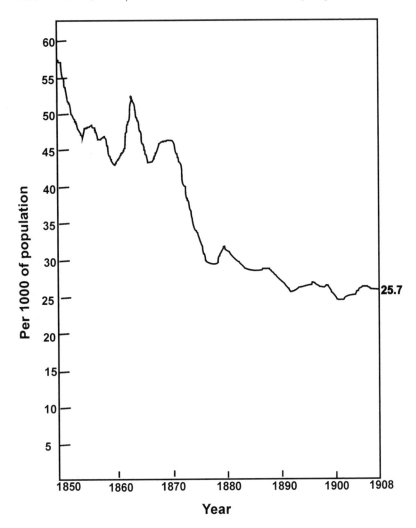

**Figure A1   Pauperism in England and Wales, 1850–1908 (average
daily numbers of paupers of all classes relieved per 1000
of population).**

Source: Local Government Board, *Statistical Memoranda on Public Health and Social
Conditions*, Section 4, Cd 4671 (1909).

NOTES

(Please note that places of publication are London unless otherwise stated)

1 A Mixed Economy of Welfare

1. P. Thane, 'Government and society in England and Wales, 1750–1914', in F. M. L. Thompson, ed., *The Cambridge Social History of Britain, 1750–1950*, vol. 3 (Cambridge, 1990), pp. 1–2; J. Harris, 'Society and state in twentieth-century Britain', in ibid., pp. 67–8.
2. G. Finlayson, *Citizen, State, and Social Welfare in Britain, 1830–1990* (Oxford, 1994), p. 98.
3. For the phrase 'mixed economy of welfare', see G. Finlayson, 'A moving frontier: Voluntarism and the state in British social welfare, 1911–1949', *Twentieth Century British History*, 1 (1990), pp. 183–206; J. Innes, 'The "mixed economy of welfare" in early modern England', in M. Daunton ed., *Charity, Self-Interest and Welfare in the English Past* (1996).
4. For the phrase 'economy of makeshifts' see O. Hufton, *The Poor of Eighteenth-Century France, 1750–1789* (Oxford, 1974).
5. S. G. and E. O. A. Checkland, eds, *The Poor Law Report of 1834* (Harmondsworth, 1974), p. 9.
6. For what are now classic variations on this theme, see K. Polany, *The Great Transformation* (New York, 1944); and G. V. Rimlinger, *Welfare Policy and Industrialisation* (1971).
7. This is persuasively argued in J. Harris, *Private Lives, Public Spirit: A Social History of Britain, 1870–1914* (Oxford, 1993), esp. p. 238.
8. A. J. Kidd, 'How the Webbs wrote their History of the English Poor Laws', *Economic History Review*, 2nd ser. 40 (1987), pp. 400–17; A. J. Kidd, 'The state and moral progress: The Webbs' case for social reform *c.* 1905 to 1940', *Twentieth Century British History*, 7 (1996), pp. 189–205. On the whole, the earliest of their volumes, *English Poor Law Policy* (1910), is the most accessible and useful source of information. The *English Poor Law History*, 3 vols, (1927–30), adds less than at first appears.
9. The most obvious exception is the excellent study by the late Geoffrey Finlayson, without which it would have been much harder to attempt this overview. Finlayson, *Citizen, State, and Social Welfare.*

2   The State and Pauperism

1. P. Lindert, 'Towards a comparative history of income and wealth inequality', in Y. S. Brenner, H. Kaelble and M. Thomas, eds, *Income Distribution in Historical Perspective* (Cambridge, 1991), pp. 212–31.
2. For the basis on which Poor Law statistics were gathered, see P. F. Aschrott, *The English Poor Law System* (1902), pp. 328–51; S. and B. Webb, *English Poor Law History, Part II. The Last Hundred Years*, vol. 2 of 2 (1929), pp. 1036–55; the most detailed analytical tables are in K. Williams, *From Pauperism to Poverty* (1981).
3. For a discussion of these, see Webbs, *English Poor Law History*, pp. 1050–1; BPP, *Royal Commission on the Poor Laws and Relief of Distress, Majority Report*, Cd. 4499/1909, pp. 1–2.
4. P. M. Solar, 'Poor relief and English economic development before the industrial revolution', *Economic History Review*, 2nd ser. 48 (1995); see also J. Innes, 'The State and the poor: Eighteenth-century England in European perspective', in J. Brewer and E. Hellmuth eds, *Rethinking Leviathan* (Oxford, forthcoming).
5. For the early history of English poor relief, see P. Slack, *The English Poor Law 1531–1782* (1990).
6. For the administrative structure of poor relief before 1834, see G. W. Oxley, *Poor Relief in England and Wales, 1601–1834* (Newton Abbot, 1974).
7. L. Bonfield, R. Smith and K. Wrightson, eds, *The World We Have Gained: Histories of Population and Social Structure* (Cambridge, 1986), p. 201.
8. Slack, *English Poor Law*, pp. 29 and 36–7. See also K. D. M. Snell, *Annals of the Labouring Poor: Social Change in Agrarian England, 1660–1900* (Cambridge, 1985), p. 72; J. R. Poynter, *Society and Pauperism: English Ideas on Poor Relief, 1795–1834* (1969), p. 4. The poor certainly held such notions of right, see for example several of the essays in T. Hitchcock, P. King and P. Sharpe, eds, *Chronicling Poverty: The Voices and Strategies of the English Poor 1640–1840* (1997).
9. T. Wales, 'Poverty, poor relief and the life cycle' in R. M. Smith, ed., *Land, Kinship and Life Cycle* (Cambridge, 1984), pp. 351–404.
10. M. Blaug, 'The myth of the Old Poor Law and the making of the New', *Journal of Economic History*, 23 (1963); M. Blaug, 'The Poor Law Report re-examined', *Journal of Economic History*, 24 (1964).
11. G. R. Boyer, *An Economic History of the English Poor Law, 1750–1850* (Cambridge, 1990).
12. Williams, *Pauperism to Poverty*, p. 151; Boyer, *Economic History of the Poor Law*, p. 15.
13. See S. G. and E. O. Checkland, *Poor Law Report of 1834*, p. 114.
14. Blaug, 'Poor Law Report re-examined', p. 229.
15. See, for example, Snell, *Annals*, pp. 105–10.
16. S. King and A. Gritt, 'Which way to welfare? The poor and the Old Poor Law 1700–1820', forthcoming; see also S. King, 'Poor relief and English economic development reappraised', *Economic History Review*, 50 (1997), pp. 360–8.
17. King and Gritt, 'Which way to welfare?'.

18. J. Caird, *English Agriculture in 1850–51* (1852); W. A. Armstrong and J. P. Huzel, 'Food, shelter and self help, the Poor Law and the position of the labourer in rural society', in G. Mingay, ed., *The Agrarian History of England and Wales, VI, 1750–1850* (Cambridge, 1989), pp. 741, 762–3.

19. Williams, *Pauperism to Poverty*, pp. 149–50.

20. S. G. and E. O. Checkland, *Poor Law Report of 1834*, pp. 82, 334.

21. The best discussion remains Poynter, *Society and Pauperism*.

22. For classical political economy, see D. Winch, *Riches and Poverty: An Intellectual History of Political Economy in Britain, 1750–1834* (Cambridge, 1996); R. Cowherd, *Political Economists and the English Poor Laws* (Athens, Ohio, 1977); G. Himmelfarb, *The Idea of Poverty* (1984).

23. Edmund Burke, *Letters on a Regicide Peace* [1797], in *Works*, vol. 5 (1818), pp. 321–2.

24. T. R. Malthus, *An Essay on the Principle of Population* (1803 edn), ed. D. Winch (Cambridge, 1992), p. 100.

25. Ibid., p. 101.

26. Ibid., p. 262.

27. B. Hilton, *The Age of Atonement: The Influence of Evangelicalism on Social and Economic Thought 1785–1865* (Oxford, 1988).

28. Ibid., pp. 69–70.

29. Thomas Chalmers, *The Christian and Civic Economy of our Large Towns* (1821–6). This was a development of the *Edinburgh Review* articles and was reissued several times in the nineteenth century under the title, *The Christian and Economic Polity of a Nation*. For Chalmers, see S. J. Brown, *Thomas Chalmers and The Godly Community* (Oxford, 1982); B. Hilton, 'Chalmers as a political economist', in A. C. Cheyne, ed., *The Practical and the Pious* (Edinburgh, 1985), pp. 141–56; Hilton, *Age of Atonement*, pt 1.

30. P. Mandler, 'Tories and paupers: Christian political economy and the making of the New Poor Law', *Historical Journal*, 33 pp. 81–103; see also P. Mandler, 'The making of the New Poor Law, *Redivivus*', *Past and Present*, 117 (1987).

31. Blaug, 'Myth of the Old Poor Law', p. 176.

32. Blaug, 'Myth of the Old Poor Law'; D. M. McCloskey, 'New perspectives on the Old Poor Law', *Explorations in Economic History*, 10 (1973), pp. 419–36; D. A. Baugh, 'The cost of poor relief in south-east England, 1790–1834', *Economic History Review*, 2nd ser., 28 (1975), pp. 50–68; J. P. Huzel, 'Malthus, the Poor Law and population in early nineteenth-century England', *Economic History Review*, 2nd ser., 22 (1969), pp. 430–52; J. P. Huzel, 'The demographic impact of the Old Poor Law: More reflections on Malthus', *Economic History Review*, 2nd ser., 33 (1980), pp. 367–81; Boyer, *Economic History of the Poor Law*, ch. 5. Discussions of much of the above can be found in J. D. Marshall, *The Old Poor Law*, 2nd edn (1985); Armstrong and Huzel, 'Food, shelter and self help, the Poor Law and the position of the labourer in rural society', in G. Mingay, ed., *The Agrarian History of England and Wales, VI, 1750–1850* (Cambridge, 1989); and Boyer, *Economic History of the Poor Law*, pp. 75–83.

33. Williams, *Pauperism to Poverty*, pp. 19–31; see also A. J. Kidd, 'The invention

of poverty', *Labour History Review*, 56 (1991), pp. 39–43.

34. Poynter, *Society and Pauperism*, p. 248.

35 P. Dunkley, *The Crisis of the Old Poor Law in England, 1795–1834* (1982); A. Brundage, *The Making of the New Poor Law: The Politics of Inquiry, Enactment and Implementation, 1832–39* (1978); Mandler, 'Making of the New Poor Law, *Redivivus*'; Mandler, 'Tories and paupers'; Hilton, *Age of Atonement;* Poynter, *Society and Pauperism*.

36. Boyer, *Economic History of the Poor Law*, p. 197, Table 7.1; A. Digby, *The Poor Law in Nineteenth-century England* (Historical Association, 1985), p. 9.

37. E. J. Hobsbawm and G. Rude, *Captain Swing* (1969), pp. 53–4.

38. Compare the maps in Hobsbawm and Rude, *Captain Swing*, pp. 167 and 170, with those in Boyer, *Economic History of the Poor Law*, p. 111.

39. S. G. and E. O. Checkland, *Poor Law Report of 1834*, p. 123.

40. Dunkley, *Crisis of the Old Poor Law*, p. 166.

41. Mandler, 'Tories and paupers', p. 99.

42. S. G. and E. O. Checkland, *Poor Law Report of 1834*, pp. 334, 335.

43. Ibid., p. 338.

44. Ibid., p. 375.

45. Ibid., pp. 418–9, 438–9.

46. S. Leon Levy, *Nassau W. Senior, 1790–1864* (Newton Abbot, 1970), pp. 255–62.

47. As indeed did the bastardy clauses of the 1834 Act, particularly during their passage through the Lords, see Brundage, *Making of the New Poor Law*, pp. 65–6 and 71–2. The retention in the Report and in the New Poor Law of settlement law might seem an anomaly in a system designed to free up the movement of labour, but can be put down to the survival of parish rates as the source of funds. Despite the strictures of Adam Smith over half a century before, the practices and litigation of settlement and removal survived to blight the lives of the poor throughout the nineteenth century. See M. E. Rose, 'Settlement, removal and the New Poor Law', in D. Fraser, ed., *The New Poor Law in the Nineteenth Century* (1976), also see D. Ashforth, 'Settlement and removal in urban areas: Bradford, 1834–71', in M. E. Rose, ed., *The Poor and the City* (Leicester, 1985).

48. The Poor Law Commission lasted until 1847 when its responsibilities were given to a new government department, the Poor Law Board. Finally, in 1870, the central administration of the Poor Law was subsumed into the newly created Local Government Board, with its President sitting in the Cabinet.

49. N. C. Edsall, *The Anti-Poor Law Movement* (Manchester, 1971); M. E. Rose, 'The Anti-Poor Law movement', in J. T. Ward, ed., *Popular Movements, 1830–1850* (1970); D. Williams, *The Rebecca Riots: A Study in Agrarian Discontent* (Cardiff, 1955); A. Charlesworth, ed., *An Atlas of Rural Protest in Britain 1548–1900* (1983), includes essays by J. Lowerson on the southeast and by A. Digby on East Anglia.

50. Williams, *Pauperism to Poverty*, p. 220, Table 4.33(b); R. Boyson, 'The New Poor Law in north-east Lancashire, 1834–71', *Transactions of the Lancashire and Cheshire Antiquarian Society*, 70 (1960), pp. 35–57; J. Cole, *Down*

Poorhouse Lane: The Diary of a Rochdale Workhouse (Littleborough, 1994).

51. Chiefly M. E. Rose, 'The allowance system under the New Poor Law', *Economic History Review,* 2nd ser., 19 (1966); A. Digby, 'The labour market and the continuity of social policy after 1834', *Economic History Review*, 2nd ser., 28 (1975), pp. 69–83; Boyer, *Economic History of the Poor Law*.

52. Digby, in Fraser, ed., *Poor Law in the Nineteenth Century*, p. 170. For the 'subterfuges' mentioned, see J. V. Mosley, 'Poor Law Administration in England and Wales, 1834–1850, with Special Reference to the Problem of Able-Bodied Pauperism', unpubl. Ph.D. thesis, University of London, 1975; and Digby, 'The labour market and the continuity of social policy'.

53. Williams, *Pauperism to Poverty*, pp. 59 and 231.

54. M. E. Rose, *The English Poor Law 1780–1930* (Newton Abbot, 1971), pp. 140, 150–1; Williams, *Pauperism to Poverty*, p. 65.

55. S. and B. Webb, *English Poor Law Policy* (1910), p. 84; F. Driver, *Power and Pauperism: The Workhouse System, 1834–1884* (Cambridge, 1993), map on p. 50.

56. W. Apfel and P. Dunkley, 'English rural society and the New Poor Law: Bedfordshire, 1834–47', *Social History*, 10 (1985), pp. 41, 47, 68.

57. Compare P. Dunkley, 'The hungry forties and the New Poor Law: A case study', *Historical Journal* 17 (1974) pp. 329–46; M. E. Rose, 'The Anti-Poor Law Movement in the North of England', *Northern History*, 1 (1966), pp. 70–91; and Boyson, 'New Poor Law in North East Lancashire'. For 'organised diversity', see Driver, *Power and Pauperism*, p. 53, and map on p. 51.

58. Dunkley, 'The hungry forties and the New Poor Law'.

59. See tables in M. E. Rose, *The Relief of Poverty, 1834–1914*, 2nd edn (1986), p. 50; Williams, *Pauperism to Poverty*, Table 4.5, pp. 158–63.

60. *First Annual Report of the Poor Law Commissioners for England and Wales*, 1835, Appendix A, Documents Issued by the Central Board, No. 9, Workhouse Rules, Clauses IX and X.

61. See *Annual Reports of the Poor Law Commissioners;* and Williams, *Pauperism to Poverty*, pp. 109–113; Driver, *Power and Pauperism*, pp. 59–64.

62. M. Foucault, *Discipline and Punish* (Harmondsworth, 1979). However, the extent and meaning of this transformation has been questioned; see, for example, M. J. Wiener, *Reconstructing the Criminal: Culture, Law and Policy in England, 1830–1914* (Cambridge, 1990), esp. pp. 101–3.

63. *First Annual Report of the Poor Law Commissioners*, Appendix A, Clause XXII.

64. M. A. Crowther, *The Workhouse System, 1834–1929* (1981), pp. 52–3. See also Cole, *Down Poorhouse Lane*.

65. P. Thane, 'Women and the Poor Law in Victorian and Edwardian England', *History Workshop Journal*, 6 (1978), p. 32.

66. See Rose, 'Settlement, removal and the New Poor Law'.

67. Williams, *Pauperism to Poverty*, pp. 196 and 199.

68. Rose, 'Allowance system under the New Poor Law', p. 617.

69. U. Henriques, 'Bastardy and the New Poor Law', *Past and Present*, 37 (1967), pp. 103–29; K. D. M. Snell and J. Millar, 'Lone parent families

and the welfare state: past and present', *Continuity and Change*, 2 (1987), pp. 387–422; S. and B. Webb, *English Poor Law Policy* (1909), chs 2 and 3; Thane, 'Women and the Poor Law', p. 32.

70. D. Thomson, 'The welfare of the elderly in the past: a family or community responsibility?', in M. Pelling and R. M. Smith, eds, *Life, Death and the Elderly: Historical Perspectives* (1991), pp. 194–221; D. Thomson, 'The decline of social security: falling state support for the elderly since early Victorian times', *Ageing and Society*, 4 (1984), pp. 451–82; P. Thane, 'Old people and their families in the English past', in M. Daunton, ed., *Charity, Self Interest and Welfare in the English Past* (1996), pp. 113–138. See also the critique of Thomson, in P. Lindert, 'Towards a comparative history of income and wealth inequality', pp. 227–8.

71. Thane, 'Old people and their families', p. 121.

72. Calculated from Williams, *Pauperism to Poverty*, Table 4.27 on p. 208; see ibid., Tables 4.24, 4.25 on pp. 205–7 for other data referred to in this paragraph.

73. R. G. Hodgkinson, *The Origins of the National Health Service: The Medical Services of the New Poor Law, 1834–71* (1967).

74. R. Pinker, *English Hospital Statistics, 1861–1938* (1966), pp. 8, 91–5; Williams, *Pauperism to Poverty*, Table 4.28 on p. 209.

75. M. W. Flinn, 'The medical services under the New Poor Law', in D. Fraser, ed., *The New Poor Law in the Nineteenth Century* (1976), pp. 49–50; Crowther, *Workhouse System*, pp. 158 and 160.

76. Flinn, 'Medical services', p. 51.

77. S. G. and E. O. Checkland, *Poor Law Report of 1834*, pp. 437, see also p. 430. *First Annual Report of the Poor Law Commissioners*, Appendix A Workhouse Rules, Clause XVIII.

78. *Fourth Annual Report of the Poor Law Commissioners* (1838)pp. 228–65. For Kay, see R. Selleck, *John Kay Shuttleworth: Journey of an Outsider* (Ilford, 1994).

79. R. Johnson, 'Educational policy and social control in early Victorian England', *Past and Present*, 49 (1970); Driver, *Power and Pauperism*, pp. 95–9. Kay argued that in the district schools, pupils would be freed from the 'moral contamination' of their parents and other paupers. Quoted in Digby, *Pauper Palaces*, p. 189; see also F. Duke, 'Pauper education', in Fraser *New Poor Law in the Nineteenth Century*.

80. F. Crompton, *Workhouse Children: Infant and Child Paupers under the Worcestershire Poor Law, 1780–1871* (Stroud, 1997), p. 47.

81. Digby, *Pauper Palaces*, p. 191; E. Higgs, 'Domestic service and household production', in A. V. John, ed., *Unequal Opportunities: Women's Employment in England, 1800–1914* (1986), p. 133.

82. BPP, 'Returns of Children Chargeable to the Poor Rates', 1870, LVIII, pp. 65–9, 561.

83. J. M. Robson and A. Brady, eds, *Collected Works of J. S. Mill* (Toronto, 1977), vol. XVIII, p. 170; vol., III, p. 763; vol. IV, p. 368.

84. H. Fawcett, *Manual of Political Economy*, 2nd. edn, (1865), p. 587; L. Stephen, *Life of Henry Fawcett*, 3rd. edn, (1886), ch. 4; L. Goldman, ed., *The Blind Victorian: Henry Fawcett and British Liberalism* (Cambridge,

1989), p. 45.

85. H. Fawcett, *Pauperism: Its Causes and Remedies* (1871), pp. 8–9, 42–4, 78, 121. These lectures greatly influenced the Poor Law inspectorate and the first generation of COS activists, see T. Mackay, *History of the English Poor Laws* (1899), p. 569. The poor relief chapter in the fourth edition of Fawcett's *Manual of Political Economy* in 1874 was substantially revised along the lines of his *Pauperism*.

86. H. Sidgewick, *The Principles of Political Economy* (1883), pp. 534–5.

87. Fawcett, *Pauperism*, p. 47; see also Stephen, *Life of Henry Fawcett*, p. 153.

88. M. E. Rose, 'The crisis of poor relief in England 1860–1890', in W. J. Mommsen, ed., *The Emergence of the Welfare State in Britain and Germany* (1981), pp. 50–70.

89. J. Hollingshead, *Ragged London in 1861* (Everyman edn, 1986), pp. 5–6.

90. G. S. Jones, *Outcast London: A Study in the Relationship between Classes in Victorian Society* (Harmondsworth, 1984), ch. 13; J. H. Treble, *Urban Poverty in Britain, 1830–1914* (1979), ch. 2; J. Harris, *Unemployment and Politics, 1886–1914* (Oxford, 1972), pp. 7–20; A. J. Kidd, 'Outcast Manchester: Voluntary charity, poor relief and the casual poor 1860–1905', in A. J. Kidd and K. W. Roberts, eds, *City, Class and Culture* (Manchester, 1985).

91. The terms 'voluntary' and 'involuntary' poor are from Fawcett, *Pauperism*, pp. 8–9; for the use of 'clever pauper' and 'Pauper Frankenstein', see Jones, *Outcast London*, pp. 245–6.

92. *Twenty-Second Annual Report of the Poor Law Board* (1869–70), Appendix A, No. 4.

93. Ibid., pp. x–xvii.

94. *First Annual Report of the Local Government Board*, (1871–72), App. A, No. 20. The fullest account remains, S. and B. Webb, *English Poor Law Policy*, ch. 4.

95. Thane, 'Women and the Poor Law', p. 39.

96. Flinn, 'Medical services', pp. 65–6; S. and B. Webb, *English Poor Law Policy*, pp. 207–10; Thomson, 'Decline of social security'.

97. Williams, *Pauperism to Poverty*, p. 102, and Table 4.5 on pp. 158–63.

98. For the 'Manchester Rules', see Rose, *English Poor Law*, pp. 230–1.

99. R. H. Crocker, 'The Victorian Poor Law in crisis and change: Southampton, 1870–1895', *Albion*, 19 (1987), p. 30.

100. H. Longley, *Outdoor Relief in the Metropolis*, 1874; BPP, *Report from the Select Committee of the House of Lords on Poor Relief*, 1888, p. 43, para. 330; Kidd, 'Outcast Manchester', p. 55; P. Ryan, 'Politics and relief: East London unions in the later nineteenth and early twentieth centuries', and K. Gregson, 'Poor Law and organised charity: The relief of exceptional distress in North-East England, 1870–1910', both in Rose, ed., *Poor and the City*; Crocker, 'The Victorian Poor Law', pp. 27–8.

101. M. Mackinnon, 'English Poor Law policy and the crusade against outrelief', *Journal of Economic History*, 47 (1987), pp. 603–25; M. Caplan, 'The New Poor Law and the struggle for union chargeability', *International Review of Social History*, 23 (1978), pp. 267–300; P. Wood, 'Finance and the urban Poor Law: Sunderland Union, 1836–1914', in Rose, *Poor and the City*, esp. pp. 34–5.

102. Ryan, 'Politics and relief', p. 147.
103. Kidd, 'Outcast Manchester', esp. pp. 56–7; Ryan, 'Politics and relief', p. 150. The most extensive use of the 'test workhouse' was for seven years in the 1870s and 1880s, when several London unions sent their able-bodied paupers to the Poplar 'test workhouse', see Webbs, *English Poor Law Policy*, pp. 159–64.
104. *Report of the Lancet Sanitary Commission for Investigating the State of the Infirmaries of Workhouses*, 1866; BPP, H. C. Sess. Paper, 4, 1867–8, *Report of Dr Edward Smith, Medical Officer to the Poor Law Board on . . . the Care and Treatment of the Sick Poor in Forty-Eight Provincial Workhouses*. Details of the investigations can be found in B. Abel-Smith, *The Hospitals* (1964), ch. 4 and P. Wood, *Poverty and the Workhouse in Victorian Britain* (Stroud, 1991), pp. 131–7.
105. G. M. Ayers, *England's First State Hospitals 1867–1930* (1971), chs 1 and 2; J. E. O'Neill, 'Finding a policy for the sick poor', *Victorian Studies*, 7 (1964), pp. 265–84.
106. Pinker, *Hospital Statistics*, pp. 49–51 and 75, Tables I, II, III and XII. Pinker follows *Burdett's Hospital and Charities* (1913) in classifying 'separate workhouse infirmaries' as those with a training school for nurses attached, *Hospital Statistics*, p. 7.
107. J. Pickstone, *Medicine and Industrial Society: A History of Hospital Provision in Manchester and its Region, 1752–1946* (Manchester, 1985), pp. 122–7.
108. Abel-Smith, *The Hospitals*, pp. 84–94; Webbs, *English Poor Law Policy*, pp. 207–10; Flinn, 'Medical services'; S. Cherry, *Medical Services and the Hospitals in Britain, 1860–1939* (1996), p. 43.
109. Williams, *Pauperism to Poverty*, Tables 4.32 and 4.35 on pp. 218–9, 221.
110. R. Vorspan, 'Vagrancy and the New Poor Law in Late-Victorian and Edwardian England', *English Historical Review*, 92 (1977), pp. 59–81; Williams, *Pauperism to Poverty*, Table 4.15 on pp. 187–8; Crowther, *Workhouse System*, ch. 10.
111. Webbs, *English Poor Law Policy*, pp. 235–40; Rose, *English Poor Law*, pp. 252–4; Crowther, *Workhouse System*; Horn, *Labouring Life*, ch. 10.
112. Williams, *Pauperism to Poverty*, Table 4.31 on p. 215; K. Jones, *Mental Health and Social Policy, 1845–1959* (1961); Ayers, *England's First State Hospitals*, ch. 4; J. K. Walton, 'The treatment of pauper lunatics in Victorian England', in A. Scull, ed., *Madhouses, Mad–Doctors and Madmen* (1981); B. Forsythe et al., 'The New Poor Law and the county pauper lunatic asylum', *Social History of Medicine*, 9 (1996), pp. 335–55; J. Melling et al., '"A proper lunatic for two years": Pauper lunatic children in Victorian and Edwardian England', *Journal of Social History*, 31(1997), pp. 371–405.
113. H. Hendrick, *Child Welfare: England, 1872–1989* (1994), p. 74.
114. Calculated from the figures in Hendrick, *Child Welfare*, p. 76 and Williams, *Pauperism to Poverty*, p. 197, Table 4.18.
115. G. S. Jones, *Outcast London*; J. Harris, *Unemployment and Politics: A Study in English Social Policy, 1886–1914* (Oxford, 1972). The best discussion of the notion of a *residuum* in late-Victorian social thought is J. Harris, 'Between civic virtue and Social Darwinism: the concept of the residuum', in D. Englander and R. O'Day, eds, *Retrieved Riches: Social Investigation*

in Britain, 1840–1914 (Aldershot, 1995). For a case study of street politics and the unemployed, see A. J. Kidd, 'The Social Democratic Federation and popular agitation among the unemployed in Edwardian Manchester', *International Review of Social History*, 29 (1984), pp. 336–58.

116. *Pauperism and Distress: Circular Letter to Boards of Guardians* (Chamberlain Circular), 15 March 1886.
117. Harris, *Private Lives, Public Spirit*, pp. 226, 241–2.
118. Numerous references, but see esp. Marshall, *Principles of Economics*, pp. 1–3 and A. C. Pigou, ed., *Memorials of Alfred Marshall* (1925), p. 462.
119. Harris, *Private Lives, Public Spirit*, pp. 248–50; Finlayson, *Citizen, State, and Social Welfare*, pp. 177–82.
120. William Beveridge, in *Sociological Papers*, 3 (1906), p. 325. Both Hobson and the Webbs employed the same argument see Kidd, 'State and moral progress', p. 198.
121. J. R. Hay, *The Origins of the Liberal Welfare Reforms* (1975), pp. 34 and 35.

3 Voluntary Charity and the Poor

1. J. Habermas, *The Structural Transformation of the Public Sphere: An Inquiry into a Category of Bourgeois Society*, Eng. trans. (1989); R. J. Morris 'Clubs, societies and associations', in F. M. L. Thompson, ed., *Cambridge Social History of Britain, 1750–1950*, vol. 3 (Cambridge, 1990); P. Langford, *Public Life and the Propertied Englishman, 1689–1798* (Oxford, 1991).
2. See, for example, N. McCord, 'The Poor Law and philanthropy' in D. Fraser, ed., *The New Poor Law in the Nineteenth Century* (1976); G. Best, *Mid-Victorian Britain, 1851–1875* (1971), p. 138, *et seq.*
3. M. Gorsky, 'Charity, Mutuality and Philanthropy: Voluntary Provision in Bristol 1800–70', unpubl. Ph.D. thesis, Bristol University, 1995; P. Shapely, 'Voluntary Charities in Nineteenth Century Manchester: Structure, Social Status and Leadership', unpubl. Ph.D. thesis, Manchester Metropolitan University, 1994.
4. R. J. Morris, *Class, Sect and Party* (Manchester, 1990), p. 184.
5. For the historiography of charitable motives, see A. J. Kidd, 'Philanthropy and the social history paradigm', *Social History*, 21 (1996), pp. 180–92.
6. See P. Shapely, 'Charity, status and leadership: Charitable image and the Manchester man', *Journal of Social History*, 32 (1998), pp. 157–77; 'Charity, status and parliamentary candidates in Manchester', *International Review of Social History* (1999, forthcoming); *Charity and Power in Victorian Manchester* (Manchester, 1999, forthcoming).
7. See P. Mandler, ed., *The Uses of Charity: The Poor on Relief in the Metropolis* (Philadelphia, Penn., 1990), pp. 15, 33 n. 52.
8. F. K. Prochaska, *Women and Philanthropy in Nineteenth Century England* (Oxford, 1980). Prochaska should be complemented by other studies on women in middle-class culture such as, C. Hall and L. Davidoff, *Family Fortunes: Men and Women of the English Middle Class, 1780–1850* (1987); J. Parker, *Women and Welfare* (1988); A. Summers 'A home from home:

Women's philanthropic work in the nineteenth century', in S. Burman, ed., *Fit Work for Women* (1979); M.Vicinus, *Independent Women: Work and Community for Single Women, 1850–1920* (1985); E. Yeo, *The Contest for Social Science: Relations and Representations of Gender and Class* (1996).

9.   See Hilton, *Age of Atonement*; Prochaska, *Women and Philanthropy*; F. K. Brown, *Fathers of the Victorians* (Cambridge, 1961); K. Heasman, *Evangelicals in Action: An Appraisal of their Social Work in the Victorian Era* (1962); I. Bradley, *The Call to Seriousness* (1972).

10. T. Haskell, 'Capitalism and the origins of the humanitarian sensibility', *American Historical Review*, 40 (1985), pp. 551.

11. D. Andrew, *Philanthropy and Police: London Charity in the Eighteenth Century* (Princeton, NJ, 1989), p. 169.

12. Hilton, *Age of Atonement*, pp. 100–08; Prochaska, *Women and Philanthropy*, pp. 8–9.

13. Andrew, *Philanthropy and Police*; M. J. D. Roberts, 'Reshaping the gift relationship: The London Mendicity Society and the suppression of begging in England, 1818–1869', *International Review of Social History*, 37 (1991), pp. 205–6; *idem*, 'Head versus heart? Voluntary associations and charity organisation in England, c. 1700–1850', in H. Cunningham and J. Innes, eds, *Charity, Philanthropy and Reform from the 1690s to 1850* (1998).

14. T. Malthus *An Essay on the Principle of Population*, ed. D. Winch (Cambridge, 1992), pp. 281 and 283.

15. For the SBCP, see Poynter, *Society and Pauperism*, esp. pp. 91–8; Andrew, *Philanthropy and Police*, esp. pp. 174–7; Owen, *English Philanthropy*, pp. 106–8.

16. Roberts, in Cunningham and Innes, *Charity, Philanthropy and Reform*.

17. Prochaska, *Women and Philanthropy*, p. 9.

18. Brown, *Fathers of the Victorians*; M. Simey, *Charity Rediscovered: A Study of Philanthropic Effort in Nineteenth Century Liverpool* (Liverpool, 1992); G. B. Hindle, *Provision for the Relief of the Poor in Manchester, 1754–1826* (Manchester, 1975); Innes, 'A mixed economy of welfare', pp. 145–6.

19. J. Aston, *A Picture of Manchester* (Manchester, 1816), pp. 137–8.

20. Brown, *Fathers of the Victorians*, p. 238; Hindle, *Relief of the Poor in Manchester*, pp. 82 and 83.

21. Roberts, in Cunningham and Innes, *Charity, Philanthropy and Reform*.

22. Roberts, 'Reshaping the gift relationship', pp. 201–3; Owen, *English Philanthropy*, pp. 109–13.

23. *Bath Society for the Suppression of Vagrants, Annual Report for 1812*.

24. Yeo, *The Contest for Social Science*.

25. Prochaska, *Voluntary Impulse*, p. 43.

26. For Chalmers, see the references in ch. 2, note 29. In addition, A. F. Young and E. T. Ashton, *British Social Work in the Nineteenth Century* (1956), ch. 4 is still useful. An interesting contemporary account of the Elberfeld scheme is in A. Emminghaus, ed., *Poor Relief in Different Parts of Europe* (1873), ch. 4.

27. *District Visitors' Record for 1832*, cited in Brown, *Fathers of the Victorians*, p. 241. See also H. D. Rack, 'Domestic visitation: A chapter in early nineteenth-century evangelicalism', *Journal of Ecclesiastical History*, 24 (1973);

D. M. Lewis, *Lighten Their Darkness: The Evangelical Mission to Working-Class London, 1828–1860* (New York, 1986).

28. Simey, *Charity Rediscovered*, p. 30.
29. *Manchester and Salford District Provident Society, First Annual Report* (1833), p. 6.
30. Sampson Low, *Charities of London*, pp. 127–8, cited in Prochaska, *Women and Philanthropy*, p. 104.
31. Young and Ashton, *Social Work in the Nineteenth Century*, p. 188.
32. For Louisa Twining, see T. Deane, 'Late nineteenth-century philanthropy: The case of Louisa Twining', in A. Digby and J. Stewart, eds, *Gender, Health and Welfare* (1996).
33. *Manchester & Salford District Provident Society, Fifth Annual Report* (1837), p. 5; and *37th Annual Report* (1869), p. 6. See also M. Hewitt, 'The travails of domestic visiting: Manchester, 1830–70', *Historical Research*, 71 (1998), pp. 196–227.
34. Prochaska, *Women and Philanthropy*, p. 128.
35. W. Rathbone, *The History and Progress of District Nursing*, 1890, p. 25, cited in Simey, *Liverpool*, p. 72. For voluntary health visiting and its absorption by public bodies, see C. Davies, 'The health visitor as mother's friend: A woman's place in public health, 1900–14', *Social History of Medicine*, 1 (1988), pp. 39–59.
36. Prochaska, *Voluntary Impulse*, p. 49. See also Prochaska, 'Body and soul: Bible nurses and the poor in Victorian London', *Historical Research*, 60 (1987), pp. 336–48.
37. H. Thompson, *Life of Hannah More* (1838), p. 99.
38. P. Horn, *Children's Work and Welfare, 1780–1890* (Cambridge, 1994), pp. 1–4; H. Cunningham, *The Children of the Poor: Representations of Childhood Since the Seventeenth Century* (Oxford, 1991), pp. 3, 48, 54, 90–1.
39. J. S. Mill, *On Liberty*, ed. Mary Warnock (Collins, 1979), p. 238.
40. Mary Carpenter, *Reformatory Schools for the Children of the Perishing and Dangerous Classes and for Juvenile Offenders* (1851), pp. 2–3, emphasis in the original.
41. E. Bradlow, 'Children's Friend Society at the Cape of Good Hope', *Victorian Studies*, 27 (1984), pp. 155–77; E. Hadley, 'Natives in a strange land: The philanthropic discourse of juvenile emigration in mid-nineteenth-century England', *Victorian Studies*, 33 (1990), pp. 411–36; J. Parr, *Labouring Children: British Immigrant Apprentices to Canada, 1869–1924* (1980).
42. E. Clark, 'The early ragged schools and the foundation of the Ragged School Union', *Journal of Educational Administration and History*, 1 (1969).
43. *Speeches of the Earl of Shaftesbury upon Subjects Relating to the Claims and Interests of the Labouring Classes* (1868), p. 253, quoted in Hadley, 'Natives in a strange land', p. 418.
44. A. M. Babler, *Education of the Destitute. A Study of London Ragged Schools, 1844–1874* (Ann Arbor, Mich., 1986).
45. G. K. Behlmer, *Child Abuse and Moral Reform in England, 1870–1908* (Stanford, Calif., 1982), pp. 174–5, 181 *passim*.
46. Parr, *Labouring Children*, pp. 66–9; G. Wagner, *Barnado* (1979), pp. 233–6.

47. Ellice Hopkins, *Notes on Penitentiary Work* (1879), p. 5, cited in Prochaska, 'Philanthropy', p. 376. The best introduction to rescue work with prostitutes is Prochaska, *Women and Philanthropy*, ch. 6.

48. F. Finnegan, *Poverty and Prostitution: A Study of Victorian Prostitutes in York* (1979), p. 211.

49. B. Harrison, 'For Church, Queen and Family: The Girls' Friendly Society, 1874–1920', *Past and Present*, 61 (1975), p. 116.

50. Pinker, *Hospital Statistics*, p. 57.

51. M. E. Fissell, 'The "sick and drooping poor" in eighteenth-century Bristol and its region', *Social History of Medicine*, 2 (1989), pp. 35–58.

52. J. Woodward, *To Do the Sick No Harm: A Study of the British Voluntary Hospital System to 1875* (1974), pp. 18, 38–43.

53. J. Stonhouse, *Friendly Advice to a Patient*, quoted in Woodward, *To Do the Sick No Harm*, p. 20; for sick visiting, Prochaska, *Women and Philanthropy*, pp. 141 and 158.

54. Bristowe and Holmes, *The Hospitals of the United Kingdom* (1864), cited in Abel-Smith, *The Hospitals*, p. 37.

55. H. Marland, *Medicine and Society in Wakefield and Huddersfield, 1780–1870* (Cambridge, 1987), pp. 119 and 121.

56. Woodward, *To Do the Sick No Harm*, pp. 43–4; Abel-Smith, *The Hospitals*, p. 41.

57. An exception is R. P. Hastings, 'A nineteenth-century dispensary at work', *Local Historian*, 10 (1973), pp. 221–6.

58. Pickstone, *Medicine and Industrial Society*, p. 16.

59. Quoted in Marland, *Medicine and Society*, p. 262.

60. A. Digby, *Making a Living: Doctors and Patients in the English Market for Medicine, 1720–1911* (Cambridge, 1994), p. 252.

61. Abel-Smith, *Hospitals*, ch. 9; S. Cherry, 'Before the National Health Service: Financing the voluntary hospitals, 1900–1939', *Economic History Review*, 2nd ser., 50 (1997), p. 314, Table 5.

62. A. D. Gilbert, *Religion and Society in Industrial England: Church, Chapel and Social Change, 1740–1914* (1976), pp. 187–98.

63. F. K. Prochaska, 'A mother's country: Mother's meetings and family welfare in Britain, 1850–1950', *History*, 74 (1989), pp. 379–99.

64. Quotations cited in K. Woodroofe, *From Charity to Social Work in England and the United States* (1962), pp. 26 and 27.

65. See esp. C. L. Mowat, *The Charity Organisation Society, 1869–1913* (1961); Woodroofe, *Charity to Social Work*, ch. 2; Young and Ashton, *Social Work in the Nineteenth Century*, ch. 6; Owen, *English Philanthropy*, ch. 8. And more recently, the analysis and bibliographies in A. W. Vincent, 'The Poor Law Reports of 1909 and the social theory of the Charity Organisation Society', *Victorian Studies*, 27 (1984); R. Humphreys, *Sin, Organised Charity and the Poor Law in Victorian England* (1995); J. Lewis, *The Voluntary Sector, the State and Social Work in Britain: The Charity Organisation Society/Family Welfare Association since 1869* (Aldershot, 1995).

66. Humphreys, *Sin, Organised Charity and the Poor Law*; Lewis, *Voluntary Sector, the State and Social Work*, pp. 56–7.

67. Mowat, *Charity Organisation Society*, p. 58.

68. Vincent, 'Social theory of the Charity Organisation Society'; see also R. Plant and A. W. Vincent, *Philosophy, Politics and Citizenship* (Oxford, 1984).
69. Lewis, *Voluntary Sector, the State and Social Work*, esp. pp. 34, 36, 59–60.
70. Harris, *Unemployment and Politics*, pp. 106, 109–10.
71. A. M. McBriar, *An Edwardian Mixed Doubles: The Bosanquets Versus the Webbs. A Study in British Social Policy, 1890–1929* (Oxford, 1987).
72. Quoted in A. Briggs and A. Macartney, *Toynbee Hall: The First Hundred Years* (1984), p. 6.
73. J. N. Tarn, *Five Per Cent Philanthropy: An Account of Housing in Urban Areas between 1850 and 1914* (Cambridge, 1973); S. M. Gaskell, *Model Housing from the Great Exhibition to the Festival of Britain* (1986); R. Rodger, *Housing in Urban Britain 1780–1914* (1989).
74. See her letter to *The Times* of 4 March 1901, reprinted in R. Whelan, ed., *Octavia Hill and the Social Housing Debate* (1998), pp. 111–13.
75. See M. Daunton, 'Housing' in Thompson, ed., *Cambridge Social History of Britain*, vol. 2, pp. 235–6.
76. A point made in Henry Mayhew, *London Labour and the London Poor*, vol. I, (1851) p. 416; see also Kidd, 'Outcast Manchester', pp. 63–4.
77. Harris, *Unemployment and Politics*, p. 107.
78. G. S. Jones, *Outcast London*, ch. 16.
79. W. Booth, *In Darkest England and the Way Out* (1890), p. 14. The most detailed study of the rescue work of the Salvation Army remains R. Sandall, *The History of the Salvation Army, Volume III, Social Reform and Welfare Work* (1955).
80. *In Darkest England*, p. 18.
81. Finlayson, *Citizen, State and Social Welfare*, ch. 2.
82. Harris, *Unemployment and Politics*, pp. 128–9.
83. K. Laybourn, *The Guild of Help Movement and the Changing Face of Edwardian Philanthropy* (Lampeter, 1994).
84. See, for example, M. J. Moore, 'Social work and social welfare: The organisation of philanthropic resources in Britain, 1900–1914', *Journal of British Studies*, 16 (1977), esp. p. 68.
85. M. Cahill and T. Jowitt, 'The new philanthropy: The emergence of the Bradford City Guild of Help', *Journal of Social Policy*, 9 (1980), p. 376.
86. *Hints to Helpers*, quoted in Kidd, 'Charity organisation and the unemployed', p. 64.
87. Finlayson, *Citizen, State and Social Welfare*, p. 176.

4   The Working Class, Self-Help and Mutual Aid

1. Friendly societies have been curiously neglected in several of the histories of the working class widely used by students. See, for example, J. Rule, *The Labouring Classes in Early Industrial England, 1750–1850* (1986); J. Belchem, *Industrialisation and the Working Class: The English Experience, 1750–1900* (1990); J. Benson, *The Working Class in Britain, 1850–1939* (1989). P. H. G. H. Gosden, *Friendly Societies in England, 1815–1875* (1961),

is the standard work on the friendly societies, yet deals only with the registered societies and says little about the later part of the century, see also his *Self Help: Voluntary Institutions in the Nineteenth Century* (1973); P. Johnson, *Saving and Spending: The Working-class Economy in Britain, 1870–1939* (Oxford, 1985), deals with the post-1875 period; B. Supple, 'Legislation and virtue: An essay in working-class self help and the state in the early nineteenth century', in N. McKendrick ed., *Historical Perspectives* (1974), is useful on official attitudes; E. Hopkins, *Working-Class Self Help in Nineteenth-Century England* (1995), is the most recent general survey. D. Green, *Working Class Patients and the Medical Establishment: Self Help in Britain from the Mid-Nineteenth Century to 1948* (1985), has some single-minded arguments, but can be cavalier in the handling of evidence. There are several useful local studies which will be referred to below.

2. M. Gorsky, 'The growth and distribution of English friendly societies in the early nineteenth century', *Economic History Review*, 2nd ser., 51 (1998), p. 507 *passim*; Gosden, *Friendly Societies*, pp. 21–4; Hopkins, *Working-Class Self Help*, p. 10.

3. E. J. Hobsbawm, *Labouring Men* (1964), ch. 4; H. Southall, 'The tramping artisan revisits: Labour mobility and economic development in early Victorian England', *Economic History Review*, 2nd ser., 44 (1991), pp. 272–96.

4. Gosden, *Self Help*, p. 70; see also Gosden, *Friendly Societies*, p. 34.

5. Both cited in T. R.Tholfsen, *Working Class Radicalism in Mid-Victorian England* (1976), p. 294.

6. S. G. and E. O. Checkland, *Poor Law Report of 1834*, p. 346; *First Annual Report of the Poor Law Commissioners* (1835), pp. 55-6; *Fourth Annual Report of the Poor Law Commissioners* (1838), pp. 84-7.

7. For Pratt, see Gosden, *Friendly Societies*, pp. 190–7.

8. BPP, *Royal Commission on Friendly and Benefit Building Societies, Fourth Report and Appendix*, XXIII, Sir George Young's Report, C. 997, 1874, p. 7.

9. T. Laqueur, 'Bodies, death and pauper funerals', *Representations*, 1 (1983); R. Richardson, *Death, Dissection and the Destitute* (1988); Thomas Noel, 'The Pauper' drive' in *Rhymes and Roundelays* (1841).

10. Maud Pember Reeves, *Round About a Pound a Week* [1913] (Virago edn, 1979), pp. 66–72. In London, the average cost of burying a working-class adult in 1870 was £5. 9s.; the funeral of a child cost £2. 2s.

11. See BPP, *Royal Commission on Friendly and Benefit Building Societies, Fourth Report and Appendix*, XXIII, App. IV, C. 961, 1874.

12. F. M. L. Thompson, *The Rise of Respectable Society* (London, 1988), pp. 201–2.

13. G. Crossick, *An Artisan Elite in Victorian Society: Kentish London, 1840–1880* (1978), pp. 181–2.

14. D. Jones, 'Did friendly societies matter? A study of friendly society membership in Glamorgan 1794–1910', *Welsh History Review*, 12 (1985), p. 336.

15. *Saving and Spending*, Table 3. 3 on p. 57.

16. Evidence for the early to mid nineteenth century is sparse. Gorsky con-

jects a membership involving up to one third of English households in 1815; see Gorsky, 'Growth and distribution of English friendly societies', p. 507. On the basis of Poor Law returns for Scotland in 1843, up to 1 working man in 4 may have belonged to a friendly society, see I. Levitt and C. Smout, *The State of the Scottish Working Class in 1843* (Edinburgh, 1979), pp. 132, 142, 147.

17. BPP, *Royal Commission on Friendly and Benefit Building Societies, Fourth Report and Appendix*, XXIII, Sir George Young's Report, C. 997, 1874, p. 2.

18. Gosden, *Friendly Societies*, Table 12 on p. 75. Surveys such as that undertaken by the MUOF in the 1840s are rare and later ones less than reliable, see ibid., pp. 229–30 for example.

19. See R. Q. Gray, *The Labour Aristocracy in Victorian Edinburgh* (Oxford, 1976), pp. 122–3; Crossick, *Artisan Elite*, Table 9.1 on p. 183.

20. Johnson, *Saving and Spending*, pp. 58–60; BPP, *Royal Commission on the Poor Laws and Relief of Distress*, App. Vol. VII, Cd. 5035/1910, pp. 224, 492, 495, 504.

21. Johnson, *Saving and Spending*, pp. 62–3; see also G. Anderson, *Victorian Clerks* (Manchester, 1976).

22. See E. Higgs, 'Household and work in the nineteenth-century censuses of England and Wales', *Journal of the Society of Archivists*, 11:3 (1990), pp. 73–7; E. Higgs, *A Clearer Sense of the Census* (1996), pp. 136–8; S. R. S. Szretser, 'The genesis of the Registrar General's social classification of occupations', *British Journal of Sociology*, 35 (1984), pp. 522–46.

23. See W. A. Armstrong, 'The use of information about occupation', in E. A. Wrigley, ed., *Nineteenth Century Society* (Cambridge, 1972), pp. 212–3, 215–23.

24. J. A. Banks, 'The social structure of nineteenth-century England as seen through the Census', in R. Lawton, ed., *The Census and the Social Structure* (1978).

25. From G. D. H. Cole, *Studies in Class Structure* (1955), pp. 55–8; to E. Evans *The Forging of the Modern State: Early Industrial Britain, 1783–1870*, 2nd edn, (1996), p. 133.

26. Cole, *Studies in Class Structure*, p. 57; F. Bedarida, *A Social History of England, 1851–1990* (1991), p. 61.

27. N. Kirk, *The Growth of Working-Class Reformism in Mid-Victorian England* (1985), p. 198.

28. See S. and B. Webb, *The History of Trade Unionism, 1666–1920* (1920), p. 445; see also M. F. Robinson, *The Spirit of Association* (1913), p. 289.

29. However, see C. G. Hanson, 'Craft unions, welfare benefits and the case for trade union law reform, 1867–75', *Economic History Review*, 2nd ser., 28 (1975), pp. 243–59.

30. S. and B. Webb, *History of Trade Unionism*, p. 219.

31. BPP, *Royal Commission on Friendly and Benefit Building Societies, Fourth Report and Appendix*, XXIII, Sir George Young's Report, C. 997, 1874, p. 30; R. Glen, *Urban Workers in the Early Industrial Revolution* (1984), p. 110; A. Clark, *The Struggle for the Breeches: Gender and the Making of the British Working Class* (1995), pp. 35–6, 290–1.

32. Gosden, *Friendly Societies*, devotes one page to female societies. For some

evidence from the rules of early female societies, see Clark, *Struggle for the Breeches*, pp. 35–8.

33. D. Jones, 'Self help in nineteenth century Wales: The rise and fall of the female friendly society', *Llafur*, 4 (1984), pp. 14–26.
34. Clark, *Struggle for the Breeches*, pp. 36–7.
35. D. Jones, 'Rise and fall of the female friendly society', pp. 23–4.
36. Gosden, *Friendly Societies*, p. 62; Jones, 'Rise and fall of the female friendly society', p. 25.
37. M. Boddy, *The Building Societies* (1980); Gosden, *Self Help*, p. 147; Johnson, *Saving and Spending*, pp. 117–8
38. For the savings bank movement, see H. O. Horne, *A History of Savings Banks* (Oxford, 1947); Gosden, *Self Help*, ch. 8.
39. A. Scratchley, *A Practical Treatise On Savings Banks* (1861), p. xxviii; A. Fishlow, 'The Trustee Savings Banks, 1817–1861', *Journal of Economic History*, 21(1961), pp. 26–40.
40. See Johnson, *Saving and Spending*, Table 4.1 on pp. 91–2.
41. BPP, *Royal Commission on Friendly and Benefit Building Societies, Fourth Report*, XXXIII, pt. 1, C. 961, App. 1, p. 14, cited in Johnson, *Saving and Spending*, p. 94.
42. The data are variously represented and discussed in Gosden, *Self Help*, pp. 239–40; and Johnson, *Saving and Spending*, pp. 94–5. The analysis which follows is my own.
43. The standard modern study remains G. D. H. Cole, *A Century of Co-operation* (1944); but see S. Pollard, 'Nineteenth-century co-operation: From community building to shopkeeping' in A. Briggs and J. Saville, eds, *Essays In Labour History. Vol. I* (1960); M. Purvis, 'Co-operative retailing in England, 1835–1850', *Northern History*, 22 (1986), pp. 198–215; M. Purvis, 'The development of co-operative retailing in England and Wales, 1851–1901: A geographical study', *Journal of Historical Geography*, 16 (1990), pp. 314–31.
44. Purvis, 'Development of co-operative retailing', p. 316.
45. Cole, *Century of Co-operation*, p. 9.
46. Crossick, *Artisan Elite*, pp. 165–8.
47. Kirk, *Working Class Reformism*, p. 201.
48. Purvis, 'Development of co-operative retailing'.
49. Quoted in Crossick, *Artisan Elite*, p. 169.
50. See Johnson, *Saving and Spending*, pp. 133–4.
51. J. O. Foster, 'Nineteenth-century towns: a class dimension', in H. J. Dyos, ed., *The Study of Urban History* (1968), p. 284; *idem, Class Struggle and the Industrial Revolution* (1974), p. 96; Crossick, *Artisan Elite*, pp. 112, 174.
52. For the development of actuarial science in the friendly society movement, see Gosden, *Friendly Societies*, pp. 100–12.
53. Hopkins, *Working-Class Self Help*, p. 51.
54. For discussions of the data and the various assessments of the historians, see R. Floud and D. McCloskey, eds, *The Economic History of Britain Since 1700*, 2nd edn, 3 vols, (Cambridge, 1994), vol. 1, ch. 14; and vol. 2, ch. 11.
55. For a good survey see, ibid., vol. 1, pp. 361–81.

56. Burnett, *Idle Hands*, pp. 91, 106.

57. BPP, *Royal Commission on the Poor Laws, Minority Report, Part II, The Unemployed*, Cd. 4499/1909, p. 1147.

58. G. S. Jones, *Outcast London*, is invaluable on London's casual-labour market.

59. Thomas Carter, *Memoirs of a Working Man* (1845), p. 163. For Mayhew, see E. P. Thompson and E. Yeo, eds, *The Unknown Mayhew: Selections from the Morning Chronicle, 1849–50* (Harmondsworth, 1984).

60. J. Gutteridge, *Lights and Shadows in the Life of an Artisan* (1893). The edition used here is that reprinted in V. E. Chancellor, ed., *Master and Artisan in Victorian England* (New York, 1969), esp. pp. 119–28, 143, 178–9.

61. E. Ross, *Love and Toil: Motherhood in Outcast London, 1870–1918* (Oxford, 1993), p. 198; Hendrick, *Child Welfare*, pp. 93–100.

62. H. Bosanquet, *Rich and Poor*, 2nd edn, (1898), p. 81.

63. E. Roberts, *A Woman's Place: An Oral History of Working-Class Women, 1890–1940* (1984), p. 203.

64. See E. Roberts, *Women's Work, 1840–1940* (1988), p. 44.

65. Bosanquet, *Rich and Poor*, p. 80.

66. See G. E. Mingay, ed., *The Victorian Countryside*, 2 vols, (1981), vol. 1, pp. 131–2.

67. Quoted in P. Horn, *Victorian Countrywomen* (Oxford, 1991), p. 20.

68. *The Autobiography of Joseph Arch*, [1898], Fitzroy edn, (1966), pp. 23–4.

69. Horn, *Victorian Countrywomen*, p. 18.

70. For useful overviews, see J. Lewis, *Women in England, 1870–1950* (Brighton, 1984); C. Chinn, *They Worked All Their Lives: Women of the Urban Poor in England, 1880–1939* (Manchester, 1988); Roberts, *A Woman's Place*; Roberts, *Women's Work*.

71. M. Tebbutt, *Making Ends Meet: Pawnbroking and Working Class Credit* (Leicester, 1983), p. 38.

72. E. Roberts, 'Women's strategies, 1890–1940', in J. Lewis, ed., *Labour and Love: Women's Experience of the Home and Family, 1850–1940* (1986), p. 226.

73. Roberts, 'Women's strategies', pp. 229–30; L. Tilley, J. Scott and M. Cohen, 'Women's work and European fertility patterns', *Journal of Interdisciplinary History*, 6 (1976), esp. pp. 458–63.

74. Higgs, *Census*, pp. 97–9; Roberts, *Women's Work*, p. 45; Chinn, *They Worked All Their Lives*, p. 85.

75. J. Humphries, 'Enclosures, common rights and women: The proletarianisation of families in the late eighteenth and early nineteenth centuries', *Journal of Economic History*, 50 (1990), pp. 117–42; D. Valenze, *The First Industrial Woman* (Oxford, 1995); N. Reed, 'Gnawing it out: A new look at economic relations in nineteenth-century rural England', *Rural History*, I (1990), pp. 83–94.

76. R. Samuel, *East End Underworld: Chapters in the Life of Arthur Harding* (1981); Henry Mayhew, *The Morning Chronicle Survey of Labour and the Poor: The Metropolitan Districts*, 6 vols, Caliban edn, (Horsham, 1982), vol. 5, pp. 209–10; Roberts, *Women's Work*, pp. 40–1; Lewis, *Labour and Love*, p. 222.

77. J. Benson, *The Penny Capitalists: A Study of Nineteenth-Century Working-Class Entrepreneurs* (1983), p. 130 *passim*.
78. Joseph Adshead, *Distress in Manchester: Evidence of the State of the Labouring Classes in 1840–42* (1842), p. 43.
79. Charles Dickens, 'The Pawnbroker's Shop', *Sketches By Boz* (1836).
80. Adshead, *Distress in Manchester*, p. 20; Tebbutt, *Making Ends Meet*, p. 6; Johnson, *Saving and Spending*, p. 170.
81. Tebbutt, *Making Ends Meet*, p. 9; Johnson, *Saving and Spending*, p. 167.
82. Robert Roberts, *The Classic Slum* (Harmondsworth, 1973), p. 25.
83. Adshead, *Distress in Manchester*, pp. 20–1.
84. For general discussions of the issues, see J. H. Johnson and C. G. Pooley, eds, *The Structure of Nineteenth-Century Cities* (1982); R. Dennis, *English Industrial Cities of the Nineteenth Century: A Social Geography* (Cambridge, 1984).
85. See, for example, the discussion in B. S. Rowntree, *Poverty: A Study of Town Life* (1901), ch. 6.
86. See, M. Tebbutt, *Women's Talk?: A Social History of 'Gossip' in Working Class Neighbourhoods, 1880–1960* (Aldershot, 1995).
87. E. Ross, 'Survival networks: Women's neighbourhood sharing in London before World War I', *History Workshop Journal*, 15 (1983), p. 6.
88. Compare M. Anderson, *Family Structure in Nineteenth Century Lancashire* (Cambridge, 1971), p. 178 with Roberts, *A Woman's Place*, pp. 171–2.
89. For a useful discussion, see M. Bulmer, *Neighbouring: The Work of Philip Abrams* (Cambridge, 1986).
90. Agnes Hunt, *Reminiscences* (Shrewesbury, 1935), p. 78.
91. See A. Digby, *British Welfare Policy: Workhouse to Workfare* (1989), pp. 90–3; Ross, 'Survival networks'; A. Davin, *Growing up Poor: Home, School and Street in London, 1870–1914* (1996); J. Lewis, 'Family provision of health and welfare in the mixed economy of care in the late nineteenth and twentieth centuries', *Social History of Medicine*, 8 (1995).
92. M. Young and P. Willmott, *Family and Kinship in East London* (1962).
93. See esp. Roberts, *A Woman's Place*; Ross, *Love and Toil*; Tebbutt, *Women's Talk*.
94. Anderson, *Family Structure*, pp. 40, 154.
95. Ibid., pp. 57–8, 171.
96. S. Meacham, *A Life Apart: The English Working Class, 1890–1914* (1977), pp. 45–52; C. Chinn, *Poverty Amidst Prosperity: The Urban Poor in England, 1834–1914* (Manchester, 1995), pp. 131–2.
97. H. M. Boot, 'Unemployment and poor relief in Manchester, 1845–50', *Social History*, 15 (1990), pp. 217–28.
98. P. Wilmott, *Kinship and Urban Community: Past and Present* (Leicester, 1987), pp. 8–15.
99. C. Lis and H. Soly, 'Neighbourhood social change in Western European cities, sixteenth to nineteenth centuries', *International Review of Social History*, 38 (1993), p. 13 (my emphasis).
100. Anderson, *Family Structure*, p. 42.
101. P. Rushton, 'Family survival strategies in mid-Victorian Ancoats', *Manchester Region History Review*, 7 (1993), pp. 36–44; J. Emerson, 'The

lodging market in a Victorian city: Exeter', *Southern History*, 9 (1987), pp. 103–13; A. Bowley and A. R. Burnett-Hurst, *Livelihood and Poverty: A Study of the Economic Conditions of Working-Class Households* (1915).
102. Lis and Soly, 'Neighbourhood social change', p. 14.
103. Boot, 'Unemployment and poor relief', p. 225.
104. See, for example, Rose, *Poor and the City*, p. 3; Fraser, *New Poor Law*, p. 21.
105. See ch. 2 and Harris, *Unemployment and Politics*, pp. 148–50.
106. See Mandler, *Uses of Charity*, Introduction and essays by Lynn Hollen Lees and Ellen Ross.
107. G. Wagner, *Children of Empire* (1982), pp. 121–2.

5 Poverty and Welfare in Historical Perspective

1. For the social theory of New Liberalism, see M. Freeden, *The New Liberalism: An Ideology of Social Reform* (Oxford, 1978); P. Weiler, *The New Liberalism: Liberal Social Theory in Great Britain, 1889–1914* (New York, 1982).
2. The importance of the friendly societies as a model for health insurance is stressed in E. P. Hennock, *British Social Reform and German Precedents: The Case of Social Insurance, 1880–1914* (Oxford, 1987), p. 189.
3. See Johnson, *Saving and Spending*, pp. 207–9, 215–6; and *idem*, 'Self help versus state help: Old age pensions and personal savings in Great Britain, 1906–1937', *Explorations in Economic History* (1984), pp. 329–50.
4. See, for example, M. Loney, ed., *The State or the Market: Politics and Welfare in Contemporary Britain* (1987).
5. Charities Aid Foundation, *Dimensions of the Voluntary Sector: Key Facts, Figures, Analysis and Trends* (West Malling, Kent, 1997), p. 164; J. Kendall and M. Knapp, *The Voluntary Sector in the United Kingdom* (Manchester, 1996), p. 111.
6. For 'citizenship', see T. H. Marshall, *Citizenship and Social Class* (Cambridge, 1950). For current views on poverty, see for example, B. Nolan and C. Whelan, *Resources, Deprivation and Poverty* (Oxford, 1996); D. Gordon and C. Pantazis, eds, *Breadline Britain in the 1990s* (Aldershot, 1997).

FURTHER READING

This is not meant to be a comprehensive bibliography since much of the historiography has been discussed in the text and references can be found in the notes to each chapter. It is confined to secondary works and several of the titles listed themselves contain bibliographies. To avoid repetition, items have been cited only once even if they are of value in more than one of the sections. Places of publication are London unless otherwise stated.

The traditional emphasis in the historiography which looked to the nineteenth century for the 'origins of the welfare state' has been challenged most successfully by G. Finlayson, *Citizen, State, and Social Welfare in Britain, 1830–1990* (Oxford, 1994). The longer history of the 'mixed economy of welfare' is discussed in M. Daunton, ed., *Charity, Self-Interest and Welfare in the English Past* (1996). Helpful (and brief) introductory overviews are A. Digby, *British Welfare Policy: Workhouse to Workfare* (1989); and M. E. Rose, 'Poverty and self help: Britain in the nineteenth and twentieth centuries', in A. Digby et al., *New Directions in Economic and Social History Volume 2* (1992).

The State and Pauperism

Apfel, W., and P. Dunkley, 'English rural society and the New Poor Law: Bedfordshire, 1834–47', *Social History*, 10 (1985).
Armstrong, W. A., and J. P. Huzel, 'Food, shelter and self help, the Poor Law and the position of the labourer in rural society', in G. Mingay, ed., *The Agrarian History of England and Wales, VI, 1750–1850* (Cambridge, 1989).
Ayers, G. M., *England's First State Hospitals, 1867–1930* (1971).
Blaug, M., 'The myth of the Old Poor Law and the making of the New', *Journal of Economic History*, 23 (1963).

Blaug, M., 'The Poor Law Report re-examined', *Journal of Economic History*, 24 (1964).

Boyer, G. R., *An Economic History of the English Poor Law, 1750–1850* (Cambridge, 1990).

Brundage, A., 'The landed interest and the New Poor Law: A reappraisal of the revolution in government', *English Historical Review*, 87 (1972).

Brundage, A., *The Making of the New Poor Law: The Politics of Inquiry, Enactment and Implementation, 1832–39* (1978).

Checkland, S. G., and E. O. Checkland, eds, *The Poor Law Report of 1834* (Harmondsworth, 1974), editors' introduction.

Crocker, R. H., 'The Victorian Poor Law in crisis and change: Southampton, 1870–1895', *Albion*, 19 (1987).

Crowther, M. A., *The Workhouse System, 1834–1929* (1981).

Digby, A., 'The labour market and the continuity of social policy after 1834', *Economic History Review*, 28 (1975).

Digby, A., *Pauper Palaces* (1978).

Driver, F., *Power and Pauperism: The Workhouse System, 1834–1884* (Cambridge, 1993).

Dunkley, P., 'The hungry forties and the New Poor Law: A case study', *Historical Journal*, 17, (1974).

Dunkley, P., *The Crisis of the Old Poor Law in England, 1795–1834* (1982).

Edsall, N. C., *The Anti Poor Law Movement* (Manchester, 1971).

Englander, D., and R. O'Day, eds, *Retrieved Riches: Social Investigation in Britain, 1840–1914* (Aldershot, 1995).

Englander, D., *Poverty and Poor Law Reform in 19th Century Britain, 1834–1914* (1998).

Fraser, D., ed., *The New Poor Law in the Nineteenth Century* (1976).

Gilbert, B. B., *Evolution of National Insurance in Great Britain: Origins of the Welfare State* (1966).

Harris, J., *Unemployment and Politics: A Study in English Social Policy 1886–1914* (Oxford, 1972).

Harris, J., *Private Lives, Public Spirit: A Social History of Britain, 1870–1914* (Oxford, 1993).

Hay, J. R., *The Origin of the Liberal Welfare Reforms* (1975).

Hendrick, H., *Child Welfare: England, 1872–1989* (1994).

Hennock, E. P., 'Poverty and social theory in England', *Social History*, 1 (1976).

Hennock, E. P., 'The measurement of urban poverty: from metropolis to the nations, 1880–1920', *Economic History Review*, 40 (1987).

Henriques, U., 'Bastardy and the New Poor Law', *Past and Present*, 37 (1967).

Henriques, U., 'How cruel was the Victorian Poor Law?', *Historical Journal*, 11 (1968).

Hilton, B., *The Age of Atonement: The Influence of Evangelicalism on Social and Economic Thought, 1785–1865* (Oxford, 1988).

Himmelfarb, G., *The Idea of Poverty* (1984).

Hodgkinson, R. G., *The Origins of the National Health Service: The Medical Services of the New Poor Law, 1834–71* (1967).

Kidd, A. J., 'How the Webbs wrote their History of the English Poor Laws', *Economic History Review*, 40 (1987).

Kidd, A. J., 'The state and moral progress: The Webbs' case for social reform, *c.* 1905–1940', *Twentieth Century British History*, 7 (1996).

King, S., 'Poor relief and English economic development reappraised', *Economic History Review*, 50 (1997).

King, S., and A. Gritt, 'Which way to welfare? The poor and the Old Poor Law, 1700–1820', forthcoming.

Mackinnon, M., 'English Poor Law policy and the crusade against out–relief', *Journal of Economic History*, 47 (1987).

Mandler, P., 'The making of the New Poor Law *Redivivus*', *Past and Present*, 117 (1987).

Mandler, P., 'Tories and paupers: Christian political economy and the making of the New Poor Law', *Historical Journal*, 33 (1990).

Marshall, J. D., *The Old Poor Law*, 2nd edn (1985).

Melling, J. et al., '"A proper lunatic for two years": Pauper lunatic children in Victorian and Edwardian England', *Journal of Social History*, 31 (1997).

Midwinter, E., *Social Administration in Nineteenth Century Lancashire* (1969).

Oxley, G. W., *Poor Relief in England and Wales, 1601–1834* (Newton Abbot, 1974).

Poynter, J. R., *Society and Pauperism: English Ideas on Poor Relief, 1795–1834* (1969).

Roberts, D., 'How cruel was the Victorian Poor Law?', *Historical Journal*, 4 (1963).

Rose, M. E., 'The allowance system under the New Poor Law', *Economic History Review*, 19 (1966).

Rose, M. E., 'The Anti-Poor Law movement', in J. T. Ward, ed., *Popular Movements, 1830–1850* (1970).

Rose, M. E., ed., *The English Poor Law, 1780–1930* (Newton Abbot, 1971).

Rose, M. E., 'The crisis of poor relief in England 1860–1890', in W. J. Mommsen, ed., *The Emergence of the Welfare State in Britain and Germany* (1981).

Rose, M. E., ed., *The Poor and the City: The English Poor Law in its Urban Context, 1834–1914* (Leicester, 1985).

Rose, M. E., *Relief Of Poverty: 1834–1914*, 2nd edn (1986).

Snell, K. D. M., *Annals of the Labouring Poor: Social Change in Agrarian England 1660–1900* (Cambridge, 1985).

Solar, P. M., 'Poor relief and English economic development before the industrial revolution', *Economic History Review*, 48 (1995).

Thane, P., 'Non-contributory versus insurance pensions 1878–1908', in Thane, ed., *The Origins of British Social Policy* (1978).

Thane, P., 'Women and the Poor Law in Victorian and Edwardian England', *History Workshop Journal*, 6 (1978).

Thane, P., 'The working class and state "welfare" in Britain, 1880–1914', *Historical Journal* (1984).

Thane, P., 'Gender, welfare and old age in Britain, 1870s–1940s', in A. Digby and J. Stewart, eds, *Gender, Health and Welfare* (1996).

Thomson, D., 'The decline of social welfare: falling state support for the elderly since early Victorian times', *Ageing and Society*, 4 (1984).

Vorspan, R., 'Vagrancy and the New Poor Law in Late-Victorian and Edwardian England', *English Historical Review*, 92 (1977).

Webb, S., and B. Webb, *English Poor Law Policy* (1910).

Webb, S., and B. Webb, *English Poor Law History, Part II. The Last Hundred Years*, 2 vols, (1929).

Williams, K., *From Pauperism to Poverty* (1981).

Winch, D., *Riches and Poverty: An Intellectual History of Political Economy in Britain, 1750–1834* (Cambridge, 1996).

Wood, P., *Poverty and the Workhouse in Victorian Britain* (Stroud, 1991).

Charity and the Poor

Abel-Smith, B., *The Hospitals, 1800–1948* (1964).

Andrew, D. T., *Philanthropy and Police: London Charity in the Eighteenth Century* (Princeton, 1989).

Babler, A. M., *Education of the Destitute. A Study of London Ragged Schools, 1844–1874* (1986).

Behlmer, G. K., *Child Abuse and Moral Reform in England, 1870–1908* (Stanford, Calif., 1982).

Brown, F. K., *Fathers of the Victorians* (Cambridge, 1961).

Cherry, S., *Medical Services and the Hospitals in Britain, 1860–1939* (1996)

Cunningham, H., *The Children of the Poor: Representations of Childhood since the Seventeenth Century* (Oxford, 1991).

Cunningham, H., and J. Innes, eds, *Charity, Philanthropy and Reform* (1998).

Davies, S., 'Two conceptions of welfare: Voluntarism and incorporationism', *Social Philosophy and Social Policy*, 14 (1997).

Evans, N., 'Urbanisation, elite attitudes and philanthropy: Cardiff, 1850–1914', *International Review of Social History*, 27 (1982).

Hadley, E., 'Natives in a strange land: The philanthropic discourse of juvenile emigration in mid-nineteenth century England', *Victorian Studies*, 33 (1990).

Hall, C., and L. Davidoff, *Family Fortunes: Men and Women of the English Middle Class, 1780–1850* (1987).

Harrison, B., *Peaceable Kingdom: Stability and Change in Modern Britain* (Oxford, 1982), ch. 5.

Harrison, B., 'For Church, Queen and Family: The Girls' Friendly Society, 1874–1920', *Past and Present*, 61(1975).

Heasman, K., *Evangelicals in Action: An Appraisal of their Social Work in the Victorian Era* (1962).

Horn, P., *Children's Work and Welfare, 1780–1890* (Cambridge, 1994).

Humphreys, R., *Sin, Organised Charity and the Poor Law in Victorian England* (1995).

Inglis, K. S., *Churches and the Working Classes in Victorian England* (1968).

Jones, G. S., *Outcast London* (Harmondsworth, 1984).

Kidd, A. J., 'Charity organisation and the unemployed in Manchester', *Social History*, 9 (1984).

Kidd, A. J., 'Outcast Manchester: Voluntary charity, poor relief and the casual poor, 1860–1905', in A. J. Kidd and K. W. Roberts, eds, *City, Class and Culture* (Manchester, 1985).

Kidd, A. J., 'Philanthropy and the social history paradigm', *Social History*, 21 (1996).

Lewis, D. M., *Lighten Their Darkness: The Evangelical Mission to Working-class London, 1828–1860* (New York, 1986).

Lewis, J., *The Voluntary Sector, the State and Social Work in Britain: The Charity Organisation Society/Family Welfare Association since 1869* (Aldershot, 1995).

Mandler, P., ed., *The Uses of Charity: The Poor on relief in the Metropolis* (Philadelphia, Penn., 1990).

Meller, H., *Leisure and the Changing City, 1870–1914* (1976).

Morris, R. J., 'Clubs, societies and associations', in F. M. L. Thompson, ed., *Cambridge Social History of Britain*, vol. 3 (Cambridge, 1990).

Morris, R. J., 'Voluntary societies and urban elites, 1780–1850', *Historical Journal*, 26 (1983)

Mowat, C. L., *The Charity Organisation Society, 1869–1913* (1961).

Owen, D., *English Philanthropy, 1660–1960* (Cambridge, Mass., 1964).

Parker, J., *Women and Welfare: Ten Victorian Women in Public Social Welfare* (1988).

Parr, J., *Labouring Children: British Immigrant Apprentices to Canada, 1869–1924* (1980).

Pickstone, J., *Medicine and Industrial Society: A History of Hospital Development in Manchester and its Region, 1752–1946* (Manchester, 1985).

Prochaska, F. K., *Women and Philanthropy in Nineteenth-century England* (Oxford, 1980).

Prochaska, F. K., 'Body and soul: Bible nurses and the poor in Victorian London', *Historical Research*, 60 (1987).

Prochaska, F. K., 'A mother's country: mother's meetings and family welfare in Britain, 1850–1950', *History*, 74 (1989).

Prochaska, F. K., *The Voluntary Impulse: Philanthropy in Modern Britain* (1988).

Prochaska, F. K., 'Philanthropy', in Thompson, ed., *Cambridge Social History*, vol. 3.

Rack, H. D., 'Domestic visitation: A chapter in early nineteenth-century evangelicalism', *Journal of Ecclesiastical History*, 24 (1973).

Roberts, M. J. D., 'Reshaping the gift relationship: The London Mendicity Society and the suppression of begging in England, 1818–1869', *International Review of Social History*, 36 (1991).

Shapely, P., 'Charity, status and leadership: Charitable image and the Manchester man', *Journal of Social History*, 32 (1998).

Shapely, P., *Charity and Power in Victorian Manchester* (Manchester, 1999).

Simey, M. B., *Charity Rediscovered: A Study of Philanthropic Effort in Nineteenth Century Liverpool* (Liverpool, 1992).

Summers, A., 'A home from home: women's philanthropic work in the nineteenth century', in S. Burman, *Fit Work for Women* (1979).

Tarn, J. N., *Five Percent Philanthropy: An Account of Housing in Urban Areas between 1850 and 1914* (Cambridge, 1973).

Vicinus, M., *Independent Women: Work and Community for Single Women 1850–1920* (1985).

Vincent, A. W., 'The Poor Law Reports of 1909 and the social theory of the Charity Organisation Society', *Victorian Studies*, 27 (1984).

Wagner, G., *Barnado* (1979).

Woodward, J., *To Do the Sick No Harm: A Study of the British Voluntary Hospital System to 1875* (1974).

Yeo, E., The *Contest for Social Science: Relations and Representations of Gender and Class* (1996).

Yeo, S., *Religion and Voluntary Organisations in Crisis* (1976).

Working-Class Self-Help and Mutual Aid

1 Formal Institutions

Clark, A., *The Struggle for the Breeches: Gender and the Making of the British Working Class* (1995).

Cole, G. D. H., *A Century of Co-operation* (1944).

Crossick, G., *An Artisan Elite in Victorian Society: Kentish London 1840–1880* (1978).

Fishlow, A., 'The Trustee Savings Banks, 1817–1861', *Journal of Economic History*, 21(1961).

Gorsky, M., 'The growth and distribution of English friendly societies in the early nineteenth century', *Economic History Review*, 51 (1998).

Gosden, P. H. G. H., *Friendly Societies in England, 1815–1875* (1961).

Gosden, P. H. G. H., *Self Help: Voluntary Institutions in the Nineteenth Century* (1973).

Gray, R. Q., *The Labour Aristocracy in Victorian Edinburgh* (Oxford, 1976).

Green, D., *Working-Class Patients and the Medical Establishment: Self help in Britain from the Mid-Nineteenth Century to 1948* (1985).

Green, D. R., *From Artisans to Paupers: Economic Change and Poverty in London, 1790–1870* (Aldershot, 1995).

Hanson, C. G., 'Craft unions, welfare benefits and the case for trade union law reform, 1867–75', *Economic History Review*, 28 (1975).

Hastings, R. P., 'A nineteenth-century dispensary at work', *Local Historian*, 10 (1973).

Hastings, R. P., *Essays in North Riding History* (Northallerton, 1981) ch. 7.

Hopkins, E., *Working-Class Self Help in Nineteenth Century England* (1995).

Horne, H. O., *A History of Savings Banks* (Oxford, 1947).

Johnson, P., *Saving and Spending: The Working-Class Economy in England 1870–1939* (Oxford, 1985).

Jones, D., 'Self help in nineteenth century Wales: The rise and fall of the female friendly society', *Llafur*, 4 (1984).

Jones, D., 'Did friendly societies matter? A study of friendly society membership in Glamorgan, 1794–1910', *Welsh History Review*, 12 (1985).

Kirk, N., *The Growth of Working Class Reformism in Mid-Victorian England* (1985).

Musson, A. E., *British Trade Unions, 1800–1875* (1972).

Purvis, M., 'Co-operative retailing in England, 1835–1850', *Northern History*, 22 (1986).

Purvis, M., 'The development of co-operative retailing in England and Wales, 1851–1901: A geographical study', *Journal of Historical Geography*, 16, (1990).

Tholfsen, T. R., *Working Class Radicalism in Mid-Victorian England* (1976).

Webb, S., and B. Webb, *The History of Trade Unionism, 1666–1920* (1920).

2 'Neighbourhood' Survival Strategies

Anderson, M., *Family Structure in Nineteenth-Century Lancashire* (Cambridge, 1971).

Benson, J., *The Penny Capitalists: A Study of Nineteenth-Century Working-Class Entrepreneurs* (1983).

Burnett, J., *Idle Hands: The Experience of Unemployment, 1790–1990* (1994).

Chinn, C., *They Worked All Their Lives: Women of the Urban Poor in England, 1880–1939* (Manchester, 1988).

Chinn, C., *Poverty Amidst Prosperity: The Urban Poor in England, 1834–1914* (Manchester, 1995).

Crowther, M. A., 'Family responsibility and state responsibility in Britain before the welfare state', *Historical Journal*, 25 (1982).

Davin, A., *Growing up Poor: Home, School and Street in London, 1870–1914* (1996).

Horrell, S., and J. Humphries, 'The origin and expansion of the male breadwinner family: The case of nineteenth-century Britain', *International Review of Social History*, 42 (1997), Supplement.

Lewis, J., 'Family provision of health and welfare in the mixed economy of care in the late nineteenth and twentieth centuries', *Social History of Medicine*, 8 (1995).

Lis, C., and H. Soly, 'Neighbourhood social change in Western European cities, sixteenth to nineteenth centuries', *International Review of Social History*, 38 (1993).

Meacham, S., *A Life Apart: The English Working Class, 1890–1914* (1977).

Roberts, E., *A Woman's Place: An Oral History of Working-Class Women, 1890–1940* (1984).

Roberts, E., 'Women's strategies, 1890–1940', in J. Lewis, ed., *Labour and Love: Women's Experience of the Home and Family, 1850–1940* (1986).

Roberts, R., *The Classic Slum* (Harmondsworth, 1973).

Ross, E., 'Survival networks: Women's neighbourhood sharing in London before World War I', *History Workshop Journal*, 15 (1983).

Ross, E., 'Hungry children: Housewives and London charity, 1870–1918', in P. Mandler, ed., *The Uses of Charity* (1990).

Ross, E., *Love and Toil: Motherhood in Outcast London, 1870–1918* (Oxford, 1993).

Rushton, P., 'Family survival strategies in mid-Victorian Ancoats', *Manchester Region History Review*, 7 (1993).

Tebbutt, M., *Making Ends Meet: Pawnbroking and Working Class Credit* (Leicester, 1983).

Tebbutt, M., *Women's Talk?: A Social History of 'Gossip' in Working-Class Neighbourhoods, 1880–1960* (Aldershot, 1995).

INDEX